"Morgan and Easley have assembled a w   d
Christian scholars with complementary are   n
and theology, the history of Christian thoug.   .d
missiology—to produce this comprehensive volume on the doctrine of the church. A
much-needed resource for lay people, clergy, and scholars alike!"

Gregg R. Allison, professor of Christian Theology, The Southern Baptist Theological
Seminary

"This comprehensive biblical theology of the church has contributions by leading
evangelical Baptist scholars whose integrity, scholarship, and insight are remarkable.
Biblical theology is enlightening because its material is drawn from the Word itself.
Even though the role the church might play in a future millennial kingdom is intentionally omitted, much can be gained from this study, and I heartily recommend it.
This book sharpens our thinking, delights our souls, and encourages us as we move
forward in the twenty-first century of the church."

James A. Borland, professor of New Testament and Theology, Liberty University

"This collection of essays is a welcome addition to ecclesiological scholarship in
the Baptist tradition. The authors, mostly younger scholars, bring together an
impressive array of recent literature that informs several angles of debate about the
church. Especially strong are the chapters exhibiting biblical material and discussion. Baptist theologians should definitely add this book to their research tools and
course bibliographies."

William Brackney, Millard R. Cherry Distinguished Professor of Christian
Thought and Ethics, Director of Acadia Centre of Baptist and Anabaptist Studies,
Acadia Divinity College

"The last few decades have witnessed voluminous writings on the church. Few of
these publications, however, have approached the subject in the way this volume
does: begin with exegetically grounded biblical theology, gain at least some insights
from the history of how "church" has been understood across two millennia, and
only then venture a synthesis. This is surely methodologically right: we ought to
listen attentively to the diverse, complementary voices of Scripture, and learn from
the theological reflections of Christians who have gone before, prior to venturing a
stable, constructive ecclesiology. Drs. Easley and Morgan and their contributors have
accomplished this in a winsome and accessible way."

D. A. Carson, research professor of New Testament at Trinity Evangelical Divinity
School

"This is a book to deepen your love for the bride of Christ and to strengthen your
commitment to the body of Christ. The only true world superpower is the church
—because it is the only institution that will last into eternity. The healthy theology of
the church in *The Community of Jesus* is crucial to our day, as it is through the church
that the message of Christ is shared and the mission of Christ is accomplished."

Tom Holladay, teaching pastor, Saddleback Church

"The church is the Spirit's creation, Jesus' bride, the consummation of God's plan for the ages. Therefore, living, loving, and serving the church must be our passion. These days, the church is often either denigrated as an out-of-date institution or over-simplified as a few believers gathering for coffee. This book will help you develop a more robust ecclesiology, going beyond doctrinal degrees to creating healthy models for church life in any context. Those of us who love and serve the church long for this kind of rich rediscovery of what churches can be today."

Dr. Jeff Iorg, president, Golden Gate Baptist Theological Seminary

"*The Community of Jesus* helps to fill a significant gap in theological reflection on the church in the evangelical world. With thoroughness, clarity, and a pastoral touch, the contributors offer a well-rounded and thoroughly biblical view of the church with fresh applications for evangelicals today. In an age when the church is increasingly marginalized, criticized, and maligned, *The Community of Jesus* reminds us that the church is still the bride of Christ with an unfinished task and mission in the world today. This work represents the best of evangelical thinking on an often overlooked but critically important component of our faith—the identity and mission of the Triune God's church. It will inspire the heart and inform the head of every pastor, layperson, seminary professor, theological student, and vocational Christian minister. A must read for the church of the twenty-first century!"

John D. Massey, associate professor of Missions, Southwestern Baptist Theological Seminary

"As a church planter, my job (to be honest, my life) needs to be shaped by a robust and thoroughly biblical ecclesiology. On the flip side, I also need resources that serve me well in the trenches of day-to-day church leadership. *The Community of Jesus* gives me scholarship that I can trust, with a view of the church that is beautiful, grand, and cosmic in scale. But I also know that I have a volume written by men who don't just love the idea of the church, but love and serve real local churches filled with real people and real problems. I am grateful for both their precision and passion."

Jonathan McIntosh, lead pastor, Christ City Church, Memphis, Tennessee

"The renewed interest in ecclesiology is one of the most encouraging developments of our times. With this new interest come new questions, and *The Community of Jesus: A Theology of the Church* is addressed to several of those most pressing questions. Furthermore, this is a book that is rich in biblical content and deep in theological reflection. Those who love the church will welcome this new volume."

R. Albert Mohler, Jr., president, The Southern Baptist Theological Seminary

"This thoughtful introduction to the doctrine of the church rightly roots its system-atic theology in biblical theology."

Andy Naselli, assistant professor of New Testament and Biblical Theology, Bethlehem College and Seminary

"The church is not an afterthought in the plan and purposes of God. The glory of God in the formation of a missionary people who show and share the love of God is the goal of the gospel. This book gives us a biblical theology of the church and offers insights into historical and contemporary concerns related to God's people. The pastor or church leader who desires to keep the church at the forefront of their theology and practice will benefit from these essays."

Trevin Wax, managing editor of The Gospel Project, LifeWay Christian Resources

"Seldom do readers encounter a volume about Christ's church that is as satisfying as this one. The book's distinguished editors believe the church of Jesus Christ is the most important institution in the world and say so. The book's competent authors offer informed biblical, historical, theological, and missional studies that provide powerful evidence supporting the editors' claim. Many folks today indicate they love Jesus but hate the church. This book serves as a much-needed and persuasive corrective for this unbiblical and spiritually harmful way of thinking. Pastors and lay persons alike will profit greatly from reading this instructive and encouraging book about Christ's church."

John D. Woodbridge, research professor of Church History and Christian Thought, Trinity Evangelical Divinity School

THE
COMMUNITY
OF JESUS

A Theology

of the Church

Kendell H. Easley
Christopher W. Morgan
Editors

Nashville, Tennessee

Contents

To Chelsey, Jordan, and Leah,
cherished blessings from the Lord

Acknowledgments

Shelley and Nancy—thank you for your love, patience, and encouragement.

California Baptist University and Union University and our respective presidents, Dr. Ron Ellis and Dr. David Dockery—thank you for your creativity, diligence, and vision.

Andreas Köstenberger, Jim Baird, Chris Cowan, Terry Wilder, and the team from B&H—thank you for believing in this project and for taking such good care of us. It is a pleasure to serve the Lord with you.

Tony Chute, for reading and offering insightful feedback on parts of the manuscript.

Joe Slunaker, for assistance in editing the bibliography.

To students in Chris's ecclesiology courses at California Baptist University, Golden Gate Baptist Theological Seminary, and Southern Baptist Theological Seminary, for your diligence, enthusiasm, and desire to serve Christ through the church.

To students in Ken's master's courses and doctor of ministry seminars at Union University, for your role in helping me "keep it real" regarding your churches.

To Helendale Community Church and Christ City Church: it is a joy to share life with you.

Introduction

Kendell H. Easley and Christopher W. Morgan

When the word "church" is mentioned, wide-ranging reactions surface. For some, it brings back nostalgic memories of childhood, of a quaint building and singing old gospel songs with grandparents. For others, "church" makes them cringe, as they think of hypocrisy or toxic personal relationships from which they fled. Still others see "church" as that conservative subculture or institution that judges them and resists their ways. They like Jesus but hate the church.[1]

Even pastors and church leaders have varied reactions. Many seasoned pastors picture particular congregations and their lives' work in serving them. They recall the church at its best, times when people came to Christ, were captured by God's Word, lived in community with one another, and genuinely cared for the lost. Some pastors have also experienced the church at its most frustrating, encountering people who promote hidden agendas or refuse to move past petty grievances. New pastors with freshly minted seminary degrees may tend to think of church as an idea, doctrine, or ideal—because sometimes it takes a while to shift from loving the idea of the church to loving the church itself.

Some may be like me (Kendell), having seen the landscape of North American evangelical (and Baptist) churches shift steadily over the past forty years. The style and ministry approach of some contemporary

---

[1] This expression seems valid if used to mean that people respect Jesus but have been turned off by a Christian subculture or particular churches. But so often, the question needs to be asked: do they really like the biblical Jesus, the exclusive Lord who demands sole allegiance?

churches are vastly different from anything I envisioned when I attended seminary in the 1970s. For example (although I have mainly led, participated in, and worshipped in traditional Baptist churches), I have witnessed—with both curiosity and admiration—the rise of seeker sensitive and emerging (or emergent) churches. For the past three years, I have become deeply immersed in the life of a newly planted urban congregation, Christ City Church in Memphis, which has intentionally embraced an "ancient-future" and "missional" orientation. My paradigm for the local church is being wonderfully—and sometimes painfully—stretched. (Change often comes hard for this baby boomer who longs for the fourth quarter of life and ministry to matter deeply for God's church and kingdom.) Moreover, I cannot project what the church in North America will look like during the next half century. The rate of cultural change keeps increasing, and the church struggles to respond well.

Others may be like me (Chris), who as a young pastor and seminary student loved church people but grew weary *with ecclesiology*. Though I loved (and still love) theology—enough to obtain a PhD in systematic theology—I was frustrated with never-ending theological discussions about important, but not ultimate, questions of ecclesiology. Sad to say, my first exposure to discussions of ecclesiology was in a church whose pastor majored on obscure debates. For instance, should a Southern Baptist church accept the baptism of a person who was immersed as a believer by a nondenominational church whose theology is baptistic? Was that truly a church, and could that be baptism? Or consider this scenario: when a missionary Baptist church wanted to join our local Southern Baptist association, my pastor contended that the missionary Baptist pastor and all the members must be baptized (not kidding). As some pastors go overboard with their view of Calvinism or eschatology, some do with their particular ecclesiologies.

But as I pastored churches in Catron, Missouri, and Barstow, California, and as I taught ministry students courses in systematic theology, pastoral leadership, and preaching, I found myself drawn to ecclesiology—not to the obscure, though. I kept seeing how central the church is to God's eternal plan. I began to see the church in conjunction with the glory of God; salvation history; the kingdom of God; the attributes of God; the image of God; the mission of God; and the call to love, holiness, unity, and truth. The Sermon on the Mount, Acts, Ephesians, and James came alive. Seeing the New Testament as written by church leaders for the sake of helping churches captured me. Seeing how a careful, biblical view of the church drives pastoral leadership, ministry, evangelism, and preaching has clarified my thinking and honed my approach to ministry.

We (Kendell and Chris) see the importance of the disputed questions but in a healthy theological and pastoral perspective. Baptism, the Lord's Supper, church discipline, the relationship of Israel and the church, denominations, ecumenism[2]—their importance, in our experience, is best seen through a broader, salvation historical lens on the theology of the church framed by a context of the nature and mission of God. Seeing the church this way recasts our perspective on pastoral ministry, preaching, leadership, worship, evangelism, fellowship, discipleship, youth ministry, counseling, church planting, missiology, social justice, denominations, ecumenism, hermeneutics, theological method, and much of systematic theology.

In this volume, we do not attempt to address all these issues but to lay a theological foundation that will help readers sort through them. Our focus is to work toward a biblical, historic, systematic, missional theology of the church.

Our approach is to do this as a team, composed of an OT scholar, four NT scholars, two theologians, one historian, and one philosopher/missiologist. The contributors possess significant pastoral, teaching, missions, administrative, and denominational experience.

Our structure is twofold. The first five chapters (written by Paul House, Andreas Köstenberger, Kendell Easley, David Dockery, and Ray Van Neste respectively) carefully set forth biblical teachings concerning the church. The next four chapters (written by James Patterson, Steve Wellum, Chris Morgan, and Bruce Ashford) build on this core biblical

---

[2] Helpful books on such topics include Mark Dever, *Nine Marks of a Healthy Church* (Wheaton: Crossway, 2000); Thomas R. Schreiner and Shawn Wright, ed., *Believer's Baptism: Sign of the New Covenant in Christ* (Nashville: B&H, 2008); Thomas R. Schreiner and Matthew Crawford, ed., *The Lord's Supper: Remembering and Proclaiming Christ Until He Comes* (Nashville: B&H, 2011); Christopher W. Morgan and Robert A. Peterson, ed., *The Kingdom of God*, Theology in Community 4 (Wheaton: Crossway, 2012); Peter Gentry and Stephen J. Wellum, *Kingdom through Covenant: A Biblical–Theological Understanding of the Covenants* (Wheaton: Crossway, 2012); and Anthony L. Chute, Christopher W. Morgan, and Robert A. Peterson, eds., *Why We Belong: Evangelical Unity and Denominational Diversity* (Wheaton: Crossway, 2013).

material, relating the theology of the church to church history, salvation history, God's glory, and God's mission.

We invite readers to join us on this biblical, historical, systematic, missional journey investigating a magnificent theme: the church of our Lord Jesus Christ. Our prayer is that along the way we all will be captured by the astonishing significance of the church in God's eternal purpose, sense the great privilege it is to be a part of Christ's church, and grow in our love for Christ and his church. Such a robust vision of Christ's church surely shaped John Piper's bold words:

> The church of Jesus Christ is the most important institution in the world. The assembly of the redeemed, the company of the saints, the children of God are more significant in world history than any other group, organization, or nation. The United States of America compares to the church of Jesus Christ like a speck of dust compares to the sun. The drama of international relations compares to the mission of the church like a kindergarten riddle compares to Hamlet or King Lear. And all pomp of May Day in Red Square and the pageantry of New Year's in Pasadena fade into a formless grey against the splendor of the bride of Christ. . . . The gates of Hades, the powers of death, will prevail against every institution but one, the church. . . . Lift up your eyes, O Christians! You belong to a society that will never cease, to the apple of God's eye, to the eternal and cosmic church of our Lord, Jesus Christ.[3]

---

[3] John Piper, "The Cosmic Church," sermon on Eph 3:10 preached March 22, 1981; http://www.desiringgod.org/resource-library/sermons/the-cosmic-church.

Abbreviations

AB	Anchor Bible
BBR	*Bulletin for Biblical Research*
BDAG	Danker, R. W., W. Bauer, W. F. Arndt, and F. W. Gringrich. *Greek-English Lexicon of the New Testament and Other Early Christian Literature.* 3rd ed. Chicago, 2000
BECNT	Baker Exegetical Commentary on the New Testament
BI	*Biblical Illustrator*
BST	The Bible Speaks Today
BTNT	Biblical Theology of the New Testament
CH	*Church History*
DJG	*Dictionary of Jesus and the Gospels.* Edited by J. B. Green, S. McKnight, and I. H. Marshall. Downers Grove, 1997
DPL	*Dictionary of Paul and His Letters.* Edited by G. F. Hawthorne, R. P. Martin, and D. G. Reid. Downers Grove, 1995
EBC	*The Expositor's Bible Commentary*
EDNT	*Exegetical Dictionary of the New Testament.* Edited by H. Balz, G. Schneider. English translation. Grand Rapids, 1990–1993
ExpTim	*Expository Times*
IBC	Interpretation: A Bible Commentary for Teaching and Preaching
Int	*Interpretation*
IJST	*International Journal of Systematic Theology*
JETS	*Journal of the Evangelical Theological Society*
JPS	Jewish Publication Society
JTS	*Journal of Theological Studies*
L&N	*Greek-English Lexicon of the New Testament: Based on Semantic Domains.* Edited by J. P. Louw and E. A. Nida. 2nd ed. New York, 1989

LXX	Septuagint
MJT	*Midwestern Journal of Theology*
NAC	New American Commentary
NDBT	*New Dictionary of Biblical Theology*. Edited by B. S. Rosner, T. D. Alexander, G. Goldsworthy, and D. A. Carson. Downers Grove, 2004
NICNT	New International Commentary on the New Testament
NICOT	New International Commentary on the Old Testament
NIDNTT	*New International Dictionary of New Testament Theology*. Edited by C. Brown. 4 vols. Grand Rapids, 1975–1985
NIDOTTE	*New International Commentary on the Old Testament Theology and Exegesis*. Edited by W. A. VanGemeren. 5 vols. Grand Rapids, 1997
NIGTC	New International Greek Testament Commentary
NIVAC	The NIV Application Commentary
NSBT	New Studies in Biblical Theology
OBT	Overtures to Biblical Theology
PNTC	Pelican New Testament Commentaries
RB	*Revue biblique*
SBJT	*Southern Baptist Journal of Theology*
SBT	Studies in Biblical Theology
SE	*Studia evagelica I, II, III* (= TU 73 [195], 87 [1984], 88 [1964], etc.)
SJT	*Scottish Journal of Theology*
SwJT	*Southwestern Journal of Theology*
TDNT	*Theological Dictionary of the New Testament*. Edited by G. Kittel and G. Friedrich. Translated by G. W. Bromiley. 10 vols. Grand Rapids, 1964–1976
TJ	*Trinity Journal*
TLOT	*Theological Lexicon of the Old Testament*. Edited by E. Jenni, with assistance from C. Westermann. Translated by M. E. Biddle. 3 vols. Peabody, MA, 1997
TynBul	*Tyndale Bulletin*
VT	*Vetus Testamentum*
WBC	World Biblical Commentary
WTJ	*Westminster Theological Journal*

CHAPTER 1

God Walks with His People: Old Testament Foundations

Paul R. House

The OT begins the Bible's long, multifaceted story of God's relationship with "his people." Defined simply, they are persons in right relationship with God, in contrast to those who are not (see Ps 1:1–6; Eph 2:1–10). The Bible calls them many things that highlight their close bond with him: God's friends (Exod 33:11; Isa 41:8), God's son (Exod 4:22; Jer 31:9; Hos 11:1–9), God's priests (Exod 19:1–6; Isa 61:6), God's assembly (Num 16:3; Deut 23:2–4; Neh 13:1), God's people (Exod 6:7; 8:23; Deut 7:6; Pss 53:6; 81:11; 100:3; Hos 1:10), God's bride (Isa 54:1–7; 62:4–5; Jeremiah 2–3; Ezekiel 16; Hosea 1–2), God's flock (Pss 77:20; 78:52; 100:3), God's servants (Isa 56:1–8; 66:14–23), and subjects in God's kingdom (Isa 4:2–6; 11:1–12:6; 65:1–66:24). Because it appears often in the OT and because it links many other images, the term "God's people" is probably the best summative concept to use. As Charles Scobie writes, "The actual phrase 'people of God' appears only eleven times, but phrases such as 'my people,' 'your people,' and 'his people' are frequent (c. 300 times)."[1]

---

[1] Charles H. H. Scobie, *The Ways of Our God: An Approach to Biblical Theology* (Grand Rapids: Eerdmans, 2003), 469.

As it progresses, the Bible presents God and his people in a connected plot in which they walk together from creation in Genesis 1–2 to new creation in Revelation 21–22, via promise texts such as Isa 65:17–25.[2] These people are one because they are God's, and he is one (Deut 6:4–9; Mark 12:28–32). No fissure exists between the people of God in the Old and New Testaments. God's ways become clearer as the Bible unfolds, but his saving work with, for, and by his people in the Old and New Testaments varies by degree, not by substance.

In this chapter I will seek to provide a foundation for a biblical theology of the church by outlining the identification and mission of God's people in the OT. I will argue that God calls his people to walk with him so they can be priests for the whole world, thereby sharing his redemptive mission to humanity. He creates his people by bringing them into covenant relationship with him. Though they often rebel against him and his covenant, he does not allow his covenant to fail. He preserves a people on his mission so the Messiah can complete the mission by walking with his people into a new creation shaped by a new covenant that completes, not replaces, all God's previous covenantal acts.

I will first analyze passages that define the mission of God's people as a kingdom of priests. By starting with foundational passages, I echo Elmer Martens's excellent OT theology, *God's Design*.[3] Second, I will trace the concept of God's walking with his people in the Law, Prophets, and Writings. Walking with God is how his people serve as his priests in his world. Their identity and mission are united. In these sections I utilize a canonical approach similar to that used by Brevard Childs, Ronald Clements, John Sailhamer, Rolf Rendtorff, and my own work.[4]

---

[2] Note this pattern in Bernhard W. Anderson, *From Creation to New Creation: Old Testament Perspective*, OBT (Minneapolis: Fortress, 1994), 233–45; William J. Dumbrell, *The Search for Order: Biblical Eschatology in Focus* (Grand Rapids: Baker, 1994), 346; and G. K. Beale, *A New Testament Biblical Theology: The Unfolding of the Old Testament in the New* (Grand Rapids: Baker, 2011), 23.

[3] Elmer Martens, *God's Design: A Focus on Old Testament Theology* (Grand Rapids: Baker, 1981).

[4] Brevard S. Childs, *Introduction to the Old Testament as Scripture* (Minneapolis: Fortress, 1980); Ronald E. Clements, *Old Testament Theology: A Fresh Approach* (London: Marshall, Morgan, and Scott, 1978); John Sailhamer, *Introduction to Old Testament Theology: A Canonical Approach* (Grand Rapids: Zondervan, 1995); Rolf Rendtorff, *The Canonical Hebrew Bible: A Theology of the Old Testament*, trans. David E. Orton (Leiden: Deo, 2005); Paul R. House, *Old Testament Theology* (Downers Grove: InterVarsity, 1998); id., "God's Character and the Wholeness of Scripture," *Scottish*

At the end of each canonical section I will present a synthesis of the major themes. These segments try to reflect thematic treatments found in volumes by H. J. Kraus, Walther Zimmerli, John Goldingay, and Robin Routledge.[5] I will at times explore or cite NT texts, which I believe have been breathed out by God, just as the OT books have been (2 Tim 3:14–17; 2 Pet 1:19–21). The NT is also valuable for examining the OT because it represents the oldest Christian interpretative traditions. I will conclude with observations about the unity of God's people in all eras.

The Mission of God's People and God's Character: Exodus 19:1–6; 1 Peter 2:9–10; and Exodus 34:6–7

God's people, like all created beings, have their origin in God. He made them; they have not made themselves (Ps 100:3). Their identity and purpose come from him. One could choose many passages to orient the discussion, but Exod 19:1–6; 1 Pet 2:9–10; and Exod 34:6–7 stand out. Written against the background of Yahweh's deliverance of Israel from Egypt, Exod 19:1–6 defines God's people and their mission. The apostle Peter uses this passage to characterize God's people and their purpose in 1 Pet 2:9–10. Written against the background of Israel's greatest sin to that point in time, Exod 34:1–27 provides Yahweh's self-definition and ongoing commitment to Israel. Several subsequent OT writers echo or quote it. Together these passages provide a framework for understanding the ongoing mission of God's people anchored in God's permanent, covenant-keeping, and covenant-preserving character.

God's People's Priestly Mission: Exodus 19:1–6

By Exod 19:1–6, Scripture has revealed much significant information about God and his people. Genesis 1–2 reveals God is the Creator of the

---

Bulletin of Evangelical Theology 23, no. 1 (Spring 2005): 4–17; and id., "Examining the Narratives of Old Testament Narrative: An Exploration in Biblical Theology," *WTJ* 67 (2005): 229–45.

[5] H. J. Kraus, *The People of God in the Old Testament*, World Christian Books 22 (London: Lutterworth Press, 1958); Walther Zimmerli, *Old Testament Theology in Outline*, trans. David E. Green (Edinburgh: T&T Clark, 1978); John Goldingay, *Old Testament Theology, Volume One: Israel's Gospel* (Downers Grove: InterVarsity, 2003); and Robin Routledge, *Old Testament Theology: A Thematic Approach* (Downers Grove: InterVarsity, 2008).

heavens, the earth, and the first human beings. Genesis 3–4 shows God loved and protected Adam and Eve even after they sinned. Genesis 5–10 demonstrates that God endured humanity's death spiral into violence and corrupt thinking, judged humanity using a great flood, and began afresh by making a covenant with Noah and his family. Furthermore, Genesis 11–36 shows that he chose and made a covenant with Abraham and his family, the descendants of Noah's son Shem, to bless the whole world. Genesis 37–50 reveals how God protected this fragile growing family by sending them to Egypt. Finally, Exodus 1–18 describes how God delivered Abraham's descendants after they were forced into slavery in Egypt and how he brought them safely into the desert to meet with him at Sinai. This deliverance occurred because of Yahweh's unbreakable determination to keep his covenant promises to Abraham (Exod 2:23–25; see Gen 12:1–9). Now Yahweh calls Abraham's whole family and those who have joined them to serve as priests for the whole world. As Deut 10:12 will point out later, Yahweh calls a whole group of people "to walk in all his ways, to love him, to serve" him with all their heart and soul (NRSV).

Exodus 19:1–4 sets this call to priesthood in the context of Yahweh's redemptive work for Israel. The account occurs "the third new moon after the people of Israel had gone out of the land of Egypt" (v. 1 NRSV). The phrase "people of Israel," or translated more woodenly "the sons [*bene*] of Israel," refers to the descendants of Jacob, Abraham's grandson, whom God renamed Israel (Gen 32:22–32). The phraseology indicates a family connection, as does the word typically translated "people" in the OT (*'am*).

Yet ancestry is not the only defining factor. When Yahweh delivered these people, the group included persons who were not Jacob's blood descendants. Moses' first and second wives were not ethnic Israelites (Exod 2:11–22; 4:24–26; Num 12:1). Caleb, who later represents a whole tribe and desires to invade Canaan when others do not (Numbers 13–14), was not of Israelite descent (13:6). In fact, Exod 12:38 states that a mixed multitude left Egypt. While it is impossible to determine the exact makeup and motives of this group, many scholars agree the phrase means persons of various racial backgrounds left with the Israelites.[6]

---

[6] See for example A. Cohen, *The Five Books of Moses with Haphtaroth*, Soncino Books of the Bible (New York: Soncino Press, 1947), 396; Walter C. Kaiser Jr., "Exodus," *EBC* 2 (Grand Rapids: Zondervan, 1990), 379–80; Nahum M. Sarna, *Exodus*, JPS Commentary (New York: Jewish Publication Society, 1991), 62; and John L. Mackay, *Exodus*, Mentor (Fearn, Scotland: Christian Focus, 2001), 226–27.

Once the group camps at Sinai (19:2–3), Yahweh gives Moses a message for the people. It unfolds in three parts. First, Yahweh reminds them what he did in Egypt and that he has brought them to Sinai, just as he promised Moses (v. 4; see 3:12). What united this assortment of people was their deliverance by and faith in Yahweh. They owed their freedom to him alone. They also owed their preservation in the desert, safety in travel, and arrival at their destination (Sinai) to God's power.[7] They had personally and corporately experienced God's kindness.[8]

Second, Yahweh promises them that if they will reflect their relationship with him by keeping his covenant,[9] they will be "My own possession out of all the peoples, although all the earth is Mine" (19:5). The word translated "own possession" originally referred to "valued property to which one has an exclusive right of possession."[10] Israel's faith in and consequent obedience to Yahweh will mark them as people who belong to him, and him alone. It will show they are happy subjects of his rule.[11] As Yahweh's subjects, they separate themselves from other gods and those who serve them.[12]

Third, Yahweh describes their function more specifically when he says their covenant faithfulness will show they are "My kingdom of priests, and My holy nation" (19:6). The word for "nation" (goy) indicates that this mixed multitude of descendants of Israel and those who join them will become a corporate entity. Though other interpretations of "kingdom of priests" are possible,[13] I think Graeme Goldsworthy's is correct: "As a people they shall then exist in a unique relationship to God while representing him to the whole world as priests (v. 6). This priestly function in a world that belongs to God gives further meaning to

---

[7] William J. Dumbrell, *Covenant and Creation: A Theology of Old Testament Covenants* (Grand Rapids: Baker, 1984), 84.

[8] See Mackay, *Exodus*, 325.

[9] The concept is that all God's covenant activity to this point is a unified whole, not a series of separate events. On this point see Dumbrell, *The Search for Order*, 44–45.

[10] Sarna, *Exodus*, 104.

[11] John Bright, *The Kingdom of God* (Nashville: Abingdon, 1953), 176.

[12] Dumbrell, *Covenant and Creation*, 85; and Zimmerli, *Old Testament Theology in Outline*, 46.

[13] See for instance Goldingay, *Old Testament Theology, Volume One*, 374. Goldingay does not think the verse indicates Israel has a ministry to the rest of the world. Nonetheless, he thinks Exod 19:4–6 reflects the inclusive vision of Gen 12:3. Israel does not exist solely for itself.

the original covenant promise that all the nations of the earth would be blessed through Abraham's descendant (Gen 12:3)."[14]

Priests were to "approach God on behalf of others and to approach people on behalf of God . . . that the blessings of the covenant would one day overflow through them into the whole world."[15] This priestly ministry included teaching God's word accurately (Hos 4:1–14; Mal 2:7–9), praying for others (Jer 15:1–2), and helping people worship God through offering sacrifices appropriately (see Mal 1:6–14).[16]

The Priestly Mission of God's People: 1 Peter 2:9–10

First Peter 2:9–10 affirms this interpretation of Israel's priestly mission and connects it to NT believers. Like the people gathered at Mount Sinai, Peter's readers probably included both Jews and Gentiles.[17] The apostle calls them to godly living under persecution (1:1–25). He tells them to put away malice, deceit, hypocrisy, and envy in favor of the pure milk of God's word (2:1–3). He reminds them that though they are "rejected by men" (v. 4), God is building them into a "holy priesthood to offer spiritual sacrifices acceptable to God through Jesus Christ" (v. 5). Others stumble over Jesus, the cornerstone of their faith, because they disobey God's word (vv. 6–8). Peter's readers do not.

To contrast his readers and those who reject Jesus, Peter uses several OT passages in 2:9–10. First, he tells them they are "a chosen race," probably citing Isa 43:20,[18] a passage that highlights God's deliverance of his people from trouble and exile, and "a royal priesthood a holy nation" (1 Pet 2:9), citing Exod 19:6. Like their predecessors, their election by God is for the purpose of serving God. Second, Peter states they are "a people for His possession," a concept found in Exod 19:5; Isa 43:21; and Mal 3:17. These passages describe Israel as a separated covenant people

---

[14] Graeme Goldsworthy, *According to Plan: The Unfolding Revelation of God in the Bible, An Introduction to Biblical Theology* (Downers Grove: InterVarsity, 1991), 141. See also Dumbrell, *The Search for Order*, 45–46; Zimmerli, *Old Testament Theology in Outline*, 45; and Walter Brueggemann, *Theology of the Old Testament: Testimony, Dispute, Advocacy* (Minneapolis: Fortress, 1997), 431.

[15] Goldsworthy, *According to Plan*, 141.

[16] For a summary of these priestly activities, see Routledge, *Old Testament Theology*, 180–85.

[17] See Thomas R. Schreiner, *1, 2 Peter, Jude*, NAC (Nashville: B&H, 2003), 37–41.

[18] Alan M. Stibbs, *The First Epistle General of Peter: A Commentary* (London: Tyndale, 1959), 103.

serving as God's witnesses among the nations.[19] Third, Peter writes that their mission is to "proclaim the praises of the One who called you out of darkness into His marvelous light." Here he cites Isa 43:21 (or perhaps Isa 42:12) and Gen 1:1–3 to tie his readers to Israel's mission and to God's new creation work in the world through Jesus Christ.[20] Paul includes similar "light from darkness" and new creation imagery in 2 Corinthians 4–5 and Gal 6:17. Fourth, in 2:10, Peter cites Hos 1:6–10 and 2:23 when he observes his readers were once not a people and without mercy. In Hosea both Israelites and non-Israelites are included in this imagery,[21] so Peter and Paul (see Rom 9:25–26) have reason to cite this passage when addressing Jews and Gentiles serving Christ together.

God's Enduring Character and the Enduring Mission of God's People: Exodus 34:6–7

Exodus 34:6–7 occurs after the sordid golden calf incident, when Israel breaks its covenant with Yahweh after mere weeks (contrast Exod 24:1–8 and 32:1–35). If anything could revoke the people's priestly status and mission, surely this sorry episode would. But God's character does not allow this to occur. After sustained intercession by Moses in Exod 33:1–17, Yahweh starts over with the people. This act of grace makes Moses want to know more about Yahweh (vv. 18–23). Yahweh agrees yet does not grant Moses' request to experience his full presence (vv. 18–23).

Yahweh explains his character through several key phrases in 34:6–7.[22] He is "gracious and merciful" (v. 6).[23] These conjoined terms[24] reflect Yahweh's parental kindness (see 1 Kgs 3:26). They also demonstrate his

---

[19] Ibid., 104.

[20] See Beale, *A New Testament Biblical Theology*, 741, and Schreiner, *1, 2 Peter, Jude*, 116.

[21] This is not the majority opinion on Hosea 1–2. I think Hos 1:6–10 deals with northern Israel's estrangement from Yahweh. Their renewal in 2:21–23 is set within a renewal of heaven and earth, however, which I take to mean that all peoples will be included in their renewal, as is the case in Isaiah 65–66; Amos 9:11–15; and Zeph 3:9–20.

[22] On the importance of Exod 34:6–7 for biblical theology and systematic theology, see House, "God's Character and the Wholeness of Scripture," 4–17; and Graham A. Cole, "Exodus 34, the Middoth and the Doctrine of God: The Importance of Biblical Theology to Evangelical Systematic Theology," *SBJT* 12, no. 3 (Fall 2008): 24–37.

[23] The translations of Exod 34:6–7 in the following exposition are the author's.

[24] According to Mike Butterworth, the terms appear together eleven times in the OT. Thus, they form a liturgical formula based on common understandings of the two words. See his "*rhm*," in *NIDOTTE* 3:1094.

tendency to show mercy like a kind king,[25] or like someone who shows benevolence to the poor,[26] respectively. Furthermore, he is "slow to anger" and multiplies loyal, covenant-type[27] love and faithfulness (34:6). He is not quick to discipline his people, regardless of how it may seem to them. This slowness to anger amplifies his resolve to make covenants successful by patiently maintaining his end of the relationship. Because of his determination to fulfill his purposes, he does not allow any covenant he makes to fail. His integrity (loyal, covenant-type love) and always-reliable[28] truthfulness (faithfulness) pervade all his actions. Indeed, he is always in the process of "keeping loyal covenant love for thousands" (v. 7), which Deut 7:9–10 indicates most likely refers to thousands of generations.[29]

In Exod 34:7 Yahweh relates why he displays this type of character. It allows him to be ever "forgiving [or, "bearing with"] iniquity and transgression and sin." To explain *what* he is constantly "forgiving," or "bearing with," Yahweh mentions three specific words that help define sin in the OT.[30] These three words appear together thirteen times in the OT,[31] so placing them together is a fairly common way of expressing sin's totality. First, Yahweh forgives "iniquity" (*awon*). This word basically expresses the conscious twisting of a personality, idea, or thing.[32] Second, he forgives "transgression" (*pesa*), a word that describes rebellion against Yahweh that "breaks with him, takes away what is his, robs, embezzles, misappropriates it."[33] Third, Yahweh forgives "sin," a word that means

---

[25] See H. J. Stoebe, "*hnn*," *TLOT* 1:442–43.

[26] Robert C. Dentan, "The Literary Affinities of Exodus 34:6f," *VT* 13 (1963): 42.

[27] Not every instance of this word occurs in a covenantal context, as Dentan ("Literary Affinities," 42) observes. However, the covenant context is a strong component of the word's usage, so it is likely that passages that are not specifically covenantal in context have something like "covenant-type" love or commitment in mind.

[28] Nahum Sarna states that this word "encompasses reliability, durability, and faithfulness." See *Exodus*, 216.

[29] See Michael Fishbane, *Biblical Interpretation in Ancient Israel* (Oxford: Clarendon Press, 1988), 343.

[30] For a discussion of these three terms as foundational to the problem of sin in the Old Testament, see T. V. Farris, *Mighty to Save: A Study in Old Testament Soteriology* (Nashville: Broadman Press, 1993), 120–39; and Ludwig Kohler, *Old Testament Theology*, trans. A. S. Todd (Philadelphia: Westminster, 1957), 169–71.

[31] Alex Luc, "*awon*," in *NIDOTTE* 3:351.

[32] Rolf Knierim, "*awon*," *TLOT* 2:863–64.

[33] Rolf Knierim, "*pesa*," *TLOT* 2:1036.

"missing a goal" (*ht'*).[34] So Yahweh's compassionate and merciful nature means he must always be forgiving of the twisting of his words, of the breaching of his trust, and of the missing of his good goals. In context, these terms must be defined in light of Yahweh's covenant loyalty. By Exod 34:1–9, he has been faithful to his covenant with Abraham, Isaac, and Jacob long after they have died (see 2:23–25). He has also kept his promises to the current generation of Israelites (3:13–18).

God's forgiving nature does not mean he is unjust or indifferent toward sin, for he "will by no means clear the guilty, visiting the iniquity of the fathers on the children and the children's children, to the third and fourth generation" (34:7). Based on Exod 20:4–5, the successive generations mentioned here "hate" Yahweh. Thus, this text does not mean God punishes persons who have not sinned (see Ezek 18:17). Rather, it describes him punishing sin as long as it occurs.

God's words to Moses are not only for Moses. God commands him to write them (Exod 34:27) so that the forgiven people may know them. Though Moses pens the words, they are God's. They communicate the character of the One who gives them, as words always do. Thus, these words are personal, relational, faithful, and true. Their message is grace, forgiveness, and justice.

The use of Exod 34:6–7 in Numbers, Nehemiah, Psalms, Joel, Jonah, Micah, and other books reveals that OT writers depend on these characteristics of God when they ask forgiveness, praise God's goodness, and seek to be his people in new situations.[35] His character guarantees the covenant people's ongoing identity and mission. They are God's people "because God called them and . . . the ground of this call is to be found solely in God's character of love, justice, and mercy."[36]

Synthesis

These passages lead us to five key observations about God's people.

First, they are God's people because God seeks, redeems, and gathers them. God always finds his people. They do not take the first step to find him. According to Exod 19:1–6, Yahweh has delivered, protected,

---

[34] Rolf Knierim, "*ht'*," *TLOT* 1:406–11.

[35] See House, "God's Character and the Wholeness of Scripture," for usages in subsequent texts.

[36] D. B. Knox, *Selected Works, Volume Two: Church and Ministry* (Sydney: Mathias Media, 2003), 11.

and gathered the people Moses addresses. He has done these things because of the covenant he made with Abraham, Isaac, and Jacob through his initiative and power.[37] Similarly, 1 Pet 2:1–12 reveals that Jesus has delivered and united the apostle's readers.

Second, God's people consist of individuals gathered as a visible community from more than one ethnic background. God's deliverance and their reception of his covenant unite them. Abraham's descendants are chosen to carry God's blessings to the world, but they are not the only people God cares about.

Third, these passages stress God's reasonable relational expectations of his people. They must be holy, that is, set apart for his purposes, as he has set himself apart for them. Their fidelity to God's words reflects the relationship Yahweh has established with them through his redemptive acts and promises. Their obedience based on faith and hope does not create the relationship. Exodus 34:6–7 shows that God knows their weaknesses; he recognizes that they sin. Amazingly, he forgives and starts fresh with them, and will do so repeatedly.

Fourth, these texts do not treat the OT and NT people as two different entities. Nor do they treat the former group as a failed attempt at having a people and the latter group as a more successful attempt on God's part. Rather, 1 Pet 2:9–10 treats both Jews and Gentiles as natural successors to the people in Exodus. Jewish and Gentile OT and NT believers are inextricably linked parts of God's redemptive story.

Fifth, the success of God's people ultimately depends on God. Exodus 34:6–7 presents God as unyieldingly faithful and unbelievably tenacious where his word, covenant, and people are concerned. If Israel's individual and corporate dalliances with idolatry could have ended the covenants with Noah, Abraham, Isaac, Jacob, and David, they would have. But they cannot. If sin, heresy, divisions, greed, and cowardice could end the new covenant, they would. But they cannot. God's creating power, covenant fidelity, and unwavering determination to forge a people guarantee that his word—including his word about his people—will never fail. God's chosen nation "derive(s) its character not from its membership, but from its Head, not from those who join it but from Him who calls it into being.

---

[37] See the section on the Law below for further discussion of this covenant.

It is God's gathering."[38] All covenants need the Messiah in promise and fulfillment to succeed, and God's provision of Jesus the Christ safeguards the success of every covenant God has ever made.

Foundations of God's Walk with His People: The Law

The Law lays the foundation of a biblical understanding of God's people by displaying his desire for a close, loving relationship with men and women. God creates human beings in his image (Gen 1:26–31). This means human beings can have a meaningful relationship with God and one another (2:8–25). It also means they can reflect at "a creaturely level the holy ways of God."[39] The concept of God "walking with" people is one way these books describe this divine-human relationship. This is an evocative, enduring image.

God's Unfettered Walk with His People: Genesis 2:8–3:8

It is hard to imagine a more ideal scene than Gen 2:8–25. God places the first man and woman in a flawless setting (vv. 8–14). He gives them simple and limited standards to follow (vv. 15–18). They enjoy a full and uninhibited relationship with one another (vv. 19–25). These verses are as tantalizing as they are brief, for the situation changes drastically in the next chapter, leaving readers to wonder what might have been.

This perfect situation includes God's free relationship with Adam and Eve. According to 3:8, he walks with them and calls out to them. In short, he enjoys unfettered fellowship with them.[40] The sin described in 3:1–7 and its consequences noted in vv. 14–21 interrupt this fellowship. Adam and Eve must leave their home (vv. 22–24), the place where God walks, trusting God's plans for redemption through Eve's offspring (see v. 15). God still cares for them and speaks with them, and they call on him (v. 21; 4:25–26). He finds his people.

---

[38] Lesslie Newbigin, *The Household of God: Lectures on the Nature of the Church* (New York: Friendship Press, 1954), 21.

[39] James I. Packer, *Concise Theology: A Guide to Historic Christian Belief* (Wheaton: Tyndale, 1993), 71.

[40] Kenneth A. Mathews, *Genesis 1–11:26*, NAC (Nashville: B&H, 1996), 239.

God's Uninterrupted Walk with Enoch: Genesis 5:21–24

Despite Gen 3:1–7, walking with God remains possible because of God's grace. In the middle of the genealogy in 5:1–32, exceptional verses appear. The passage begins by listing six men, noting their ages when they fathered particular sons, and stating their ages at death. But the information about the seventh man, Enoch, follows a different pattern. Instead of stating only his lifespan after fathering a notable son, 5:22 declares, "After the birth of Methuselah, Enoch walked with God 300 years." Gordon Wenham believes "the phrase suggests a special intimacy with God and a life of piety. This is not to say that the other antediluvians mentioned in this chapter were godless: they all represent the chosen line of Seth and include Enosh and Noah as well. The double repetition of the phrase 'walks with God' indicates Enoch was outstanding in this pious family."[41]

Furthermore, instead of noting when he died, 5:24 reveals, "Enoch walked with God; and he was not there, because God took him." Though many ideas about Enoch have been offered through the centuries,[42] the passage indicates that Enoch did not die (Heb 11:5).

Enoch's walking with God reveals four important realities. First, as noted above, the ability to relate closely to God had not ceased. Second, his walk with God was consistent; it lasted at least 300 years. Third, the end of life on earth did not end this close relationship.[43] Fourth, God took the initiative in concluding Enoch's time on earth. This may imply that God took the initiative to start the relationship with Enoch, as he did with Adam and Eve.[44]

God's Creation-Redeeming Walk with Noah: Genesis 6:9

Genesis 6:1–7 records increasing violence and corruption. So God determines to cleanse the world by a flood. Yet one man, Noah, "found favor in the eyes of the LORD" (v. 8). As Kenneth Mathews explains: "This does not mean that Noah's character automatically secures divine favor, for God is under no obligation to bestow his favor. It presupposes a relationship. The proper emphasis . . . is God's gracious favor, just as we see his

---

[41] Gordon J. Wenham, *Genesis 1–15*, WBC 1 (Waco: Word, 1987), 127.

[42] For a summary of some of these, see Mathews, *Genesis 1–11:26*, 313–15; and Wenham, *Genesis 1–15*, 128.

[43] On this point see Deryck Sheriffs, *The Friendship of the Lord: An Old Testament Spirituality* (Carlisle: Paternoster, 1996), 32–33.

[44] Ibid., 33.

preservation of the human family in chapters 1–11 despite human sin."[45] Rolf Rendtorff adds, "The most important thing . . . is that the covenant is always at God's behest and on his initiative."[46]

Noah responds to God's grace appropriately. Genesis 6:9 states, "Noah was a righteous man, blameless among his contemporaries." In short, "Noah walked with God" (9c). Like Enoch, Noah walked with God in a sinful world because he received God's initiating grace by faith and obeyed God's covenant standards in his generation. God's walking with Noah endured in the midst of universal human failure. Because of their relationship, God tells Noah of his plans to destroy the world (vv. 11–17).

God also promises to "establish My covenant with you" (6:18), thereby saving Noah and his family. From this point on Scripture increasingly uses the term "covenant." As Scott Hafemann writes, "Scripture testifies to one, constant relationship between God and his people throughout redemptive history that is formalized and embodied in its successive covenants."[47] A covenant reflects, formalizes, and orders an existing relationship. At its heart a covenant is "a promise given under oath, accompanied by stipulations and sealed with a sign. The covenant binds parties together, and so is sometimes thought of as a league or agreement. . . . But the chief element, without which it could not be thought of as a covenant at all, is the promise."[48] Paul R. Williamson links the relational and promissory aspects of covenant. He defines a divine-human covenant as "the solemn ratification of an existing elective relationship involving promises or obligations that are sealed with an oath."[49] God's saving act on behalf of Noah, his family, the animals, and the human race will perpetuate the human race in a cleansed world (6:18). This covenant is therefore in continuity with God's previous creating work.[50] Noah believes God, so at

---

[45] Mathews, *Genesis 1–11:26*, 346.

[46] Rendtorff, *The Canonical Hebrew Bible*, 433.

[47] Scott J. Hafemann, "The Covenant Relationship," in *Central Themes in Biblical Theology: Mapping Unity in Diversity*, ed. Scott J. Hafemann and Paul R. House (Nottingham: Apollos; Grand Rapids: InterVarsity, 2007), 30.

[48] Peter Jensen, *The Revelation of God*, Contours of Christian Theology (Downers Grove: InterVarsity, 2002), 75.

[49] Paul R. Williamson, *Sealed with an Oath: Covenant in God's Unfolding Purpose*, NSBT (Downers Grove: InterVarsity, 2007), 43.

[50] Dumbrell, *Covenant and Creation*, 20–26; Scott W. Hahn, *Kinship by Covenant: A Canonical Approach to the Fulfillment of God's Saving Promises*, The Anchor Yale Bible Reference Library (New Haven: Yale University Press, 2009), 95–100.

God's command he builds a boat (vv. 18–22; see Heb 11:7). By faith he meets the obligations the covenant places on him.

When the flood ends, God establishes his covenant with all creation through Noah (8:20–9:17). He pledges never to destroy the world by flood again, but he holds humans accountable for perpetuating violence. Scott Hahn believes God's covenant with Noah is a "grant covenant," one of the three major types in ancient times.[51] In such covenants the "obligations of the covenant rest predominantly with the superior party, who freely accepts responsibilities toward the inferior, usually in response to the inferior's faithfulness or other meritorious qualities."[52] The lesser party's conduct is not the basis of the covenant, however, for the "initiative in establishing a covenant of this form also rests with the superior; it is generally *granted* as a reward to a faithful vassal or servant—thus the name."[53]

God's walk with Noah redeems all humanity and all creation. It begins with God's grace and culminates in God's covenant with Noah and creation. God's covenant saves his people and thereby preserves his relationship with humanity. God's covenant with creation through Noah secures the order of nature, and it reemphasizes human responsibility within that order. As Goldsworthy writes, "In both these covenant statements God makes the first move and establishes a relationship for the good of the creation. . . . God is refusing to allow human rebellion to divert him from his purpose to create a people to be *his* people in a perfect universe."[54] Noah's life indicates once again that God always finds his people, and they walk with him.

God's Humanity-Blessing Walk with Abraham: Genesis 12; 15; and 17

After God makes his covenant with Noah, sin does not cease. Noah, his descendants, and their descendants rebel against God (Gen 9:18–11:9). Then another genealogy introduces Abram (11:10–26), whom God commands to walk with him in 17:1. God forges a remarkable bond with Abram through covenant promises and personal faithfulness. Through this man Isaiah later calls God's friend (Isa 41:8), God will bless all peoples (Gen 12:1–9), eventually defeating sin through his descendant,

---

[51] Hahn, *Kinship by Covenant*, 29.
[52] Ibid.
[53] Ibid.
[54] Goldsworthy, *According to Plan*, 115.

Jesus the Christ (Matt 1:1–17). Thus, God's walk with Abram will benefit humanity, not only Abram's expanding family.

Genesis 12:1–9 recounts Yahweh's commands to Abram before he journeys to Canaan (v. 1; see 11:31–32) and Abram's response. God tells him to leave his homeland for a place God will show him (12:1). He prompts Abram's obedience[55] through the following promises:

> I will make of you a great nation,
> and I will bless you
> and make your name great,
> so that you will be a blessing.
> I will bless those who bless you,
> and him who dishonors you I will curse,
> and in you all the families of the earth
> shall be blessed. (12:2–3 ESV)

Abram believes God and goes. Once Abram reaches Canaan, God reveals that it is the land Abram's offspring will inhabit (12:7). These promises provide the foundation for the family that will become Israel, for God's protection of this family as it grows, and for the role this family will fulfill on behalf of the world's families.

Abram's walk with God by faith includes many treacherous paths. Besides enduring famine (12:10–20), separation from family (13:1–13), and military battles (14:1–16), Abram has no heir by chapter 15. He has also shown himself prone to self-serving cowardice (12:10–20). God reassures him by repeating his promises (13:14–18), protecting Abram (14:1–16), and providing fellowship with other Yahweh followers (vv. 17–20).

In 15:4–5, God again promises Abram a child. This time Abram wonders whether the promise will ever be fulfilled. When God renews the promise (vv. 4–5), Abram "believed the LORD, and He credited it to him as righteousness" (v. 6). The relationship reconfirmed by faith, God makes a covenant with Abram anchored in God's previous redemption of Abram (v. 7), promising to give Canaan to his descendants (vv. 12–21). As with the covenant made with Noah, this is a grant-type covenant. Because of his grace, God takes the initiative to promise his faithful

---

[55] Scott J. Hafemann ("The Covenant Relationship," in Hafemann and House, *Central Themes in Biblical Theology*, 44) rightly observes, "Abraham's faith is expressed in his actions."

servant Abram land and enough children to fill that land.[56] Because of
God's patience with the Amorites' sins (v. 16), Abram's descendants may
not have Canaan for 400 years (vv. 13–16).

Years later, God approaches Abram and declares, "I am God
Almighty. Live in My presence and be devout. I will establish My
covenant between Me and you, and I will multiply you greatly"
(17:1–2). Clyde T. Francisco notes that the word translated "devout" or
"blameless" means "complete, mature. It does not imply moral perfection
but a wholehearted devotion to God (see Deut 18:13). . . . Abraham is
challenged to give himself to the service of God without reservation."[57]
God pledges to make him the father of many nations, not just the
father of a single clan. Thus, God changes his name (Gen 17:3–5) from
Abram ("exalted father") to Abraham ("father of many nations"). He also
promises to continue the covenant with Abraham's offspring "throughout
their generations, as an everlasting covenant to be your God and the God
of your offspring after you" (v. 7).

To seal the covenant, God requires that Abraham and the males
in his household be circumcised (17:9–14). All comply. The covenant is
made with Abraham and his offspring, yet from the start this covenant
is not simply with them. Those joined to Abraham's family are treated
as his family. By accepting circumcision, the males represent the female
members of the household. Sarah and Hagar (see 16:1–14; 21:8–21) also
know and walk with God as they walk with Abraham. All may walk with
God and be blameless by faith in God's promises. Thus, God's covenant
with creation through Noah and God's covenant with Abraham to bless
the world are like parts of a growing single covenant.[58]

Abraham's journey does not end in Genesis 17. He finally receives
the son God promised (21:1–7), and God proves Abraham's faith yet
again (22:1–12). Ultimately, God keeps all his promises to his friend,
who lives by faith, albeit an imperfect faith, to the day he dies (25:1–11).
When he dies, Abraham's household has a covenant sign of obedience,
an heir to carry on Abraham's role, several persons outside Abraham's

---

[56] Hahn, *Kinship by Covenant*, 112–14.

[57] Clyde T. Francisco, "Genesis," *The Broadman Bible Commentary: Volume One,
Revised* (Nashville: Broadman Press, 1973), 170.

[58] On the interconnectedness of these covenants, see John H. Walton, *Covenant,
God's Purpose, God's Plan* (Grand Rapids: Zondervan, 1994), 44–49; Dumbrell,
Covenant and Creation, 73; and Hahn, *Kinship by Covenant*, 105–7.

bloodline as participants, and a history of God's preservation. They gather for ceremonies such as circumcision, and they relate to God individually through prayer. The individual and corporate nature of God's people has emerged, as have the people's liturgical and ethical functions in the world they bless.

God's Priest-Building Walk with Israel: Leviticus 26 and Deuteronomy 28

When Exodus ends, God's people have taken many strides in their walk with him. They have gone to Egypt and been delivered from slavery (Genesis 37–Exodus 15). Non-Israelites and Israelites (Exod 12:38) have journeyed through the desert and gathered at Sinai to receive God's instructions (chaps. 16–18). God has given them their mission to be a kingdom of priests (19:5–6). God has delivered commands and case laws to them (chaps. 20–24). They have betrayed their mission (32:1–6), yet God renews his walk with them (34:1–27; see v. 9). His character determines their future, for he will always find them. Renewed, they build the tabernacle, representing God's presence among them (40:34–38; see 29:45).

The rest of the Law focuses on God's preparation of Israel to be priests for the sake of the world he created. It does so by continuing to reveal his covenant standards. This growing covenant is based on God's grant-type treaty with Abraham, for these are his offspring. Yet God also incorporates covenant elements found in the major vassal treaty form in the second millennium BC. This treaty type, the Hittite Vassal treaty, was made between two nations, a greater and a lesser. It had several parts: introduction of the covenant parties, summary of past relationship, specific stipulations, general stipulations, benefits (blessings) for keeping the covenant and consequences (curses) for breaking the covenant, and oaths to keep the covenant.[59] The "blessings and curses" segment summarizes the covenant's promises, requirements, and ramifications. Therefore, this section of the chapter will discuss Leviticus 26 and Deuteronomy 28,

---

[59] The literature on this subject is vast. Experts do not agree on the specific portions of this treaty form used in the Bible, but experts representing many different theological traditions agree that some parts of the form appear. Deuteronomy is the clearest case of use of the Hittite Vassal treaty form. See Meredith Kline, *Treaty of the Great King* (Grand Rapids: Eerdmans, 1963); P. C. Craigie, *The Book of Deuteronomy*, NICOT (Grand Rapids: Eerdmans, 1976); and Kenneth A. Kitchen, "The Fall and Rise of Covenant, Law, and Treaty," *TynBul* 40 (1989): 118–35.

passages that contain the blessings and curses segment of the covenant offered to the first and second generations of Israelites after the exodus.

God's Walk with His Priestly People: Leviticus 26

Leviticus stresses that Israel is a priestly people. It sets apart a tribe of priests (the Levites) to help it make sacrifices at the tabernacle (Leviticus 1–10) and to teach it the difference between what is clean and unclean (chaps. 11–15). Yet all the people are set apart, "holy," as Exod 19:5–6 has stated. The reason they are to be holy is that their God is holy (Lev 11:44). As a holy people, they are blessed with regular avenues for repentance and renewed relationship with God through prayer and sacrifice (Leviticus 1–10). God also offers them a fresh start each year through the Day of Atonement sacrifices (chap. 16). Individual and group holiness extends beyond liturgical observance. It embraces all of daily life. Holy living includes sexual integrity (chap. 18), unswerving love for neighbors and strangers (chap. 19), gathering as one people to worship God (chap. 23), and extending rest to land, people, and the economy (chap. 25).

This kind of community existing in the heart of the ancient world would certainly draw attention to God. Their family-like treatment of strangers would highlight God's love for all. Their location on major trade routes had the potential to spread God's fame throughout the world. The priestly nation would thereby bless all nations. It would be a physical sign of God's universal kingdom.

Leviticus 26:1–13 promises several benefits Israel will experience if it lives in the manner chaps. 1–25 describe. The chief blessing is that God promises, "I will walk among you and be your God, and you will be My people" (26:12). This promise is based solely on God's grace, for God reminds them: "I am the LORD your God, who brought you out of the land of Egypt, so that you would no longer be their slaves. I broke the bars of your yoke, and enabled you to live in freedom" (v. 13). Just as God walked with Adam and Eve, Noah, and Abraham, he will walk with them. This means they will be a blessed people and will be a blessing to others. But the chief blessing is God's presence. Knowing him surpasses all other benefits.

Leviticus 26:14–39 describes what will occur if they do not walk with God. If they "act with hostility" against God (v. 21), he will discipline them to bring them back to their walk with him (vv. 14–22). If this discipline does not work and they continue to walk contrary to his word, they will experience a set of punishments that culminate in exile (vv. 23–39). The people can turn from their errant ways at any point. Loss of the land is not inevitable. They can regain the priestly mission.

Leviticus 26:40–45 promises that even if exile occurs, this is not the end. He will find them, and the people can walk with God again. The covenant is not initiated by them or sustained by them but by the redeeming and reforming grace of God, whose character guarantees the people and the covenant's future. They did not create the covenant, and they cannot end it. If they confess their contrary ways, God will forgive and restore them (vv. 40–42) for Abraham's sake. The God who led them from bondage can do so again (vv. 44–45).

God's Walk with His Beloved People: Deuteronomy 28

Deuteronomy emphasizes God's love. After describing the past to the second generation of Israelites (Deuteronomy 1–4), Moses reiterates that the Ten Commandments are the basic covenant stipulations Israel must obey (5:6–21; cf. Exod 20:1–17). He then calls the people to love their God with heart, soul, and strength and to teach his ways to their children (Deut 6:4–9). Moses declares that such love is the proper response to God, for he loved them first (7:6–11) by redeeming them in Egypt and in the desert. God expects his love to prompt their love. So Moses asks, "And now, Israel, what does the LORD your God ask of you except to fear the LORD your God by walking in all His ways, to love Him, and to worship the LORD your God with all your heart and all your soul? Keep the LORD's commands and statutes I am giving you today, for your own good" (10:12–13). Mutual love will lead to a long and fruitful walk together.

Just as Leviticus 26 did for the first generation, Deuteronomy 28 states the benefits of keeping and the consequences of breaking the covenant. Faithfulness to God will result in their needs being met and in respect among the nations (vv. 1–14). The key to fruitful life is serving Yahweh, not walking after other gods (v. 14). But the reverse will be true if they rebel. God will discipline them through many means to cause them to repent (vv. 15–51). If they do not change, their children will walk into exile (vv. 41, 52–68). Walking after other gods and the sins that accompany worshipping them will lead to a long walk out of the land.

As in Lev 26:40–45, richly deserved exile does not end God's covenant. According to Deut 30:1–10, in exile the people will realize their error and repent, and God will bring them back to the land. Deuteronomy 30:15–16 adds that God sets before them life and death. Echoing 10:12–13, Moses states that love of God and walking in his ways are the key to life. God loves and walks with his people. He delights to meet their needs and stands ready to restore them when they rebel. People such as Moses who love God find that he has not changed since he walked with Adam and Eve, Enoch, Noah, and Abraham. He still provides, corrects, and forgives.

Synthesis

The Law is foundational for the rest of the OT, revealing truths that provide a starting point for further canonical theology.

First, preserving a people for himself has been part of God's mission ever since the fall. He created people for relationship and shared work (Gen 1:26–31; 2:8–25), in short, to walk with him.[60] When Adam and Eve sinned, God moved quickly to forgive and redeem them through protection and promise (3:15–24). They responded by calling on him (4:1–7, 25–26). Enoch responded by walking with him closely (5:21–24).

Second, God has been redeeming a people for himself from the earth's nations since the days of Noah and Abraham. His chief way of relating to them was through what he called "my covenant." His character anchored his covenant, which included promises that required faith and responsibilities that required obedience born of faith. His covenant was the means of redeeming creation in Noah's time and the means of beginning to redeem humanity in Abraham's time. When Abraham died, the covenant people included both his growing blood-related family and persons unrelated to him by blood. These people existed to serve the Creator and to help those he made.

Third, since Moses' time God has been teaching his people how to demonstrate his greatness to the nations. He uses his covenant to do so. It teaches the people how to treat both one another and strangers, how to incorporate others into their company, and how to regulate a society that reflects God's character. It also provides hope and accountability. People enter into covenant with God by grace through faith, so love, faith, and

---

[60] Graham Cole, "Preaching God's Words and Walking in God's Ways: Scripture, Preaching, and the Ethical Life," in *Serving God's Words: Windows on Preaching and Ministry*, ed. Paul A. Barker, Richard J. Condie, and Andrew S. Malone (Nottingham: InterVarsity, 2011), 135.

hope work together. Loving God (Deut 6:4–9) and walking closely with him (Lev 26:12–13) are the most cherished rewards of God's people.

Fourth, from Genesis onward the people who walk with God have rarely been a majority of the world's population, or even Israel's population. There is always what later texts call a "remnant," a minority that walks with God. Covenant keepers often have to be willing to serve in the face of opposition. The promises of forgiveness after punishment and repentance in Lev 26:40–45 and Deut 30:1–10 prove that God never ceases to forge a people for ministry regardless of how small this minority becomes.

Fifth, from Abraham's time, but particularly from Exodus 19 onward, God's people have gathered to meet with him as one body. Families gather annually for Passover (Exodus 12) and more regularly for instruction (Deut 6:4–9). The nation gathers as one people for three annual festivals (16:1–17) that remind them of God's deliverance, forgiveness, and provision. They are a people of a covenant book, which they hear read every seven years at the Feast of Booths (31:9–10). A priestly tribe exists to aid in annual and daily instruction. They can walk with God both individually and as a group.

Contours of God's Walk with His People: The Prophets

The Prophets[61] depict the contours of God's walk with his people by presenting a millennium of history that highlights the land, the temple, and the priestly witness. They begin with Joshua's conquest of Canaan c. 1400 BC, include the loss of the land c. 587 BC in Jeremiah and Ezekiel, and end in Malachi with some Israelites back in Judah c. 400 BC. They describe the building of the temple in 966 BC in 1 Kings, the destruction of the temple in 587 BC in 2 Kings and Jeremiah, and the rebuilding of the temple in 520–515 BC in Haggai and Zechariah. They mention stalwart representatives of the priestly mission, such as Joshua, Deborah, David, and Elijah, and they decry wicked persons, such as Ahab, Jezebel, and Jeroboam I. They describe the conversions of Rahab and Naaman, both Gentiles (Josh 2:1–24; 2 Kgs 5:1–14), and declare that Yahweh's acts on Israel's behalf are done so the world will know he is God (1 Sam 17:46; 1 Kgs 8:41–43; Mal 1:11).

---

[61] I am following the Hebrew canon, which includes the following books in its Prophets section: Joshua, Judges, 1–2 Samuel, 1–2 Kings, Isaiah, Jeremiah, Ezekiel, and the Book of the Twelve (Minor Prophets).

Their thematic scope is expansive, including the sin, judgment, and renewal of both Israel and the nations. Given the variety of material, there are several valid ways of approaching their contribution to Scripture's portrait of God's people. Nonetheless, it is fair to conclude that the prophetic books highlight the constant need for the forming and reforming of the priestly people's walk with God. It is also fair to conclude that God never stops finding and forming his people, regardless of how far they run from him (Hos 11:1–9). The prophets tell the story of God's undying love for his people shown by his keeping of the covenant promises, just as Leviticus 26 and Deuteronomy 28 and 30 declare. I will attempt to develop this theme of God's covenantal steadfastness by discussing 2 Samuel 7, summarizing Isaiah's main themes, and exploring briefly Jer 31:31–40.

God's Everlasting Walk with David: 2 Samuel 7

By the time the events in 2 Samuel 7 unfold, centuries have passed since Moses' death. Joshua has led Israel to possess the land God promised Abraham. The Israelites have set up a sanctuary in Shiloh (Josh 18:1–3). Levites have been given lands within all the tribes, so they can teach God's word and help God's people throughout the land (21:1–42). However, as Judges reveals, Israel has spent long periods of time rejecting God and its mission as his priests. Nonetheless, God keeps reforming the people.

This redemptive reshaping includes the rise of Israel's monarchy, which fulfilled God's promise to Abraham that his descendants would include kings (Gen 17:6, 16) and reflected Moses' teaching that Israel would eventually have a king (Deut 17:14–20). Though it begins well, the reign of Israel's first king, Saul, ends badly, both religiously and militarily. Israel's second king, David, becomes the catalyst of a new beginning for the priestly people in the holy land. He conquers Jerusalem and establishes it as his capital (2 Sam 5:6–10), receives aid from Tyre's king (vv. 11–12), and defeats Israel's foes (vv. 17–25). He makes Jerusalem the permanent home of the ark of the covenant (6:1–15). God's king now reigns over God's people in God's place. As Grant D. Taylor writes, "David's kingship, therefore, completes the conquest of Canaan . . . thus fulfilling the promise of rest given to Joshua."[62]

---

[62] Grant D. Taylor, "The Abrahamic and Davidic Covenants: God's Messianic Promise for the Nations," unpublished paper, 1.

With the nation at rest, David desires to build a permanent temple for God (7:12) where priests can serve[63] and the people can gather for worship. God responds by telling David that in all the time he has walked with Israel, from the exodus (v. 6) to the era of the judges (v. 7), he has never asked for a house for himself. God notes that he made David king of Israel (v. 8), has been with David wherever he has gone (v. 9), and has defeated all David's enemies (v. 9). Ever the gracious One, he promises to do more. He will make David's name great, give the people David leads rest in the land, and build David a house—that is, a family (vv. 9–11). In short, God gives David virtually the same promises he gave Abraham.[64] Yet God does not stop here. He promises David that a son will follow him on the throne and will build the temple (vv. 12–13). Finally, God tells David his dynasty will endure forever (vv. 13, 16). David will have an everlasting walk with God through his descendants.

David's response to these promises reflects his relationship with God. He thanks God for choosing him, exalting him, and giving him long-term promises (7:18–19). Like Abraham, David recognizes that these promises are not only for Israel. These enduring promises are "a revelation for mankind" (v. 19). As Walter Kaiser writes, "All humanity can profit from what he has just been told about his house/dynasty, kingdom, and throne."[65] He confesses that God's faithfulness honors God's character, not his (vv. 20–21), and he asserts there is no other god (v. 22). He recognizes God's past, present, and future kindnesses to Israel and his family (vv. 23–27). David concludes by affirming that God's word is true and his blessing is with David's household and nation (vv. 28–29).

The promise of an eternal kingdom is the beginning of the Bible's many statements about the Messiah coming from David's lineage. God has kept all his promises to Noah, Abraham, and Israel. Now he extends and expands them through David. The word "covenant" does not appear in 2 Samuel 7, but Ps 89:1–4 declares that Yahweh made a covenant with David at this time. Certainly the elements of a covenant are present. Yet the lack of the word here highlights the continuity with God's prior covenant promises.

---

[63] That is, a place where a selected group of priests can serve. The Levites were still supposed to fulfill their local teaching and helping responsibilities throughout the land.

[64] See Robert P. Gordon, *I–II Samuel* (Grand Rapids: Zondervan, 1986), 238; and Walter C. Kaiser Jr., *The Messiah in the Old Testament,* Studies in Old Testament Biblical Theology (Grand Rapids: Zondervan, 1995), 80.

[65] Kaiser, *The Messiah in the Old Testament,* 81.

Solomon hopes for the fulfillment of Israel's mission when he dedicates the temple. He offers a seven-part prayer based on Leviticus 19 and 26 and Deuteronomy 27–28 and 30.[66] He thanks God for Israel's rest in the land and prays they may be faithful to God's covenant in six of his seven petitions (1 Kgs 8:22–40, 44–53). His fifth petition (vv. 41–43) focuses on other peoples. On such an auspicious occasion, it would be easy for Solomon to pray for only his subjects. Instead, he prays for the foreigner who will come "from a distant land because of Your name" (v. 41). He knows foreigners will hear of Yahweh's great power and come to pray (v. 42). Solomon asks that Yahweh hear their prayers so that "all the people on earth will know Your name, to fear You as your people Israel do" (v. 43). Solomon's prayer clearly reflects God's mission for Abraham's descendants.

God's Present and Future Walk with His People(s): A Summary of Isaiah

Isaiah's magnificent "vision" (Isa 1:1) cannot be exhausted in many volumes, much less a brief section of a chapter. Nonetheless, we can taste his theological breadth on the subject of the identity and mission of God's people. He has trenchant and helpful things to say to his generation (1:2–31; 5:1–30; 7:1–25; etc.), and he agrees with fellow eighth-century prophets Hosea and Amos that Israel and Judah have earned God's disciplining acts. Yet his statements about the future are especially relevant at this point of our discussion.

Stated in outline form, Isaiah envisions a forgiven and cleansed remnant of Israelites and Gentiles (11:1–16; 19:16–25) joined together through God's royal, suffering servant Messiah (7:1–25; 9:1–7; 11:1–16; 42:1–13; 49:1–13; 52:13–53:12). God's people will hail from Israel and the most distant coastlands (41:1–5; 42:12; 49:1; 60:9; 66:19). They will join him in Zion (2:1–5; 4:2–6; 12:1–6; 35:1–10; 65:17–25). They will inhabit a new heaven and earth prepared by God (11:1–9; 65:17–25). Those who refuse God's redemptive message, his gospel (40:9; 41:27; 52:7; 60:6; and 61:1),[67] will face enduring punishment (66:24) from the

---

[66] Comments on 1 Kings 8 are dependent on Paul R. House, *1, 2 Kings*, NAC (Nashville: Broadman, 1995), 141–50.

[67] For a discussion of how the New Testament utilizes these five texts as gospel texts, see C. A. Evans, "From Gospel to Gospel: The Function of Isaiah in the New

God who created the world (40:12–17; 43:1) and rules the nations (6:1–13; 13:1–27:13). Isaiah's vision includes God's covenant activity. It embraces God's promises to Abraham, God's friend (41:8); rejoices in what he did through Moses (63:7–14); and waits expectantly for his promises to David to be fulfilled (7:14; 9:1–7; 11:1–9; 55:3).

Isaiah portrays God as the unstoppable, grace-filled King. He rules the world from his temple (6:1–13), walks on the tops of the mountains (40:3–5), judges nations (13:1–27:13), inexorably brings his people to Zion, defeats sin (53:1–12), and overcomes death (25:6–12; 26:19). He declares that "everyone who is thirsty" (55:1) may "come[68] to Me" and receive "an everlasting covenant with you, the promises assured to David" (v. 3), whom God has made "a leader and commander for the peoples" (v. 4). Nations that do not know him can know him (v. 5). According to 66:18–23, many of them *will* know him. He continues to be the reason his people exist and bless the nations.

God's New Covenant Walk with His People: Explorations in Jeremiah 31:31–40

Jeremiah suffers with Judah as God executes the exile threatened in Lev 26:14–39 and Deut 28:15–68. Indeed, his ministry includes great pain from beginning (Jer 1:17–19; 11:18–20:18) to end (39:1–44:30; 52:1–34). Like Isaiah, he waits for the Messiah to deliver the people from their sin and its consequences (23:1–8; see Deut 30:1–10). God also reveals the promise of a new covenant[69] to him, so this great sufferer becomes the bearer of good news for the future. His proclamations about God's redemption after exile highlight God's determination to secure his people, no matter what happened in the past, just as Deut 30:1–10 promises.

Having declared that in coming days Yahweh will replant Israel and Judah in the land (31:27–30), Jeremiah states that in those days God will

---

Testament," in *Writing and Reading the Scroll of Isaiah: Studies of an Interpretative Tradition: Volume Two*, ed. Craig C. Broyles and C. A. Evans (Leiden: Brill, 1997), 651–91.

[68] The word translated "come" in the HCSB is the standard Hebrew word usually translated "walk."

[69] The exact meaning of the term "new covenant" and its implications has been debated since pre-New Testament times. For a survey of interpretation, see Jack R. Lundbom, *Jeremiah 21–36*, AB 21B (New York: Doubleday, 2004), 472–82.

"make a new covenant with the house of Israel and with the house of Judah" (v. 31), the people he has punished. Scattered as they are, Israel remains the focal point of God's plans for the nations. Next, he writes that this covenant will not be like the one made in Exodus in that it will not be broken (vv. 32–33). It will be kept because he will write the law on the people's hearts (v. 33).[70] Thus, they will be always faithful. In short, all the covenant partners will know him, and he will never remember their sin" (v. 34). God will never cast off the offspring of Israel (35–37) and promises that in coming days the people will have a secure and holy home in God's city (38–40).

God's new covenant people will serve him from their hearts. They will be willing to obey; they will not need external stimuli, such as laws written on tablets, lest they rebel.[71] Thus, they will also not need a priest to teach them.[72] The "most important feature"[73] of this new covenant people is that they will be forgiven; they will not need to offer sacrifices.[74] They will be secure in Zion; they will never again face exile. The new covenant begins with the same God and the same descendants of Abraham, yet they will be willing, informed, obedient, and safe without the aid of a human priest, teacher, prophet, or king. They only need Yahweh and the Davidic Messiah (23:1–8; 33:14–16). As William J. Dumbrell writes, this prophecy "points us beyond present human experience to the perfected, unfettered fellowship of the new creation, to the time when tensions within human experience have finally been overcome."[75]

Synthesis

It is easy to miss God's reforming purposes as one reads the many prophetic denunciations of sin and the several threats and descriptions of

---

[70] For a discussion of this changed heart, see Hafemann, "The Covenant Relationship," in Hafemann and House, *Central Themes in Biblical Theology*, 51.

[71] Ronald E. Clements, *Jeremiah*, IBC (Atlanta: John Knox, 1988), 191.

[72] Elmer A. Martens, "Jeremiah," in Larry Walker and Martens, *Isaiah, Jeremiah, and Lamentations*, Cornerstone Biblical Commentary, ed. Philip W. Comfort (Wheaton: Tyndale, 2005), 455–56.

[73] Lundbom, *Jeremiah 21–36*, 471.

[74] Martens, "Jeremiah," in Comfort, *Isaiah, Jeremiah, and Lamentations*, 456.

[75] William J. Dumbrell, *The Faith of Israel: A Theological Survey of the Old Testament*, 2nd ed. (Grand Rapids: Baker, 2002), 147.

exile. Yet the prophets highlight God's indomitable will to begin fresh with Israel and the nations and to bring those who believe in him to Zion. At least four points deserve mention.

First, 2 Sam 7:1–29 places David's household at the center of God's covenantal redemptive work. Isaiah, Jeremiah, Ezekiel, and several of the Minor Prophets highlight David's greatest heir. Matthew, Mark, Luke, John, Paul, James, and Jude do as well. Redemption for Israel and salvation for Gentiles comes through a Jewish Messiah. God's promises to David continue God's redemptive work begun through Noah, Abraham, and Moses.

Second, Isaiah looks forward to the Davidic heir and to the permanent new creation God will provide for his multinational people (Isa 11:1–16; 65:17–66:24), as does 2 Cor 4:16–18 and Rev 21:1–8. Isaiah and Paul believe that Jews and Gentiles will inhabit this place. Those who serve God share him to the ends of the earth (Isa 56:1–8; 66:18–24). They are new creation servants of Yahweh and the suffering Messiah.

Third, Luke, Paul, and the writer of Hebrews emphasize the new covenant in Jer 31:31–34. At the Last Supper, Jesus informs his disciples that the wine in the cup represents his blood, the blood of the new covenant (Luke 22:20). Jesus initiates this covenant by merging Passover with an even greater event, his death on the cross. He makes the crucifixion rather than the Passover the focal point, yet without obliterating the significance of Passover. What has been fulfilled is not forgotten or declared irrelevant but becomes part of something greater, something long anticipated. Paul says believers celebrate the new covenant as they take Communion (1 Cor 11:23–26). Hebrews 8:1–12 quotes Jer 31:31–34 in a discussion of the superiority of Christ's blood over all previous sacrifices, Christ's priesthood as superior to the previous priesthood, and Christ's covenant as the final covenant. Christ is superior because he fulfills all these, not because they were faulty. All the covenantal work God has done reaches its completion in Jesus.

What does this mean for the identity and the mission of God's people? Jesus' words in Luke 22:20 are given to the Jewish disciples he chose. These disciples become his apostles to the world, thus continuing Israel's mission to the nations with the climactic news that the Messiah has come to save sinners from judgment (Matt 28:16–20; Acts 1:1–8). Jesus begins the covenant as Jeremiah predicted, with the house of Israel.

Paul shares Isaiah's vision of Jews and Gentiles serving as God's servants. A Jew, Paul writes to primarily Gentile churches, so the Jewish-led apostolic ministry has been successful. Yet Paul never forgets he is Jewish or the need for evangelizing Jewish persons (see Romans 9–11). He also strives mightily to keep Gentile believers aware of what they owe to Jewish believers (see 2 Corinthians 9).

The writer of Hebrews exhorts a primarily Jewish audience to recall the great promises Jesus fulfills. They must not return to the earlier days that awaited the fulfillment of promises. Those days have grown old and are heading toward their natural end.[76] Soon enough they will be completely gathered into God's continuing covenant faithfulness (Heb 8:13).[77] Like Christians, the old facets of the covenant are dying, to be transformed in the age to come. Seen this way, the old covenant is weak like an old person, and one shows respect for the aged. Nonetheless, it is time to embrace and anticipate the new things God has done, as the believers described in Hebrews 11 did in their day.

Jesus' kingdom has indeed begun, although Luke, Paul, and the author of Hebrews all promise a greater day. All God's people are not yet safe in God's city, the place where everyone knows God through the Messiah. God's mission to the world continues until then. His people have his Spirit in them, teaching them (John 14–17; Eph 1:3–14). But he still sends the gift of pastor-teachers to his church (Eph 4:11). His people are a multiethnic kingdom of priests in the world (1 Pet 2:9–10) who have not all reached Zion but forge ahead, certain of final victory. All that Jesus has inaugurated will be completed in the new heavens and new earth.

Fourth, these passages do not reveal an "Israel vs. the church" dichotomy. They contend that Jewish and Gentile *covenant keepers* are together God's people. Both share the same identity and mission. Each has clear ethnic identity, but these differences ultimately disappear in the body of Christ. These texts do not support a replacement theory in which the church completely supplants Israel as God's people[78] or a

---

[76] For this reading of Heb 8:13, see B. F. Westcott, *The Epistle to the Hebrews: The Greek Text with Notes and Essays*, 3rd ed. (London: Macmillan, 1920), 227.

[77] Hebrews 8:13 is a much-discussed verse, to say the least. For a survey of options consult Peter T. O'Brien, *The Letter to the Hebrews*, PNTC (Grand Rapids: Eerdmans, 2010), 293–303; and David L. Allen, *Hebrews*, NAC (Nashville: B&H, 2010), 444–56.

[78] For a survey of the history of this approach, see Ronald E. Diprose, *Israel and the Church: The Origin and Effects of Replacement Theology* (Milton Keyes, UK: Paternoster,

separate, two-covenant (one for Israel and one for Gentiles) theory. They suggest a unity theory. They teach that God will bless all nations through Abraham. Peoples from the nations will then take up the mission of being a kingdom of priests with those who led them to Christ. Jews and Gentiles will then work together to complete God's mission until Jesus comes again. God will keep his word, and his people will respond as he has declared (Isaiah 65–66; Eph 1:3–14).

Windows on God's Walk with His People: The Writings

The Writings are a diverse grouping of books that have settings ranging from patriarchal to postexilic times. As such, they contain both unique and familiar concepts related to the identity and mission of God's people. The Writings embrace the Law's emphasis on God's people walking with him as priests for his glory among the nations and reflect the Prophets' highlighting of God's reforming his people's walk with him and one another. Readers look through several literary windows to gain glimpses into the lives of God's people through many centuries of worship, wisdom, and suffering.

The Kingdom of Priests and Worship: Psalms, Ezra, Nehemiah, and 1–2 Chronicles

God rules over creation in a gracious and sovereign manner. Because of this, he merits worship by all. In some manner, every book in the Writings underscores these basic principles. Yet perhaps Psalms, Ezra, Nehemiah, and 1–2 Chronicles display them most evidently. These diverse books reflect principles related to God's people and their mission found in the Law and the Prophets.

Psalms opens the Writings on a grand scale and includes every major biblical theme.[79] Psalms 1–3 define God's people as those who have nothing to do with the wicked person's way of life (1:1) but delight in "the LORD's instruction" and meditate on it "day and night" (v. 2).[80] Therefore, his people flourish (v. 3). But the wicked, who do not love him, his word,

---

2004).

[79] See H. J. Kraus, *Theology of the Psalms,* trans. Keith Crim (Minneapolis: Augsburg, 1986); and Geoffrey Grogan, *Prayer, Praise and Prophecy* (Fearn, Scotland: Christian Focus, 2001).

[80] See Gordon J. Wenham, *Psalms as Torah: Reading Biblical Song Ethically,* Studies in Theological Interpretation (Grand Rapids: Baker, 2012).

or his ways, will perish when God judges (vv. 4–6). Furthermore, God's people bow before him and his chosen king, the Messiah, while the wicked rebel (2:1–12). Sadly, they suffer at the hands of the wicked, yet they trust in God regardless (3:1–8). This basic definition never changes in Psalms. Indeed, Psalms 19 and 119 underscore the people's love for Yahweh and his word, while Psalms 110 and 143, to name only two messianic psalms, reinforce the people's commitment to living by faith as they wait for the Messiah; and dozens of laments show his people seeking God's aid.

These identity matters in place, Psalms moves to the book's main focus, the way God's people worship him.[81] In Psalms, and elsewhere in the Bible, worship means bowing down before God the king (95:6), asking for his provision (23:1–6; 95:7), requesting forgiveness of sin (51:1–19), receiving instruction from his word (19; 119), praising him for his character and gifts (8; 103; 150), and living to serve him. God's people worship him individually and corporately (25; 103; 137). The OT indicates that they did so in their cities aided by Levites (2 Chronicles 17), as well as during the great festivals (Deut 16:1–17) at the temple. This worship is not just for Israel, for Israel seeks to draw other nations to God, as Solomon prayed in 1 Kings 8 (see Pss 67:4; 96:3; 117:1).

Ezra, Nehemiah, and 1–2 Chronicles conclude the Writings by moving readers toward Jerusalem and the temple. Ezra recounts Israel's return from exile and first faltering steps back into the land (Ezra 1–5). He then describes temple rebuilding, the renewal of worship at the temple, and the reconstruction of community life (Ezra 7–10). Nehemiah focuses on rebuilding the city of Jerusalem and reestablishing godly worship. In Nehemiah 8–9, Ezra and Nehemiah help lead worship that includes prayer, instruction, and covenant renewal. In 1–2 Chronicles, worship, priestly activity, and the Davidic promise are so prevalent that Scott Hahn aptly calls these books a history of "a liturgical empire."[82]

All these books portray the Israelites as God's chastised, forgiven, and constantly reforming people. Ezra and Nehemiah credit God's grace for Israel's history, while 1–2 Chronicles does the same for world history

---

[81] See Andrew E. Hill, *Enter His Courts with Praise: Old Testament Worship for the New Testament Church* (Grand Rapids: Baker, 1993); and Allen P. Ross, *Recalling the Hope of Glory: Biblical Worship from the Garden to the New Creation* (Grand Rapids: Kregel, 2006).

[82] Scott W. Hahn, *The Kingdom of God as Liturgical Empire: A Theological Commentary on 1–2 Chronicles* (Grand Rapids: Baker, 2012), 23.

by opening with a genealogy of Adam. The Hebrew canon closes with a call to go up and build the temple (2 Chr 36:23). This is fitting, for those seeking the Messiah find the infant Messiah at the temple in Luke 2:22–38. As the aged Simeon and Anna see and believe in the infant Messiah, the continuity of God's people and their worship moves forward, as inexorably as a mighty river flows to the sea.

God's Walk with Wise Persons: Proverbs and Ruth

Discussions of wise living occur in some of humanity's most ancient literature.[83] It is hardly surprising, then, that the Hebrew canon wrestles with how to understand and navigate life's sometimes-rough waters. Though other definitions of wisdom are certainly viable, at its most basic level wisdom in the OT is faithful execution of God's Word in daily life. Wisdom comes gradually as one walks in God's instructions over a lifetime. Wise persons show others God's character through how they think and act. Though wisdom themes exist throughout the Writings, Proverbs and Ruth offer extensive principles and clear examples of wisdom respectively.

Proverbs presents a carefully developed collection (1:1; 10:1; 25:1) of wisdom exhortations, examples, and sayings. The book opens with calls to pursue wisdom instead of foolishness (chaps. 1–9). People cannot help being simple at the beginning of life, due to inexperience. But they can help becoming confirmed and contented fools.[84] Eventually Proverbs discusses leadership skills, including those needed by royalty (10:1–31:9). As is true of Yahweh, his people's character matters most. To have godly character, they must respect (1:8) and trust him (3:5). They must learn to mirror his integrity, industriousness, justice, and graciousness (see Exod 34:6–7). Proverbs spends much time depicting a worthy, or wise, man. It ends by describing a wise and thus worthy woman (31:10–31).

The short book of Ruth follows with three main characters who embody wisdom. Like Job, Ruth is not an Israelite, yet she shows her wisdom through converting to faith in Yahweh, loyalty to Naomi, and industry before Boaz (Ruth 1:16–2:23). Boaz is deemed a worthy man

---

[83] John Day, Robert P. Gordon, and H. G. M. Williamson, *Wisdom in Ancient Israel: Essays in Honour of J. A. Emerton* (Cambridge: Cambridge University Press, 1995), 17–70; and Craig G. Bartholomew and Ryan P. O'Dowd, *Old Testament Wisdom Literature: A Theological Introduction* (Downers Grove: InterVarsity, 2011), 32–46.

[84] James L. Crenshaw, *Old Testament Wisdom: An Introduction* (Atlanta: John Knox, 1981), 81.

(2:1), no doubt because he lives out the principles of loving his neighbors (including ones from other lands) found in Leviticus 19. Soon enough he sees that Ruth is a worthy woman (3:11). Naomi gives Ruth advice at crucial moments (v. 1), thereby proving herself a good wisdom counselor. The book closes by connecting these wise people to David. Ruth, Boaz, and Naomi demonstrate the best traits of God's people: love of God and love of neighbor. Israel's blessing other peoples and God's giving David a never-ending kingdom remain in plain sight.

God's Walk with His Suffering People: Job, Lamentations, and Daniel

The Law and Prophets indicate that God's people will suffer individually and collectively. Indeed, their pages are filled with suffering servants of God such as Hagar, Joseph, Moses, Elijah, Hezekiah, and Jeremiah. Israel suffers at the hand of Pharaoh in Exodus, multiple oppressors in Judges, and the Assyrians and Babylonians in 2 Kings, Isaiah, Jeremiah, Ezekiel, and the Minor Prophets. The Writings continue this trajectory through their many laments in Psalms, as was noted above, and through Job, Lamentations, and Daniel, books that highlight three quite different situations.

Job is set in ancient times, probably in the patriarchal era. Though not an Israelite, Job clearly knows God. But this faithfulness does not shield him from pain. In fact, it draws him to pain, for God uses him as an example of commitment that cannot be shaken by physical, metaphysical, emotional, or financial trauma (chaps. 1–2). The dialogue in chapters 3–37 also proves that Job's commitment to God cannot be shaken by his friends' arguments that personal suffering is always the result of personal sin. Job demonstrates absolute, ultimate trust in God's character (13:15; 16:19; 19:23–25) and raises questions about his government of the universe (21:1–34).

When God peppers Job with questions he cannot answer (38:1–40:2; 40:6–41:34), Job responds in faith, satisfied that God has given him what he needs to know (40:3–5; 42:1–6), even before God reverses his circumstances (42:7–17). Job's relationship with God endures, showing that God's character and his people's service transcend national boundaries and life's harsh circumstances.

Lamentations shows that at times suffering occurs for a different reason. In this case, Jerusalem's people have suffered the Babylonian destruction of 587 BC because of their sins. The consequences for covenant breaking outlined in Lev 26:14–39 and Deut 28:15–68 are in effect (Lam 1:18; 2:17; 5:7). These people have no one to blame but themselves. Still, they have someone to forgive, renew, and restore them. Probably citing Exod 34:6–7, the speaker in Lam 3:19–39 bases his hope for forgiveness on God's always-gracious character. The promise of forgiveness in Lev 26:40–45 and Deut 30:1–10 bolster the people, and the whole community prays for reconciliation with God in Lam 5:1–22. God walks with his people again and again, even after they have walked away from him. Only he can provide the conviction and conditions necessary for reestablishing the covenant relationship. He alone can achieve such an improbable spiritual feat.

Like Job, Daniel has not sinned personally in any way that leads to his suffering. Taken to Babylon in 605 BC, he shares in Judah's punishment for long-term covenant disobedience. He is like Ezekiel, Jeremiah, and Baruch in this regard. God's protection (Dan 1:8–21; 2:1–45; 6:1–24) and promises of a future messianic Son of Man (7:9–28), of renewal after exile (9:1–23), and of resurrection (12:1–13) sustain him through long decades of service in Babylon. As he lives, he does not languish. Rather, he blesses other nations through bearing witness to God's majesty, including to the king (2:1–45; 4:1–37). He also remains faithful in prayer, regardless of the personal cost (6:1–13). He walks with God under extraordinarily hard circumstances.

Synthesis

Because so much of what the Writings teach is in concert with the Law and Prophets, I will note only three significant points. First, the people of God in the Writings are Jews and Gentiles who know God and walk with him according to his standards for corporate and individual worship, wisdom, and redemptive suffering as they await the Messiah. Second, God seeks his people in Israel, in Babylon, and in Moab in these books. Their history depends on his call, covenant, instruction, and willingness to forgive and reform them. Third, God's people demonstrate their role as a kingdom of priests as they include others in their communities and in their worship.

Conclusion

God's people have walked with him since the garden of Eden. They have walked with faltering steps more than once, yet they walk with him nonetheless. They do so because his grace overcomes their sin. He has protected them, and he has blessed all peoples through them. He dwells with them. They respond positively to his call to walk with him by faith, and they show their relationship to him by their repentance and their obedience to his will. They constitute a kingdom of priests for God (whose character determines the success of the covenants he has made) and for the world (which needs redemption from sin).

Of course, one can tell the story from only one side and make OT believers sound worse than they are and make NT believers better than they are. One can also tell the NT story in a terribly negative way, lamenting the divisions in Corinth, the false teachers in 2 Peter, the Judaizers in Galatia, the apostates in 1 John, and the weak churches in Revelation 2–3. A much more balanced approach is to see that the Bible links the two groups through their commitment to God, God's Word, God's promises, God's Messiah, and God's promise keeping, and that the Bible does not cover up the flaws or hide the triumphs of God's people. This is the approach taken by NT authors in Romans 9–11; 1 Corinthians 10; Hebrews 11; and 1 Pet 2:9–10.

The OT indicates that God's people include individuals and assemblies who trust and walk with him as his priests in the world and thereby share his redemptive mission. The OT people of God are one with his people in the NT who share common traits. They share the same physical ancestors, Adam and Eve (Gen 5:1; Acts 17:26). They share the same Christ, for they believe and act upon God's promises concerning the Messiah and his kingdom (Isa 11:1–12:6; Heb 11:1–40). They are one gathered body before God, whether they are currently "with Christ" or "in the flesh," as Phil 1:23–24 puts it. God is One; his word is one; so his people are one, historically and theologically.

Believers today have spiritual ancestors who are their brothers and sisters in Christ. We can learn from them as we attempt to keep the Great Commission, worship and serve through local congregations, and look with hope to the day when we will all live in Zion with God in the absence of sin, death, and pain forever (Isa 65:17–25; Rev 21:1–8). Then all the new covenant promises will be realized through the work of God—Father, Son, and Holy Spirit.

CHAPTER 2

The Church According to the Gospels

Andreas J. Köstenberger

The OT looks forward to a Messiah who will establish God's kingdom and gather a faithful remnant, the new messianic community (see 2 Sam 7:14; Isa 11:1–16; Dan 7:13–14). The Gospels declare that this Messiah—Jesus—has come and that he announced the inauguration of God's kingdom (Matt 3:2; 4:17; Mark 1:15) and commissioned his twelve disciples (Matt 4:18–22; 28:18–20). Yet the church is not completely established until Pentecost (Acts 2) and the subsequent ingathering of believing Gentiles by God's Spirit (chaps. 8; 10). In fact, the word "church" (*ekklēsia*) is found only twice in all the Gospels combined (Matt 16:18; 18:17). Technically speaking, therefore, the church, as a present reality, is absent from the Gospels because they represent a transitional period between the OT and the establishment of the NT church in the book of Acts.

This absence of the church from the Gospels in a technical sense does not, however, mean that nothing can be said about it from the Gospels. In the Gospels Jesus begins to form the church as his messianic community that has roots in God's historic covenant people. And he instructs that nascent community in many ways that apply later to the fully orbed NT church. As the following discussion will show, each

Gospel provides a distinct witness to the life and ministry of Jesus and to his calling, instruction, and commissioning of the new messianic community. To this end, we will examine each Gospel in canonical order to assess its distinctive contribution to the topic at hand. This will entail an exploration of pertinent texts such as Matt 16:18; 18:17; John 10; and 15, as well as investigation of significant themes related to the church in the respective Gospel accounts.

While each canonical Gospel constitutes a distinct witness, biblical-theological themes also cut across the four Gospels and provide a common voice on the nature of the church. The Messiah and his kingdom, the gathering of the messianic community in keeping with the Messiah's mission focused on the Jews, the ethical demands of discipleship in the new messianic community, and the commissioning of Jesus' followers to carry forward his mission to the ends of the earth are prominent themes in all four Gospels. Discussions of these topics will form the basis for a concluding theological synthesis.

Greek Term	Matthew	Mark	Luke	John	Acts	Gospels Totals
ekklēsia	2	–	–	–	19	2
mathētēs	71	45	36	74[1]	28	226
mathēteuō	3	–	–	–	1	3
akoloutheō	13	11	12	13	–	49
Totals	89	56	48	87	48	280

TABLE I: THE CHURCH AND DISCIPLESHIP IN THE GOSPELS:
A LEXICAL SURVEY[2]

---

[1] Of these 74 references, 59 are in the plural and 15 in the singular (e.g., "the disciple whom Jesus loved").

[2] The data were compiled on the basis of the information provided in Andreas J. Köstenberger and Raymond Bouchoc, *The Book Study Concordance of the Greek New Testament* (Nashville: B&H Academic, 2003); and J. P. Louw and Eugene Nida, L&N, 2nd ed. (New York: United Bible Societies, 1989). The book of Acts is included for comparative purposes.

Matthew

While all four Gospels center on the earthly ministry of Jesus culminating in his passion—his crucifixion, burial, and resurrection—the individual evangelists' presentations of the person and work of Jesus bear clear marks of their distinctive theological interests and emphases. As Scot McKnight observes, "The Gospel of Matthew is a record of the life of Jesus which has been shaped by Matthew in such a way that we can detect emphases and patterns of thoughts that are the author's . . . [and] these themes contribute to our understanding of biblical theology."[3] A careful analysis of Matthew's Gospel shows that the first evangelist is chiefly concerned with the identity of Jesus as the long-expected Messiah, his calling of twelve disciples, his teaching on the kingdom of God, and his commissioning of his disciples to carry forward his mission. These prominent themes, therefore, provide the framework for Matthew's discussion of the church. In due course, I will investigate the two instances of "church" (*ekklēsia*) in Matthew's Gospel (Matt 16:18; 18:17) in the context of these larger motifs. But we commence our study of Matthew's teaching on the church where he begins his Gospel—with the Messiah, the Lord Jesus Christ.

Jesus Christ, the Son of David, the Son of Abraham

Matthew's Gospel opens with the presentation of Jesus Christ in light of OT history and messianic predictions. The Gospel identifies itself as "the historical record of Jesus Christ, the Son of David, the Son of Abraham" (1:1). Likely written primarily for Jews in the latter half of the first century,[4] Matthew claims that Jesus Christ fulfills God's promises to Israel of a coming Messiah. In Gen 12:1–3, God called Abram from Ur of the Chaldees to go to a new land and tied his call to a promise: "I will make you into a great nation, I will bless you, I will make your name great, and you will be a blessing" (v. 2). This passage is programmatic in

---

[3] Scot McKnight, "Matthew, Gospel of," in *DJG*, 532.

[4] For thorough discussions of Matthew's background, see Robert H. Gundry, *Matthew: A Commentary on His Handbook for a Mixed Church under Persecution*, 2nd ed. (Grand Rapids: Eerdmans, 1994), 599–622; Donald A. Hagner, *Matthew 1–13*, WBC 33A (Dallas: Word, 1993), xxxix–lxxvii; and Craig S. Keener, *A Commentary on the Gospel of Matthew* (Grand Rapids: Eerdmans, 1999), 16–51.

establishing the framework for the remainder of the OT[5] and lays the foundation for Matthew's salvation-historical presentation in his Gospel. By identifying Jesus Christ as the "son of Abraham," Matthew asserts that he is the One through whom God's above-stated promises to Abraham will be fulfilled. The culminating Great Commission passage in Matt 28:18–20 shows how Jesus, the "son of Abraham," fulfills the Abrahamic promise—that God would bless all nations through his descendant—by sending out the representatives of his new messianic community to take the gospel of salvation in Jesus Christ to the ends of the earth.[6]

The title "Son of David" confirms that Jesus is the rightful heir to David's throne. In 2 Sam 7:12–16, God made a covenant with David, establishing his royal dynasty and promising him an everlasting kingdom (vv. 13, 16). The promises to David were to be inherited by his son Solomon (v. 14) and his descendants.[7] Matthew highlights the legal claim Jesus has to the throne of David by tracing his lineage over three sets of fourteen generations all the way back to Abraham and David (Matt 1:17).

Matthew builds his case further by identifying Jesus as Immanuel, "God with us" (1:23 NKJV, citing Isa 7:14); as the Suffering Servant bringing justice and hope for the Gentiles (Matt 12:17–21, citing Isa 42:1–3); and as the "Son of Man" of Daniel 7.[8] Later Peter, against prevailing popular notions, testifies to Jesus' messianic identity, declaring him to be "the Messiah, the Son of the living God" (Matt 16:16). Thus, by identifying Jesus as "the son of David, the son of Abraham," Matthew claims that "Jesus, the paradigmatic, representative 'son,' is . . . both the channel of blessing for the nations and the eternal, enthroned Davidic ruler."[9] The

---

[5] See the essay in this volume by Paul R. House, p. 1; see also David J. A. Clines, *The Theme of the Pentateuch*, 2nd ed. (London: Sheffield Academic, 1997); and Kenneth A. Mathews, *Genesis 1–11:26*, NAC (Nashville: B&H, 1996).

[6] In this regard, the number of the apostles appointed by Jesus (twelve) is consciously playing off the OT connection with the twelve tribes of Israel; see further below.

[7] For other "Son of David" references, see Matt 9:27; 12:23; 15:22; 20:30–31; 21:9, 15; 22:42, 45; see also Mark L. Strauss, "David," in *New Dictionary of Biblical Theology: Exploring the Unity and Diversity of Scripture*, ed. T. Desmond Alexander and Brian S. Rosner (Downers Grove: InterVarsity, 2000), 435–43.

[8] See David Turner, *Matthew*, BECNT (Grand Rapids: Baker, 2008), 32–37; I. H. Marshall, "Jesus Christ," *NDBT*, 592–602.

[9] Andreas J. Köstenberger and Peter T. O'Brien, *Salvation to the Ends of the Earth: A Biblical Theology of Mission*, NSBT 11 (Downers Grove: InterVarsity, 2001), 89, referring also to Matt 2:5–6 citing Mic 5:2.

arrival of the Messiah, in turn, ushers in the presence of his reign, the kingdom of God.

The Messiah and the Kingdom

Matthew's Gospel contains the fullest presentation of the kingdom in any of the Gospels. Matthew uses the terms "kingdom" (*basileia*), "kingdom of heaven" (*basileia tou ouranou*), and "kingdom of God" (*basileia tou theou*).[10] Although the different expressions have led some to argue for differences in meaning, it is best to view "kingdom of heaven" and "kingdom of God" as largely synonymous expressions referring to the reign of God, with heaven, God's dwelling place, connoting God's rule over and in the world.[11]

Matthew indicates that God's kingdom is both present and future. As George Eldon Ladd argued, Matthew's eschatology is best characterized in terms of "already but not yet."[12] The kingdom is present as John the Baptist, Jesus, and the disciples preach the message, "Repent, for the kingdom of heaven is at hand" (Matt 3:2; 4:17; 10:7 NKJV), and those who repent enter the kingdom (5:3, 10). Indeed, Jesus' earthly ministry entails healing the diseased and afflicted and proclaiming "the good news of the kingdom" (*to euangelion tēs basileias*, 4:23; 9:35; 24:14). Yet the kingdom is also future, in that Jesus will return and usher in God's total rule over the entire world (7:21–23; 25:31, 34). The one universal reign of God has broken into human history in the person of Jesus Christ. Thus, "it is not that the kingdom does not involve a concrete realm. It is, rather, that the kingdom exists as a microcosm today and as a macrocosm when Jesus returns."[13] Part and parcel of the inaugurated-but-not-yet-consummated nature of the kingdom is the inclusion of a community of people who will inherit and inhabit it.

---

[10] According to C. Caragounis, "Kingdom of God/Heaven," in *DJG*, 426, Matthew uses "kingdom of heaven" thirty-two times, "kingdom of God" five times, and "kingdom" thirteen times. See Turner, *Matthew*, 37–41.

[11] Turner, *Matthew*, 39–42, traces the debate. See also Jonathan T. Pennington, *Heaven and Earth in the Gospel of Matthew* (Grand Rapids: Baker, 2009), who argues that "heaven" is not a reverent synonym for "God" but rather highlights the tension between heaven and earth while looking forward to its eschatological resolution.

[12] George E. Ladd, *The Presence of the Future: The Eschatology of Biblical Realism*, rev. ed. (Grand Rapids: Eerdmans, 1974), 105–48; see Graeme Goldsworthy, "Kingdom of God," *NDBT*, 615–20.

[13] Turner, *Matthew*, 43.

Calling the Messianic Community

Many critical studies of Matthew's Gospel dispute that Jesus ever intended his message and mission to be perpetuated in an institutional church.[14] Yet the arrival of the Messiah and his inauguration of the kingdom of heaven/God necessitate a kingdom people. As I. Howard Marshall contends, "The concept of the kingdom of God implies both the existence of a group of people who own him as king and the establishment of a realm of people within which his gracious power is manifested."[15] Indeed, several OT messianic passages speak of the people of the Messiah.[16] By calling twelve disciples (Matt 10:1–4)—whereby the number twelve plainly mirrors the number of the OT tribes of Israel (see 19:28)[17]—Jesus gathers his messianic community, the new Israel, to carry out his mission. This mission, initially directed to the Jews, will require radical discipleship and will include the Gentiles among the people of God.

Jesus Gathers the New Israel, the Twelve (Matt 4:18–22; 10:1–4)

Matthew records Jesus' call of his disciples, including Matthew himself (4:18–22; 9:9), as an injunction to follow Jesus. The command issues a radical call to discipleship, which involves forsaking all other earthly allegiances on the basis of an unconditional commitment to Jesus (10:37; see 4:22; 8:21–23; 12:46–50). Jesus' followers must take up their "cross" (10:38–39; 16:24–26) in view of promised persecution (10:16–23). At the same time, following Jesus as disciple carries the promise of being equipped to enter into his ministry (10:26–33; see 28:20).[18] In calling the Twelve, Jesus gathers a new Israel, which he commissions to carry out his messianic mission.

Jesus' Mission to the Jews (Matt 10:1–15; 15:24)

Upon gathering his messianic community, Jesus grants his followers authority over unclean spirits and diseases and charges his inner circle of the Twelve to avoid Gentile and Samaritan territories and "instead, go

---

[14] See especially C. K. Barrett, *Jesus and the Gospel Tradition* (London: S.P.C.K., 1967); and Eduard Schweizer, *Church Order in the New Testament*, SBT 32 (London: SCM, 1961).

[15] I. H. Marshall, "Church," in Green, McKnight, and Marshall, *DJG*, 123.

[16] See Isa 11:1–16; 42:1–6; Dan 7:13–18.

[17] See Keener, *Matthew*, 310; Turner, *Matthew*, 264; Hagner, *Matthew 1–13*, 265.

[18] See Köstenberger and O'Brien, *Salvation*, 93–94.

to the lost sheep of the house of Israel" (Matt 10:6). Jesus' followers are enjoined to proclaim the arrival of the kingdom of heaven (v. 7). Thus their mission and message correspond to Jesus' mission and message (4:17; 15:24).

In light of his later command to "make disciples of all nations" (Matt 28:19), how are we to explain the fact that Jesus and the disciples focused their mission on Israel? This focus reflects the salvation-historical thrust found consistently in all four Gospels and Acts: "Jesus, the Jewish Messiah offers the kingdom to Israel; Israel rejects Jesus, issuing in his crucifixion; the kingdom is offered universally to all those who believe in Jesus the Messiah, Jew and Gentile alike."[19]

Jesus and the Gentiles

In Matthew as well as the other Gospels, Jesus' relationship to Gentiles is often at their initiative. His healing of the centurion's servant is representative. After healing the servant, Jesus asserts, "I tell you that many will come from east and west, and recline at the table with Abraham, Isaac, and Jacob in the kingdom of heaven. But the sons of the kingdom will be thrown into the outer darkness" (8:11–12; see also 21:43). Clearly Jesus anticipates the Gentiles' full participation in God's promises to Abraham. The reference to the Isaianic Servant in 12:17–21 (see Isa 42:1–4), likewise, envisions the future inclusion of the Gentiles in the kingdom.

The tension between Jesus' mission first to the Jews and his ministry to a limited number of Gentiles at their initiative is likely due to the transitional nature of the period marked by Jesus' earthly ministry. The messianic community featured in Matthew consists of an already constituted Jewish core while anticipating a yet-to-be incorporated Gentile contingent. The ethical standards for membership in this community and its proper operation are addressed in Jesus' Sermon on the Mount.

---

[19] Köstenberger and O'Brien, *Salvation*, 93. It is unnecessary to posit different traditions within the "Matthean community" as some have done; see Köstenberger and O'Brien, *Salvation*, 92n21. On the history and debate of "communities" in Gospels scholarship, see Richard Bauckham, ed., *The Gospels for All Christians: Rethinking Gospel Audiences* (Grand Rapids: Eerdmans, 1997); and Edward W. Klink III, "Gospel Audience and Origin: The Current Debate," in *The Audience of the Gospels: The Origin and Function of the Gospels in Early Christianity*, ed. Edward W. Klink III (London: T&T Clark, 2010), 1–26.

The Messiah on Life in the Kingdom (Matthew 5–7)

Jesus' Sermon on the Mount harks back to the giving of the law at Mount Sinai.[20] The repeated assertion, "You have heard that it was said . . . but I tell you," indicates that Jesus is fulfilling and applying OT law to his new messianic community (see Matt 5:17–20). Jesus' message highlights "the arrival of God's kingdom and the righteousness required of those who would receive it (see esp. 5:3–12, 20; 6:33)."[21] The sermon unfolds what kingdom righteousness looks like and defines the ethical standards for membership in the messianic community.

An essential characteristic of Jesus' disciples is their humble status in this world. This is evidenced in their pure hearts, their meek positions, their peaceful spirits, and their endurance under persecution. For this reason, they will be called "blessed" (Matt 5:3–12). Another essential characteristic is their ethical distinction from the world. They are to be "salt" and "light" (5:13–16), as evidence of the glory of their heavenly Father after whom they pattern their character—perfect (v. 48), forgiving (6:14–15), and generous (7:7–11). Thus, in the messianic community, anger, lust, divorce, false oaths, retaliation, and hatred for enemies are not only matters of deficient conduct but indications of a heart not properly aligned with the heavenly Father's will (5:28). In order to live out these ethical commands and to shun sins that originate in the heart, the disciples are taught to pray. Unlike the Pharisees, they are to pray without pretense; unlike the idolators, they are to pray without many words (6:5–7). Instead, they are to pray with sincerity that the Father's will be done "on earth as it is in heaven (6:10)." The members of Jesus' new messianic community enjoy an intimacy with their heavenly Father; they can even ask him for the good things of the kingdom because he delights in giving to his children (7:11).

Jesus' teaching in the Sermon on the Mount is not deferred to a future kingdom.[22] The kingdom of heaven is at hand, and the commands he gives here are to be lived out in the messianic community of his followers. These injunctions are directly relevant for the church. Only when the community of Jesus' followers lives out these directives do they

---

[20] D. A. Carson, "Matthew," in *The Expositor's Bible Commentary* 9, rev. ed., ed. Tremper Longman III and David E. Garland (Grand Rapids: Zondervan, 2010), 53–55, 158.

[21] Köstenberger and O'Brien, *Salvation*, 91.

[22] For a survey of approaches, see Turner, *Matthew*, 143–44; Carson, "Matthew," 155–57.

demonstrate their commitment to his words (7:24–27). At that time they will be recognized by the fruit they produce (7:15–20).

The Church (Ekklēsia) in Matthew

Having surveyed the major passages in Matthew's Gospel with a bearing on his theology of the church, we come now to the two instances of the term "church" (*ekklēsia*) in the Gospels. We will discuss each of these passages in turn and note linguistic and thematic connections between them.

Peter's Confession and the Future of the Church (Matt 16:13–20)[23]

In Matthew 16, Jesus and his followers are in Caesarea Philippi, twenty-five miles north of Galilee, where Jesus devotes the bulk of his ministry to the Twelve in keeping with the Jewish focus of his mission.[24] Jesus first asks his disciples, "Who do people say that the Son of Man is?" (v. 13), to which the disciples respond with a variety of answers: Elijah, Jeremiah, or one of the prophets (v. 14). The answers indicate the wide array of end-time, messianic expectations in Jesus' day.[25] Jesus then follows up, addressing the Twelve directly, "Who do you say that I am?" (v. 15).[26] Peter's confession, "You are the Messiah, the Son of the living God," stands in marked contrast with the range of views enunciated in v. 14.[27] Declaring Jesus to be Messiah is thus an essential mark of membership in the messianic community.

Jesus responds to Peter's confession with a beatitude (Matt 16:17; see 5:3–12)[28] and elaborates on the revelatory nature of his confession (16:17). Jesus then affirms Peter's confession with a promise: "You are Peter, and on this rock I will build My church" (v. 18). Three major issues occupy our attention in the interpretation of this verse: (1) the identity of the "rock"

---

[23] For bibliographies on the literature for this passage, see Hagner, *Matthew 1–13*, 461–62; and John Nolland, *The Gospel According to Matthew*, NIGTC (Grand Rapids: Eerdmans, 2005), 655–57.

[24] Carson, "Matthew," 415.

[25] Ibid., 416; see Keener, *Matthew*, 424; Michael Bird, *Are You the One Who Is to Come? The Historical Jesus and the Messianic Question* (Grand Rapids: Baker, 2009), 31–62.

[26] The term "you" in the question is plural, indicating that Jesus' query is directed to the Twelve as a group. Thus, Peter's answer should be taken as Peter speaking on behalf of the Twelve as a whole.

[27] Carson ("Matthew," 415) notes that despite the many views, "No group was openly and thoughtfully confessing Jesus as Messiah."

[28] Turner, *Matthew*, 404.

(*petra*), (2) the use of the term "church" (*ekklēsia*), and (3) the future aspect of the "church."

First, some scholars have argued that the "rock" is the confession Peter uttered, or Jesus himself.[29] However, Jesus uses a wordplay between "Peter" (*Petros*) and "rock" (*petra*), likely making Peter, not his confession, the "rock."[30] What is more, had Jesus referred to himself as the "rock," this would unduly mix metaphors since Jesus is in the immediate context identified as the builder of his church.[31] The rock is most likely Peter, the foundation upon which Jesus will build his church (see Eph 2:20). It does not follow, however, that the passage supports a Roman Catholic view of apostolic succession with Peter as the first pope; for there is no mention of Peter's authority or infallibility in this text. Later on, Peter answers to the Jerusalem church (Acts 11:1–18), not to mention being confronted by Paul for an instance of hypocrisy (Gal 2:11–14), which contradicts the notion that Peter was viewed as infallible.[32] At the same time, this passage does assign to Peter an important place in salvation history. He is the first disciple called (Matt 4:18; see 10:2), the first to confess Jesus as Messiah (16:17), and the first to take the gospel to both Jews and Gentiles (Acts 2; 10). Thus, Peter is to be respected but not venerated for his role in the mission of the early church.

The second issue revolves around the term "church" (*ekklēsia*). A hazard to avoid when interpreting the two "church" passages in Matthew is reading later NT meanings of "church" (or worse, twenty-first-century conceptions) into Jesus' statement. It is better to examine the OT concept with which Jesus and his disciples would have been familiar at this point. In the Septuagint, the term for "assembly" or "gathering" (Hb. *qāhāl*) is translated by *ekklēsia*. Thus it would be preferable for modern English translations to render *ekklēsia* in its two Matthean instances as "messianic community" rather than church, since the latter unduly conjures up notions of a full-fledged NT (Pauline) ecclesiology. Jesus is "building" his

---

[29] See Carson's review in "Matthew," 418–19; see Turner, *Matthew*, 406, for an updated review.

[30] This is paronomasia, a common figure of speech in the Bible; see Carson, "Matthew," 419; Turner, *Matthew*, 406; and Hagner, *Matthew*, 469–72. See also the argument by Keener (*Matthew*, 427) on the use of *kai* rather than *de* in Matt 16:18.

[31] Carson, "Matthew," 419.

[32] Ibid.

messianic community, a concept with OT roots that anticipates a future completion.[33]

The third factor in the interpretation of Matt 16:18 is the future horizon of Jesus' promise to Peter. The verb "I will build" (*oikodomēsō*) is future tense. This statement likely looks forward to the time after Pentecost when the Holy Spirit will be poured out on the messianic community and empower Jesus' followers to serve as his witnesses to the ends of the earth (Acts 1–2). Yet Jesus is already gathering his messianic community, and it is to be *his* church (*mou tēn ekklēsian*, Matt 16:18), the community of Jesus. The church, then, is not the same as the kingdom, as "church" refers to the *people* of God and "kingdom" to the *reign* of God.[34] At the same time, the church has a crucial salvation-historical purpose in the kingdom. As Carson maintains, "So far as the kingdom has been inaugurated in advance of its consummation, so far also is Jesus' church an outpost in the history of the final eschatological community."[35]

The assurance of final victory for this community comes with Jesus' promise that "the forces of Hades will not overpower it" (Matt 16:18). If, as is likely, Hades refers to death,[36] Jesus' promise here is that not even death will prevail against his community of believers, the church. The promise of victory for the messianic community is also connected to the keys of the kingdom in v. 19.[37] In Luke 11:52, Jesus denounces the teachers of the law because "[they] have taken away the key to knowledge." As a result they not only failed to enter the kingdom themselves but also they "hindered those who were going in." Not so with Peter. By his confession of Jesus as Messiah, he has entered the kingdom and will be given authority by the Messiah to carry out the mission of binding and loosing. The promise, "I will give [*dōsō*] you," has a clear future dimension. That is, "by proclaiming 'the good news of the kingdom' (Matt 4:23), which, by revelation he [Peter] is increasingly understanding, he will open

---

[33] Ibid., 420; see Ruth 4:11; 2 Sam 7:13–14; 1 Chr 17:12–13; Pss 28:5; 118:22; Jer 1:10; 24:6; 31:4; 33:7; and Amos 9:11; see Turner, *Matthew*, 405n6; Keener, *Matthew*, 428.

[34] Carson, "Matthew," 420; see Ladd, *Presence*, 262–77.

[35] Carson, "Matthew," 420.

[36] Ibid., 420–21; Turner, *Matthew*, 405; Keener, *Matthew*, 428–29; see Gundry, *Matthew*, 335, who interprets this as victory over persecution, not death *per se*.

[37] A full discussion of this complex verse is beyond the scope of this study. For fuller treatments see Turner, *Matthew*, 404–8, and Hagner, *Matthew*, 472–74.

the kingdom to many and shut it against many."[38] Although Jesus issues the promise to Peter, the implications for the Twelve are taken up in Matt 18:18. If the messianic community will have the ministry of the keys of the kingdom, the discipline of the community is an essential component of carrying out this ministry.

Discipleship and Discipline in the Ekklēsia (Matt 18:15–20)

Jesus is in the midst of teaching on discipleship within the messianic community. Following Peter's confession and Jesus' promise in chap. 16, Jesus proclaims his coming death and resurrection (Matt 16:21–23; 17:22–23) and the cost of following him (16:24–28). The right conduct of the disciples within the community is essential for the messianic mission of Jesus to succeed. Hence, he tells how to address the sin of a disciple in the community, whether against another member of the community or against the community at large.[39]

The sinful disciple is to be shown his or her sin privately. Initial confrontation is "in private" (metaxu sou kai autou monou) and aims at conviction (elenchō) of sin for the purpose of reconciliation—to win the person over to the Lord.[40] If, however, private confrontation does not achieve its intended purpose, one or two other members of the community should accompany the one who confronts the sinning person in accordance with OT standards for establishing a proper witness (Matt 18:16; see Deut 19:15). This second step is meant to preclude the third stage of discipline,[41] which includes the witness of the entire church (Matt 18:17).

As in the case of 16:18, "church" (ekklēsia) should be read in light of OT conceptions of the people of God and their gathering together. If the sinning disciple is hard-hearted and unrepentant, then he or she is to be treated as a tax collector or pagan and should be cast out of the

---

[38] Carson, "Matthew," 424. Note that "whatever" (ho) refers to people, not things. Hence, the binding and loosing will be that of people. Thus the emphasis lies on the proclamation of the gospel to people.

[39] Many of the early manuscripts exclude the phrase "against you"; however, the context (Turner, Matthew, 444; Gundry, Matthew, 367) and the geographical distribution of manuscripts (Keener, Matthew, 453n20) favor the inclusion; see Carson, "Matthew," 456–57.

[40] See Carson, "Matthew," 456; Luke 17:3–4; 2 Thess 3:14–15; Jas 5:19–20; see Sir 19:13–17.

[41] See the precedent for three stages of discipline in Qumran cited in Carson, "Matthew," 456; see Turner, Matthew, 445.

congregation.[42] Such discipline is part of discipleship in the messianic community because the latter is charged with carrying out the ministry of the keys of the kingdom on earth.

As Carson states, "If the church, Messiah's eschatological people already gathered now, has to exercise the ministry of the keys, if it must bind and loose, then clearly one aspect of that will be the discipline of those who profess to constitute it."[43] Thus Matt 18:18 here represents a special application of 16:19. In this context, 18:19–20 does not offer a promise for any prayer on which two or three believers agree but rather a promise that the Father will ratify their decision in the congregation because of Jesus' presence with them—they gather in his name.[44]

Commissioning the Messianic Community (Matt 28:18–20)

The Great Commission brings together Matthew's themes and emphases in a final climactic passage. The messianic identity and mission of Jesus as the crucified but risen Lord is crystallized; he declares that all authority in heaven and on earth has been given to him. This statement echoes Daniel's messianic vision of the Son of Man enthroned as eschatological ruler over all creation (Dan 7:14).[45] Invested with this authority, Jesus commissions his disciples to carry forward his mission on earth. They will function as emissaries of the resurrected Jesus on the basis of his words. Their mission is his mission, which is to "make disciples of all nations." The making of disciples "entails the bringing of a person into the relationship of student to teacher in order to take the teacher's yoke upon himself and learn from him (Matt 11:29)."[46] What is striking here is the scope of this mission: the followers of Jesus are commanded to carry out this mission to all nations. This command anticipates the movement of the gospel beyond the bounds of Jerusalem to Samaria and the Gentiles (Acts 1:8; 8; 10) in fulfillment of God's promise to bless all nations through the

---

[42] Against Turner, *Matthew*, 445, Jesus has excommunication in mind here. See Keener, *Matthew*, 454; Carson, "Matthew," 456; see Rom 16:17; 1 Cor 5:5; 2 Thess 3:14.

[43] Carson, "Matthew," 425.

[44] So Carson, "Matthew," 456; see J. D. M. Derrett, "'Where two or three are gathered in my name . . .': A Sad Misunderstanding," *ExpTim* 91 (1979–80): 83–86.

[45] Köstenberger and O'Brien, *Salvation*, 102; Turner, *Matthew*, 689; Keener, *Matthew*, 716; against Gundry, *Matthew*, 595.

[46] Köstenberger and O'Brien, *Salvation*, 104.

offspring of Abraham (Matt 1:1; see Gen 12:1–3). Jesus' mission to the Jews will thus extend to Gentiles through his disciples.

Jesus then identifies the mode for making disciples: baptizing and teaching, complementary terms.[47] Baptism in the name of the Father, Son, and Holy Spirit is "a sign both of entrance into Messiah's covenant community and of pledged submission to his lordship."[48] Those who are baptized will submit to the Messiah's lordship by obeying all that he has commanded. Thus, the disciples are to teach others all that the Messiah has commanded them, namely, the full body of Jesus' teaching in the Gospel (esp. Matthew 5–7). Further, while the Great Commission most assuredly teaches the proclamation of the gospel to all nations, proclamation must involve the "nurturing of converts into the full obedience of faith"[49] (see Eph 4:11–16; Col 1:28). The messianic community is charged with achieving this mission by the authority of the victorious Messiah who will always be with them until the end of the age in the power of the Holy Spirit.

Jesus' Institution of the Lord's Supper and Baptism

Also significant for the doctrine of the church is Matthew's account of Jesus' institution of the Lord's Supper and baptism.[50] As Jonathan Pennington states, "The Lord's Supper is the Christian remembrance and eschatological re-appropriation of the significance and meaning of the Last Supper."[51] Jesus' institution of the Lord's Supper illustrates the transitional nature of the Gospels as he teaches his disciples to "do this in remembrance of Me" (Luke 22:19). In reference to the cup, which represents Jesus' blood instituting the new covenant (see Jer 31:31–33) and its promises, Jesus affirms that he will not drink from it again until "that day" when his followers will be with him in his Father's kingdom (Matt

---

[47] Ibid., 105.

[48] Carson, "Matthew," 668.

[49] Köstenberger and O'Brien, *Salvation*, 105.

[50] The section is indebted to my survey "Baptism in the Gospels" in *Believer's Baptism: Sign of the New Covenant in Christ*, ed. Thomas R. Schreiner and Shawn D. Wright (Nashville: B&H Academic, 2006), 11–34; see also Jonathan Pennington, "The Lord's Last Supper in the Fourfold Witness of the Gospels," in *The Lord's Supper: Remembering and Proclaiming Christ until He Comes*, ed. Thomas R. Schreiner and Matt Crawford (Nashville: B&H Academic, 2011).

[51] Pennington, "Lord's Last Supper," in Schreiner and Crawford, *The Lord's Supper*, 28–29.

26:27–29; Mark 14:24–25; see Luke 22:17–18). Pennington notes three ways in which *the* Last Supper informs the later practice of the Lord's Supper. First, the Lord's Supper is to emphasize love and service in the community of believers, emulating Jesus' love for his disciples at the Last Supper. Second, the Lord's Supper is a celebration of the grace manifested in Jesus' sacrifice, grace his followers receive and do not need to earn. Third, the Lord's Supper looks forward in hope just as the Last Supper did (see 1 Cor 11:26).

Matthew's account of Jesus' teaching about baptism suggests four ideas. First, baptism is designed for believers who have repented of their sin and put their faith in God and his Messiah. The ministry of John the Baptist (Matt 3:1–16) and the Great Commission passage (28:18–20) both presuppose this point. Second, baptism is an essential component of discipleship. Baptism is to accompany the teaching of Jesus' message in keeping with his command to make disciples (28:18–20). Third, the mode of John the Baptist's and of Jesus' baptism was most likely immersion.[52] For when Jesus was baptized, he "went up immediately from the water" (3:16). Fourth, water baptism presupposes the regenerating work of the Holy Spirit as a prior and primary work of God. John the Baptist taught that the Messiah, Jesus, would baptize with the Holy Spirit (vv. 11–12).[53]

Summary

Matthew's Gospel has much to teach us on the nature and mission of the church. Matthew demonstrates that the church is already being gathered together as the messianic community by the Messiah, Jesus, but that this community is not yet fully constituted. Jesus' disciples are those who live righteously and shun sin, who prize the kingdom and his righteousness (6:33) in keeping with all that he taught them (28:20). Matthew teaches that as the long-expected Messiah, Jesus is the One who will build his church and that the church will prevail, even over death (16:18–19). Indeed, the members of Jesus' *ekklēsia* will carry out the ministry of the kingdom, a ministry that will extend to all the nations under his authority undergirded by his permanent presence (28:18–20).

---

[52] "To baptize" (*baptizō*) is an intensive or frequentative form of the root meaning of the word "to dip" (*baptō*; e.g., Josh 3:15 LXX; Ruth 2:14 LXX).

[53] On the baptism of Jesus as one of Holy Spirit and fire, see Köstenberger, "Baptism in the Gospels," in Schreiner and Wright, *Believer's Baptism*, 18–19. Note also the OT connection between water and the Holy Spirit (see Ezek 36:22–32).

Mark

The Gospel of Mark is considerably shorter than Matthew and does not include direct references to the "church" (*ekklēsia*).[54] Much of what Mark teaches about the messianic community overlaps with Matthew's teaching. First, just as Matthew emphasizes Jesus' identity as Messiah (1:1; 12:17; 16:16), Mark writes "the gospel of Jesus Christ, the Son of God" (1:1). Robert Stein asserts that "the central and dominating theme of Mark is Christological in nature."[55] He notes three ways in which Mark points his readers to Jesus' identity as Messiah: by Jesus' miracles, by his words and actions, and by his titles.[56]

Second, just as Matthew presents the identity of Messiah in the context of the presence of the kingdom of heaven (3:2; 4:17), Mark records Jesus preaching the same message (1:14–15).[57]

Third, just as Matthew includes reference to Jesus' call of his disciples (4:18–22), so does Mark (1:16–20). Moreover, Mark contains elements of the salvation-historical tension between the Jewish identity of the messianic community and the anticipated inclusion of Gentiles. The parable of the Wicked Tenants is found in both Gospels (12:1–12; see Matt 21:33–46). Mark also evinces concern with the character of the messianic community. Stein notes that Mark teaches about discipleship by "recounting Jesus' general teaching on the subject, and . . . by narrating different accounts in which Jesus invites various individuals to follow him."[58] Mark

---

[54] In all probability, Mark was the first canonical Gospel written. Matthew likely knew of and expanded upon Mark's material. This is more plausible than Mark adapting large portions of Matthew for his audience. For a thorough discussion of Markan priority, see D. A. Carson and Douglas J. Moo, *An Introduction to the New Testament*, 2nd ed. (Grand Rapids: Zondervan, 2005), 95–98.

[55] Robert H. Stein, *Mark*, BECNT (Grand Rapids: Baker, 2010), 21; see Robert H. Gundry, *Mark: A Commentary on His Apology for the Cross* (Grand Rapids: Eerdmans, 1993), 1022–27; R. T. France, *The Gospel of Mark*, NIGTC (Grand Rapids: Eerdmans, 2002), 20–35.

[56] Stein, *Mark*, 21–22.

[57] Of Mark's fourteen uses of "kingdom of heaven/God," nine overlap with Matthew.

[58] Stein, *Mark*, 32. Stein (pp. 26–32) also includes a helpful discussion on the misunderstandings and failures of the disciples in Mark (e.g., Mark 6:52). Though redaction critics, such as T. J. Weeden, *Mark—Tradition in Conflict* (Philadelphia: Fortress, 1971); and Mark Tolbert, *Sewing the Gospel: Mark's World in Literary Historical Perspective* (Minneapolis: Fortress, 1989), ascribed this to Mark's attack on the disciples' low Christology, there are salvation-historical and literary emphases at work. The disciples portrayed by Mark are seen as confused and doubting, but they are also portrayed

records Jesus' call to radical discipleship (8:34–38) just as Matthew does (16:24–28), both following Peter's confession of Jesus as Messiah.

All the overlapping themes noted above underscore that the messianic community is already being gathered by the Messiah and instructed in the cost of following him. Like Matthew, Mark stresses the ethical obligation of the community in response to the Messiah's declaration that the "kingdom of God has come near" (1:15). But the community is not yet the recipient of the Spirit who will empower it to take the Messiah's name to the ends of the earth (Acts 1–2) and bring God-fearers and Gentiles into the kingdom by the ministry of the church. Mark's message represents a basic treatment that is more fully developed in Matthew. It also bears certain affinities with the teachings of Luke.

Luke

Luke writes his Gospel to Theophilus so that he may "know the certainty of the things about which you have been instructed" (1:4).[59] To achieve this purpose, Luke writes a well-researched, orderly account of the life and work of the Messiah (vv. 1–3), who is the linchpin in the salvation-historical plan of God. Luke's second volume—the book of Acts—will demonstrate the implications of the Messiah's mission and work, the Spirit-empowered and expanding new community of God's people. This community will include Jews and Gentiles on equal terms and will be gathered in the name of the resurrected and ascended Messiah, Jesus Christ. This reality, however, is only nascent in the Gospel, which lays the necessary Christological groundwork for the establishment of the church in the book of Acts.

In writing his orderly account, Luke therefore emphasizes the overarching plan of God in history,[60] a theme he develops more fully than either Matthew or Mark. In so doing, Luke unfolds the ministry of

---

positively as those who follow Jesus. Stein (p. 31) states, "For the historian, the question of how the disciples could be so obtuse and dull often loses sight of the pre-Pentecost situation of the disciples."

[59] On Luke's purpose for writing, see Andreas J. Köstenberger, L. Scott Kellum, and Charles L. Quarles, *The Cradle, the Cross, and the Crown: An Introduction to the New Testament* (Nashville: B&H Academic, 2009), 266–67; I. H. Marshall, *The Gospel of Luke*, NIGTC (Grand Rapids: Eerdmans, 1978), 35–36.

[60] See I. Howard Marshall, *Luke: Historian and Theologian* (Grand Rapids: Academie, 1989).

John the Baptist, Jesus' preaching of the kingdom of God, the Messiah's suffering, and his ascension as successive stages in the outworking of salvation history.[61] This unfolding pattern of salvation history has important implications for the Messiah's relationship to both Israel and the Gentiles and thus for the identity of the messianic community as a whole.

Salvation History and the Messiah (Luke 1–4; 9:51; 24)

Luke opens his Gospel with an acknowledgment that many others have written concerning the events "fulfilled among us" (1:1). That is, God has fulfilled his promises to his people through the Messiah. Hence Luke's conception of salvation history proceeds along the lines of "promise and fulfillment." John the Baptist marks the end of the period of promise (see 16:16), while Jesus' gathering of the messianic community marks the promise's fulfillment.[62] The births of John the Baptist (1:5–25) and of Jesus (vv. 26–38) are presented as fulfillments of God's promises to Israel. John will prepare the way (vv. 16–17; 3:1–20) for Jesus, the Messiah and Son of God (1:35), who is the heir of the promises to David (1:32–33, 68–70) and Abraham (1:54–55, 72–75). Mary's song, reminiscent of the song of Hannah (1 Samuel 2), anticipates a "great reversal,"[63] which the Messiah will usher in as the fulfillment of God's promises and as the Savior of Israel (Luke 1:50–55).[64]

As "Savior" (see Luke 1:47; 2:11), Jesus is the cornerstone of salvation history for Luke. Zechariah, father of John the Baptist, describes the Messiah's future ministry along these lines (1:69, 71, 77; see 19:9). What is more, Jesus' messianic mission is bound up with providing salvation—he "has come to seek and to save [sōzō] the lost" (19:10). The parables of Luke 15 picture this compassionate mission that reaches out particularly

---

[61] Darrell L. Bock, Luke, BECNT (Grand Rapids: Baker, 1994), 27.

[62] Köstenberger, Kellum, and Quarles, Cradle, Cross, and Crown, 280. See Frank S. Thielman, Theology of the New Testament: A Canonical and Synthetic Approach (Grand Rapids: Zondervan, 2005), 117, who assumes three stages while Bock, Luke, 28 argues for two due to the continuity between Jesus and the church.

[63] Bock takes the "reversal," first indicated in Luke 1:51, to be eschatological in nature. That is, "portraying the ultimate eschatological events tied to Jesus' final victory . . . The reversal of social position will occur in the final exercise of God's power" (Luke, 155–56). Marshall, Luke, 85, sees the "reversal" as having a present effect, "bringing the ordinary life of mankind into line with the will of God."

[64] See the section on "The Messiah and the Lowly" in this chapter.

to those who are far off. Jesus is the Messiah who brings salvation in ful-fillment of God's promises to Israel as recorded in the Scriptures. In this vein, Luke 24:44–49 connects the resurrected Jesus to all of Scripture—the Law of Moses, the Prophets, and the Psalms—which describes Messiah's suffering, death, and resurrection and the forgiveness of sins to be preached in his name to all the nations. In these ways, Luke frames his narrative in terms of fulfillment (1:1–4; 24:44–49).

Within this overarching framework, the structure of Luke's Gospel further accentuates the salvation-historical thrust of Jesus' mission. The book turns on the statement in 9:51, "When the days were coming to a close for Him to be taken up, He determined to journey to Jerusalem." This begins Jesus' and his disciples' journey to Jerusalem. Darrell Bock notes that "the Jerusalem journey begins as it will end—with a note of failure (19:41–44)."[65] The theme of rejection is prominent in the Gospels. As the Messiah is rejected by the world, so will his disciples be. More importantly, at the end of this journey, the Messiah will be "taken up" (*analēmpseōs*).[66] Luke is the only evangelist who mentions the ascension. In fact, references to the ascension frame the remainder of the Messiah's earthly ministry (9:51; 24:50–53), including his passion, death, and resur-rection (9:21–22, 44–45; 18:31–34). This motif links the earthly ministry of the Messiah with the ongoing mission of the church, since Acts begins with Jesus' being taken up to the Father. Only when Jesus has ascended does the Holy Spirit come on followers whom he has commissioned to carry on his mission.

The ministry of the disciples in Luke's Gospel thus anticipates the ministry of the church in the book of Acts. The Gospel recounts the send-ing out of the Twelve at which they are given authority over demons and illnesses and commanded to "proclaim the kingdom of God and to heal" (Luke 9:2; see 4:18–19; 7:22; 11:18–21). This anticipates the authority the risen Jesus will give his disciples (Acts 1:8). The Twelve's message, as well as the message of the Seventy-two (Luke 10:9, 11), centers on the king-dom of God, announcing its nearness, issuing the call for all to repent and enter the kingdom, and warning that those who refuse to listen are subject

---

[65] Bock, *Luke*, 966.

[66] This is the only instance of this word in the NT and likely refers to Jesus' ascension, not only his death. See the entry in BDAG, 67; see Bock, *Luke*, 967; Joseph Fitzmyer, *The Gospel According to Luke (i–ix)*, AB 28 (Garden City, NY: Doubleday, 1981), 828; against Marshall, *Luke*, 405.

to God's judgment. Hence, the authority and message of the disciples is already indicated in the Gospel, but it has not yet come to full fruition because Jesus' salvific mission on earth is not yet complete. Until that time (24:50–53; Acts 1:9), the disciples are instructed to travel unencumbered (Luke 9:3–5; 10:4–8) because they are as lambs among wolves (10:3) and follow Jesus at great personal cost (9:23–27, 57–62; 12:49–53; 14:25–33). However, as the successful mission of the Seventy-two demonstrates, victory is assured under the banner of the Messiah, and this victory is meant to remind his disciples that they are citizens of heaven (10:17–20).

The Messiah and the Lowly

An important component of the "great reversal" depicted in Luke's Gospel is the evangelist's portrayal of Jesus' concern for the lowly in society— Gentiles (4:25–27; 7:1–9); Samaritans (10:30–37; 17:16); the poor (7:22; see 6:20–23);[67] tax collectors and "sinners" (5:30, 32; 7:34–50; 15:1–2; see 19:10); the sick, demon-possessed, and disabled (e.g., 4:38–41; 7:1–17; 8:26–39; 18:35–43); women (7:36–50; 8:2–3; 10:38–42; 23:55–24:10);[68] and children (9:46–48; 18:15–17). Two salvation-historical points are noteworthy. First, Luke traces Jesus' genealogy back to Adam, not just to Abraham (Matt 1:1–17), emphasizing the Savior's universal effect and his concern for "all the people" (Luke 2:10). Second, Luke frames Jesus' earthly ministry in terms of his identity as Isaiah's Servant of the Lord who was sent by God to bring good news to the poor, liberty to the captives, sight to the blind, and freedom for the oppressed (4:18–19 citing Isa 61:1–2; see Isa 11:1–5; 42:1–4). When Jesus finishes his message, he affirms that the thrust of the original passage has now been fulfilled (Luke 6:24–26; 12:13–21; 16:19–31).

Luke therefore provides a hedge against the false dichotomy some make between evangelism and social action. Each of these aspects of Jesus' earthly ministry has implications for today's churches. The evangel or "good news" promised beforehand (1:19; 2:10) and proclaimed by Jesus (4:18) directly impacts the physical, emotional, material, and spiritual

---

[67] It is best to interpret this expression not in strictly material terms but in a more general sense, that is, "the dispossessed, the excluded" (Köstenberger and O'Brien, *Salvation*, 117).

[68] Luke mentions 13 women not featured in the other Gospels. See Mark Strauss, *Four Portraits, One Jesus: An Introduction to Jesus and the Gospels* (Grand Rapids: Zondervan, 2007), 339.

needs of humanity (see 7:22). This is the "good news about the kingdom of God" (see 4:43; 8:1; 16:16), and Jesus links discipleship with the practical demands of his preaching. The issue of wealth, for example, is dealt with explicitly: "In the same way, therefore, every one of you who does not say good-bye to all his possessions cannot be My disciple" (14:33). Acts describes the early church seeking to live out these demands (Acts 2:44–45; 4:32–37).[69] What is more, the lowliness and humility of children is required of all who would enter into God's kingdom (Luke 18:15–17). Discipleship in the messianic community entails taking on the Messiah's pattern of life in humble obedience to his teaching. The ethnic identity of this community is of particular concern to Luke.

Jews and Gentiles

At the time Luke writes his Gospel, the church has already become a reality—he is writing a history of the Messiah and the church. In so doing, he addresses an important question: if Jesus came to fulfill God's promises to Israel (e.g., 1:47–55, 68–79), why should the church include Gentiles? The Gospel of Luke anticipates the full inclusion of the Gentiles into the people of God, which is narrated in Acts as salvation history progresses.

When the eight-day-old Jesus is presented at the temple, Simeon recognizes the salvation God has prepared for all peoples and prophesies that Jesus will be "a light for revelation to the Gentiles and glory to Your people Israel" (Luke 2:32; see vv. 10, 31). As noted previously, Luke's genealogy traces Jesus back to Adam to underscore that his message of salvation includes all people, even Gentiles (3:23–38). During the course of his ministry, Jesus commends several Gentiles for their faith: the widow of Zarephath and Naaman the Syrian (4:25–27), the Gentile centurion (7:9), and the Samaritan who after being healed returns to give thanks (17:16). Moreover, Jesus "repeatedly hinted at the inclusion of the Gentiles in the orbit of salvation (e.g., 14:23)."[70] Luke concludes his Gospel with Jesus commissioning his disciples to all nations (24:46–48), a mission that subsequently unfolds with the inclusion of Samaritans and Gentiles (Acts 1:8; 8; 10).

---

[69] For a thorough biblical-theological treatment, see Craig L. Blomberg, *Neither Poverty nor Riches: A Biblical Theology of Material Possessions*, NSBT (Grand Rapids: Eerdmans, 1999).

[70] For the quotation and much of this section, Köstenberger, Kellum, and Quarles, *The Cradle, the Cross, and the Crown*, 282–86.

Ekklēsia *in Luke–Acts*

Luke's use (or lack thereof) of *ekklēsia* in his Gospel and Acts indicates the already/not-yet nature of the church. The expression is not found in the Gospel at all but occurs twenty-three times in Acts, nineteen of which refer to the "church" as the gathered body of Christians.[71] Other uses pertain to a gathering of people (Acts 19:32, 39, 41) or to the OT Israelites (7:38). This omission of the term "church" in Luke's Gospel coupled with the frequent use of the same term in Luke's sequel suggests that the church is not a fully constituted entity during Jesus' earthly ministry.

Summary

Luke's Gospel demonstrates the salvation-historical plan of God for humanity. This plan includes the suffering, death, resurrection, and ascension of the Messiah, who is the Savior of Jews and Gentiles alike. Jesus' earthly ministry also demonstrates a concern for the lowest in society and provides them access to the kingdom of God. The Messiah gathers and sends followers to take part in this mission of bringing salvation to all nations, a mission that will require sacrifice but will result in ultimate victory.[72] The newly gathered messianic community, in turn, constitutes the core of the church, consisting of both believing Jews and non-Jews. The church is born in the early stages of the book of Acts.

John

As in Mark and Luke, the term "church" (*ekklēsia*) is not found in John's Gospel. John is primarily concerned with the identity and mission of the Messiah, the pre-existent, incarnate Word (1:1–18), and the eternal life entered into by faith in Jesus the Messiah (20:30–31). However, like the Synoptics, John has much to say about the nature and identity of the nascent church, the new messianic community.

---

[71] Lexical data are from Köstenberger and Bouchoc, *Book Study Concordance*, 677; see BDAG, 303–4. Note perhaps the universal sense of "church" in Acts 9:31. For more on Acts, see Kendell H. Easley's chapter in this volume.

[72] On discipleship in Luke, see Richard N. Longenecker, "Taking Up the Cross Daily: Discipleship in Luke–Acts," in *Patterns of Discipleship in the New Testament* (Grand Rapids: Eerdmans, 1996), 50–76.

John highlights the initial gathering and training of Jesus' disciples. The term "disciple" (*mathētēs*) in John refers to the followers of Jesus (as distinguished from the "crowd," *ochlos*) and at times specifically the Twelve (6:67–71).[73] Jesus calls the first disciples to follow him (1:35–41). He teaches them and involves them in his earthly ministry, including his messianic signs (2:1–11; see 4:2, 8, 27, 31–38; 6:3–24, 60–71).[74] The risen Jesus appears to and commissions them (esp. 20:19–23). Generally, the Fourth Gospel's characterization of the disciples is consistent with the way in which they are cast in the Synoptics.

Yet John depicts the essence of the messianic community not primarily through descriptions of the disciples but through his distinct corporate metaphors. Unlike the Synoptic writers, he never mentions the appointment of the Twelve. The first explicit reference to the Twelve does not occur until the end of chapter 6. John assumes his readers' knowledge of the Twelve from Synoptic tradition. In this way, by largely presupposing the Synoptic pattern of Jesus' calling and gathering of the Twelve, John is able to move beyond the portrayal of the messianic community in the other Gospels.[75] Through his corporate metaphors, then, John comes closest of any Gospel writer to presenting a theology of the church at this transitional juncture in salvation history.

Metaphors for the Messianic Community

John uses the corporate metaphors of "the flock" (chap. 10) and "the vine" (chap. 15) to transfer depictions of OT Israel to Jesus and his followers. These metaphors tie together the Johannine themes of Christology, discipleship, and mission. They also balance the emphasis on individual disciples and the need for personal faith and regeneration with the communal dimension of a believer's life, in particular the vital importance of mutual love and unity.[76]

---

[73] See especially chap. 4 of my published dissertation, *The Missions of Jesus and the Disciples According to the Fourth Gospel* (Grand Rapids: Eerdmans, 1998), 142–61; see also my monograph *A Theology of John's Gospel and Letters: The Word, the Christ, the Son of God*, BTNT (Grand Rapids: Zondervan, 2009), 490–91.

[74] On Jesus' relationship with his disciples, see my article "Jesus as Rabbi in the Fourth Gospel," *BBR* 8 (1998): 97–128.

[75] For a full discussion see Köstenberger, *Theology*, 549–63.

[76] Köstenberger, *Theology*, 501. See Schnackenburg, *Gospel According to St. John*, 3:209; Dan O. Via, "Darkness, Christ and Church in the Fourth Gospel," *SJT* 14 (1961): 172–93.

The Flock (John 10:1–18)

References to God's people as his spiritual flock are frequent in the OT. Ezekiel, for example, speaks of Yahweh as the shepherd of his sheep, Israel, whom he will visit personally in the future (Ezek 34:11–24).[77] Zechariah refers to the messianic shepherd who will be struck and his sheep scattered (Zech 13:7–9). Thus, when Jesus affirms that he is the good shepherd who came to lay down his life for the sheep (John 10:11), he claims to be the fulfillment of the scriptural promises of an end-time messianic shepherd, in contrast to Israel's faithless religious leaders. The Messiah's death will bring these promises to their ultimate fruition. As D. A. Carson observes, "By the strong language Jesus uses, he points beyond the metaphorical world to himself."[78] Jesus speaks of his bodily sacrifice for his sheep, which will not only protect and deliver them but will also draw them to himself (12:32).

What is more, in John 10:16, the term "flock" is used in the context of Jesus' uniting his sheep with yet other sheep he will gather into the fold in the near future. Likely a reference to the Gentile mission, this expresses Jesus' vision of one messianic community comprised of believing Jews and Gentiles. In keeping with Ezekiel's vision, there will be one flock and a single shepherd (Ezek 34:23). In the flock are those sheep who know the Messiah and who hear his voice (John 10:14, 16; see 8:47). Thus, the messianic flock consists of the chosen people of God, called and gathered by the Messiah's voice. Conversely, those who do not follow the messianic shepherd are not part of God's flock (10:25–26). According to John, new covenant membership is not defined by ethnic identity but by faith in Jesus (20:30–31). Consequently, "One may view the entire gospel as an unfolding presentation of the movement from old definitions of discipleship and belonging to the people of God to a new understanding of such categories."[79]

The Vine and the Branches (John 15)

The second corporate metaphor, "the vine," also has OT antecedents. The vineyard was a common conception of God's people, especially in the pro-

---

[77] See Pss 77:20; 78:52; Isa 40:11; Jer 23:1.
[78] D. A. Carson, *The Gospel According to John*, PNTC (Grand Rapids: Eerdmans, 1991), 386.
[79] Köstenberger, *Theology*, 502.

phetic writings.[80] What is different and particularly noteworthy in John 15 is that the true vine is Jesus himself, the true representative of Israel. Jesus' followers, for their part, are participants—branches—in Jesus, the new Israel.[81] The corporate metaphor of "the vine" and "the branches" highlights the organic, intimate relationship between the Messiah and his followers. Jesus' disciples find their life in him as they spiritually remain (*menō*) in him and thereby produce spiritual fruit befitting his people (15:4–5). This means that to believe in Jesus entails not simply profession of faith but reliance on Jesus as "the continuing source of nurture and strength in the life of individual believers and of the community."[82] Abiding in "the vine" organically yields love for the Father in and through Jesus the Son (vv. 9–10) and love for fellow believers as a witness to the surrounding unbelieving world (v. 12; 17:23–25; see 13:35).

In this regard, John makes clear that members of the new messianic community are not self-appointed. Rather, the Messiah has called them in keeping with the Father's will, and their election is for the purpose of bearing fruit in the world (15:16). The establishment of the new messianic community is set in the larger framework of John's missional emphasis. These corporate metaphors identify God's people, the new messianic community, as being bound together by faith in Jesus the Messiah. This one true flock of God moves beyond the ethnic boundaries of Israel to include believing Gentiles as well (10:16; see 12:37–43). This inclusive, universal vision is given vivid expression in the Messiah's final prayer for the messianic community and those who believe on account of their proclamation.

The Messiah's Prayer for His Community (John 17)

Jesus' prayer for his messianic community follows his teaching on the imminent coming of the Holy Spirit and the community's future mission. Although commonly referred to as the "high priestly prayer," Jesus' final prayer may rightfully serve as a model prayer—"the Lord's Prayer"—for his disciples (see Matt 6:9–13; Luke 11:2–4). In this prayer, Jesus prays

---

[80] See Ps 80:8–16; Isa 5:1–7; 27:2–6; Jer 2:21; Ezekiel 15; 19:10–14; Hos 10:1.

[81] Köstenberger, *Theology*, 502–3; see Carson, *John*, 511–12, on the connection to Synoptic parallels.

[82] Köstenberger, *Theology*, 503.

first for himself (John 17:1–5), then for his disciples (vv. 6–19), and finally for later generations of believers (vv. 20–26).

Jesus' prayer for himself is not focused on himself. Rather, it recognizes what God the Father has done and will do in and through him, that is, bring eternal life to those who believe in him (John 17:2–3). Moreover, it rejoices in the successful completion of the mission, which his Father had sent him to accomplish (vv. 4–5; see Isa 55:11–12). Jesus "the Son" is cast as the model of obedient submission to the Father's will.

In John 17:6–19, Jesus prays for his followers, concerned that they understand the relationship between God the Father and him. Indeed, their mission will depend on this (vv. 7–9, 18). What is significant salvation-historically here is that Jesus is praying for his disciples because they will remain in the world while he returns to the Father (v. 11). They will need the empowerment of the Holy Spirit to carry forward Jesus' mission as he had promised (14:15–17; see 16:7–11). Jesus therefore prays for their consecration just as he had been consecrated by the Father before coming into the world (17:17–19). Their witness to Jesus will depend on the sustaining grace of God.

Finally, Jesus prays for those who will believe in generations to come. His overriding concern in this prayer is for his disciples' unity (John 17:21, 23). This is because he is concerned with carrying forward his mission from the Father (v. 4). Only when the disciples are unified as the Father and the Son are unified will they be able to accomplish the mission. Rather than jockey for position, as many did during Jesus' earthly ministry (e.g., Matt 20:20–28; Mark 9:33–37), the disciples are to be unified in their witness to the world (John 17:23). Chiefly, this witness consists of loving one another (v. 26). Any community bearing the name of Christ must be characterized by love if it is to be faithful in its witness to the world.

The Gospel of John portrays this witness—the continuing mission of Jesus' disciples—in vivid terms. John presents the sending of the disciples as an extension of Jesus' sending by the Father. They are sent into the world as Jesus was sent into the world (John 17:8; 20:21), to bring in the harvest (4:38) and to bear fruit (15:16). The disciples' mission is to be characterized by an obedient relationship to their sender Jesus, by a separation from the world, and by an inaugurated, even realized, eschatological outlook (e.g., 5:19–29).

This realized eschatology of John's Gospel is related to what we might call his realized *ecclesiology*. The "flock" already *constituted* will have one

Shepherd in the future (John 10:16). Jesus does not receive the Greeks—Gentiles—yet (12:20–26), though he already speaks of, and prays for, their future ingathering (13:32; 17:20–21). Thus, the already constituted messianic community anticipates the inclusion of future believers on the basis of Jesus' impending glorification (see 12:23; 17:1–5, 22–23). This eschatological and missional perspective sets the framework for the church's ingathering of believers into the messianic community.

Summary

John depicts Jesus' new messianic community in vivid metaphorical terms that are nonetheless real theologically and spiritually. The terminology of "the flock" and "the vine" presents the new messianic community as eternally called and chosen by God the Father, obedient to the teaching of the Messiah, and remaining in him and in his teaching by the Holy Spirit. Grounded in the unity and love existing among the members of the Godhead, believers are prepared for their mission to the world. This mission, John makes clear, in keeping with Jesus' own vision, will move beyond the boundaries of ethnic Israel to include "other sheep," Gentiles, as well. Thus, John's purpose for writing is for both Jews and Gentiles to come to know the Messiah's identity and work, to believe in his name, and by believing to have eternal life (20:30–31).[83]

Conclusion

The foregoing survey of the four Gospels' distinct contributions to a biblical theology of the church has yielded common biblical-theological themes. The Messiah and his kingdom, the identity of the messianic community, the nature of discipleship in the community, and the commissioning of that community for the Messiah's mission are prominent overlapping themes in all four Gospels.

The Messiah, Jesus Christ, is the consistent focus of all the Gospels. Each is concerned with presenting him as the Son of God. It is this Messiah who announces the arrival of the kingdom of God (e.g., Mark 1:15). Matthew, Mark, and Luke present an already-not yet eschatology with regard to the gathering of the new messianic community, while

---

[83] For a fuller treatment, see Köstenberger, *Theology*, 481–500.

John's eschatology, as mentioned, is more realized in nature. The Gospels uniformly portray the Twelve as the New Israel, gathered by the Messiah. The OT promises of a Messiah and his gathered people are being brought together in the Gospels in anticipation of the sending of the Holy Spirit and the resulting mission of the church.

The four Gospels all describe the identity of the gathered messianic community that will become the foundation of the church. In each Gospel, Jesus calls disciples to himself and involves them in his ministry. He also teaches them about the nature of their community, which is rooted in its identity as his followers (e.g., Matt 16:18; John 15:1–10). Moreover, the Gospels anticipate an extension of the messianic community beyond the ethnic boundaries of Israel to the Gentiles (e.g., Matt 12:17–21; see Isa 42:1–4; Mark 12:1–12; Luke 2:28–32; see Isa 42:6; 49:6; John 10:16; 11:51–52). Although Jesus' earthly mission was first to the Jews, his mission will extend to the Gentiles through the ongoing ministry of his disciples.

The character of the messianic community will be essential to its present and future mission. Thus, Jesus teaches his disciples throughout the Gospels about the nature of discipleship. His Sermon on the Mount sets forth the type of love and unity that should be exemplified by his community (Matthew 5–7). Following Jesus means seeking his righteousness as members of his kingdom (6:33) and keeping his commands (5:19; John 14:15). As John elaborates, this is done by a spiritual union with the exalted Jesus that bears fruit for the entire world to see (15:1–17). Jesus' followers will bear fruit by their faith and obedience and through those who trust in the Messiah based on their testimony.

The fourfold Gospel canon uniformly affirms Jesus' expectation that the church will carry out its mission after his exaltation (e.g., Matt 28:18–20). The mission of the Messiah will be carried out by Jesus' followers in the power of the Holy Spirit (John 17:18; 20:21; see Luke 24:49; John 14:15–17; 16:7–11). This ministry will extend to all nations (Matt 28:19; see Gen 12:1–3), incorporating Gentiles into the people of God. The Messiah's victory over sin and death made possible the reconciliation of Jew and Gentile in the church. The mission of Jesus' messianic community is ultimately a victorious ministry, for not even death will overcome it (Matt 16:18).

When the fourfold Gospel canon closes, we have the messianic community gathered, commissioned, and poised to embark on the mission of the Messiah in the power of the Holy Spirit. The mission of the Messiah will continue in the establishment and growth of his church by his word and his Spirit. The book of Acts seamlessly continues the NT presentation of God's plan as this sequel of Luke's Gospel narrates the exaltation of Jesus, the pouring out of the Holy Spirit, and the church's establishment in the power of the Spirit from Jerusalem and Judea to Samaria and to the ends of the earth.[84]

[84] I am grateful to Grant Taylor for his assistance in preparing this essay. Under my close supervision, and based on a series of extensive conversations and my previous published work, Mr. Taylor wrote first drafts of respective portions of this essay.

CHAPTER 3

The Church in Acts and Revelation: New Testament Bookends

Kendell H. Easley

This study examines the church in the NT book that describes its historical inception (Acts) and the book that tells about its future consummation (Revelation). We will mine these bookends to help today's followers of Jesus understand ourselves as sharing in the life of a congregation.

Studies of the church in the NT often take Acts[1] into account briefly but then move on quickly to consider the epistles, especially Paul's. The contribution of Revelation to ecclesiology is often overlooked, perhaps because it emphasizes Christ and his victory, or perhaps due to an assumption (in some eschatological views) that the church is mostly absent during the events described in Revelation.[2] When additional terms

---

[1] The literature on Acts is immense. The following are highly recommended: Darrell L. Bock, *Acts*, BECNT (Grand Rapids: Baker, 2007); F. F. Bruce, *The Acts of the Apostles* (Grand Rapids: Eerdmans, 1951); John Polhill, *Acts*, NAC (Nashville: B&H, 1992); John Stott, *The Spirit, the Church, and the World* (Downers Grove: InterVarsity, 1990); Ben Witherington, *Acts: A Socio-Rhetorical Commentary* (Grand Rapids: Eerdmans, 1998).

[2] For example, Arthur G. Patzia's otherwise outstanding study of the emergence of the church gives detailed attention to the growth and diversity of early Christianity but almost completely ignores the church in Revelation. Arthur G. Patzia, *The Emergence*

for Jesus' covenant community in Acts and Revelation are included, a broader picture emerges. Though "the church" has been written about extensively, few studies have targeted "the church in Acts" or "the church in Revelation," and no study narrows in on "the church in Acts and Revelation." This study focuses especially on the varied Greek vocabulary for "church" in these two books.

Church and Churches in Acts: *Ekklēsia* Vocabulary

Elsewhere in this book, the extent to which it is appropriate to consider the church (*ekklēsia*) as present in the OT is considered. It is well known that the only specific references to church in the Gospels are Jesus' words in Matt 16:18; 18:17, though this volume elsewhere shows that the Gospels reference the church in many other ways. Yet the church first appears as a self-conscious Christian entity in the book of Acts. We begin by looking at the variety of ways Luke uses *ekklēsia* in Acts.

Ekklēsia *as a Specific, Intentional, Regularly Meeting, Local Association of Jesus' Followers*

Of the seventeen times that *ekklēsia* (singular) is used in Acts in a Christian sense,[3] nine refer to the Jerusalem congregation:

"Fear came on the whole church" (5:11).

"Persecution broke out against the church in Jerusalem" (8:1).

"Saul, however, was ravaging the church" (8:3).

"The report about them reached the ears of the church in Jerusalem" (11:22).

---

of the Church: Context, Growth, Leadership and Worship (Downers Grove: InterVarsity, 2001).

[3] The four non-Christian instances of *ekklēsia* in Acts confirm the Israelite background of "church" as related to the Hebrew *qāhāl*, "a (religious) assembly of Israelites," usually rendered *ekklēsia* in LXX, but sometimes *sunagogē*—"[Moses] was in the congregation [*ekklēsia*] in the desert," Acts 7:38, alluding to Deut 9:10. (See also Heb 2:12 [*ekklēsia*], quoting Ps 22:22 [*qāhāl*].) Of interest is *qĕhal YHWH* (LXX, *ekklēsia kuriou*, congregation of Yahweh), for example, Num 16:3; 20:4; Deut 23:2–4. On the other hand Luke used *ekklēsia* secularly to refer to "a (purposeful) assembly of persons," so three times: "the assembly was in confusion" (19:32); "decided in a legal assembly" (19:39); "he dismissed the assembly" (19:41).

"Herod cruelly attacked some who belonged to the church" (12:1).

"Prayer was being made earnestly to God for him by the church" (12:5).

"They were welcomed by the church, the apostles, and the elders" (15:4).

"The apostles and the elders, with the whole church, decided to select men from among them" (15:22).

"He went up and greeted the church" (18:22).

This congregation was comprised of baptized followers of Jesus, described as those who "devoted themselves to the apostles' teaching, to the fellowship, to the breaking of bread, and to prayers" (2:42). Because Luke did not use the term *ekklēsia* for this body until it faced and overcame a threat, the first church may have formed part of its identity *as church* in the face of difficulty. As John Polhill writes concerning Acts 5:11:

> It might be noted that this is the first time the word "church" (*ekklēsia*) occurs in Acts, which denotes the people of God gathered as a religious community. Perhaps it is not by accident that it occurs in the context of this [Ananias and Sapphira] story. The church can only thrive as the people of God if it lives within the total trust of all its members. . . . Where there is duplicity and distrust, its witness fails.[4]

The leadership of the Jerusalem congregation consisted of apostles and elders[5] (15:2, 4, 6, 22–23; 16:4). The only other church organization noted is the (possibly temporary) service of the Seven (6:3–6; 21:8).[6]

As believers took the message of Jesus elsewhere, they followed the Jerusalem pattern. Four of the *ekklēsia* occurrences in Acts refer to the mixed-race congregation in Antioch of Syria:

---

[4] Polhill, *Acts,* 160.

[5] Elder (*presbutertos*) in Acts can also refer to Jewish religious leaders: 4:5, 8, 23; 6:12; 23:14; 24:1; 25:15.

[6] There is no textual evidence that the work of the Seven was reconstituted after the Saul persecution subsided. By the time of the council in Acts 15, "apostles and elders" were functioning there again. While many trace the origin of church deacons to the Seven, this is historically not provable.

"For a whole year they met with the church" (11:26).

"In the local church at Antioch there were prophets and teachers" (13:1).

"After they arrived and gathered the church together . . ." (14:27).

"When they had been sent on their way by the church . . ." (15:3).

An additional two occurrences refer to the church in Ephesus:

"He sent to Ephesus and called for the elders of the church" (20:17).

"The Holy Spirit has appointed you as overseers, to shepherd the church of God" (20:28).

Two ideas are noteworthy. First, the leaders are called both "elders" and "overseers," with a responsibility to shepherd or pastor their flock. Second, Luke uses the same term to refer to the Gentile congregations (*ekklēsia*) that he used earlier to refer to the all-Jewish church in Jerusalem.

This same meaning ("local assembly") is found in the plural instances of *ekklēsia* in Acts. There are only two such occurrences:

"He traveled through Syria and Cilicia, strengthening the churches" (15:41).

"So the churches were strengthened in the faith" (16:5).

Thus, the principal way Luke uses *ekklēsia* is to refer to local, self-conscious groups of Jesus' followers. John Stott describes the first such congregation in Jerusalem as: (1) learning (commitment to apostolic teaching and Scripture), (2) loving (mutual concern and fellowship), (3) worshipping (prayer and the Lord's Supper), and (4) evangelizing (sharing the good news).[7] This surely was the model followed by other congregations mentioned in Acts.

Ekklēsia *as the Widespread, Intentional Association of Jesus' Followers*

This leaves only two other instances of *ekklēsia* (singular) in Acts. Each is instructive. First is Acts 14:23: "When they had appointed elders in every

---

[7] Stott, *The Spirit, the Church, and the World*, 81–87, commenting on Acts 2:42–47.

church and prayed with fasting, they committed them to the Lord in whom they had believed."[8] Thus, as early as the end of Paul's first church-planting journey, a pattern of identifying and commissioning reliable leaders for each congregation was established. These churches were alike in other regards as well: They were comprised of believers in the Lord who practiced prayer and fasting. Likely they were aware of one another, but the extent of cooperation is unknown.

The other instance of *ekklēsia* (singular) to be considered is in Acts 9:31: "So the church throughout all Judea, Galilee,[9] and Samaria had peace, being built up and walking in the fear of the Lord and in the encouragement of the Holy Spirit, and it increased in numbers." Here for the only time in Acts, *ekklēsia* (singular) is found where we might have expected Luke to use the plural—as he did in 15:41 and 16:5. Yet the singular form stubbornly remains.[10] Luke used *ekklēsia* (singular) at this point in his narrative to refer to all of Jesus' followers in many places (who met intentionally and regularly with other believers in their own cities). In addition to signifying a local congregation of believers, it appears that *ekklēsia* was a manner of referencing all believers in all the cities mentioned in Acts 9:31.[11]

This falls short of the full-orbed doctrine of the church as Paul later developed it. However, it shows the beginning of thinking about *ekklēsia* as both a city-specific association of believers led by local elders (or pastors or overseers) and the widespread association of Jesus' followers (the worldwide body of Christ). It is instructive that Luke generally referred to "the church" without modifiers. He never used such terms as "Paul's church" or "large church," as we do. The only exceptions are "the whole church" and "every church" (5:11; 14:23; 15:22), as well as Paul's

---

[8] This instance of *ekklēsia* might have been included in the previous category, except that we cannot identify the specific locations for these churches.

[9] There is no other information about the establishment of congregations in Galilee.

[10] Although most MSS read the plural (*ekklēsiai*), as does the KJV, the earliest and best evidence (including P74, Aleph, A, B, C, and 36) supports the singular. The UBS4 Greek NT editors are "certain" the original reading in Acts 9:31 was singular (*The Greek New Testament*, 4th rev. ed., ed. B. Aland, K. Aland, J. Karavidopoulos, C. M. Martini, and B. M. Metzger [United Bible Societies, 1993]).

[11] *TDNT* 3:505.

important reference to "the church of God"[12] (20:28). Paul later picked up the phrase "church of God" in his writing (1 Cor 1:2 ESV; 10:32; 15:9; 2 Cor 1:1 ESV; Gal 1:13 ESV).

Jesus' Covenant Community in Acts: Singular Nouns

In addition to *ekklēsia* language, Luke used other key terms when referring to Jesus' followers. We begin with collective (singular) nouns that focus attention on the unified identity all Christians shared. These include the Way, the company, the kingdom, the people [of God], and the flock.

The Way (Hodos)

In Acts (but never elsewhere) "the Way" (*hodos*) is used six times as a name for Jesus' followers,[13] always in contexts distinguishing them from Jews:

"If he found any who belonged to the Way . . ." (9:2).

"Some became hardened and would not believe, slandering the Way" (19:9).

"There was a major disturbance about the Way" (19:23).

"I persecuted this Way to the death" (22:4).

"According to the Way, which they call a sect . . ." (24:14).

"Felix was accurately informed about the Way" (24:22).

Like the instances of *ekklēsia*, these are used absolutely. The group was never called "the Way of Jesus" or "Way of Life" or anything similar. Further, this usage differs from Luke's nontechnical and figurative use[14] of *hodos* as a "manner of believing or behaving" (for example, 16:17; 18:25–26). No one knows why this synonym for *ekklēsia* was not used in the epistles.

---

[12] The Greek manuscript evidence is in fact divided. Some contain the reading "the church of the Lord" or "the church of the Lord and God." The UBS4 editors had difficulty determining which variant to put in the text but opted for "church of God."

[13] "It [*hodos*] probably corresponds to Hb. *halakhah* ('walk,' 'rule of life')" (Bruce, *Acts*, 197).

[14] Literally *hodos* meant a road (such as a street or highway) or a journey.

*The Company (*Plēthos*)*

In five cases in Acts, *plēthos* ("a company or multitude") refers descriptively to a Christian group that had gathered to consider a particular matter or course of action:

> "Now the multitude of those who believed were of one heart" (4:32).

> "Then the Twelve summoned the whole company of the disciples" (6:2).

> "The proposal pleased the whole company" (6:5).

> "Then the whole assembly fell silent and listened" (15:12).

> "And after gathering the assembly, they delivered the letter" (15:30).

These uses do not rise to the level of a name for the believers (as if they designated themselves "the company"). In fact *plēthos* occurs in several places in the sense of an ad hoc crowd (2:6; 5:16; 14:4; 21:36). Nevertheless, the term can reference a local fellowship of Christians called together for a specific purpose.

*The Kingdom (*Basileia*)*

The kingdom of God in the preaching of Jesus is well known, if not well understood. There is no need to review that "reign/rule of God" is preferable to "kingdom of God" in English translation or that Jesus' teaching about *basileia* included both "already" and "not yet" elements (or present and eschatological aspects).[15] All these emphases may be assumed in Luke's use of *basileia* in Acts (eight instances). These all refer unquestionably to God's rule:

> ". . . speaking about the kingdom of God" (1:3).

> "Lord, at this time are You restoring the kingdom to Israel?" (1:6).

---

[15] Generations of evangelical NT scholars and theologians have been deeply impacted along these lines by the seminal thinking of George Eldon Ladd, notably *The Gospel of the Kingdom* (Grand Rapids: Eerdmans, 1959) and *A Theology of the New Testament,* 2nd ed., ed. Donald A. Hagner (Grand Rapids: Eerdmans, 1993).

"He proclaimed the good news about the kingdom of God" (8:12).

". . . pass through many troubles on our way into the kingdom of God" (14:22).

"Persuade them about things related to the kingdom of God" (19:8).

". . . among whom I went about preaching the kingdom" (20:25)

"He expounded and witnessed about the kingdom of God" (28:23).

". . . proclaiming the kingdom of God" (28:31).

The kingdom thus remained a primary topic of early Christian discussion and preaching. This term is generally connected with an eschatological element of the church. As John Polhill summarizes:

> The book [of Acts] begins with Jesus sharing the message of God's kingdom with his disciples (1:3). It quickly raises the burning question, "Are you at this time going to restore the kingdom to Israel?" (1:6). That question has now been answered. God has indeed restored his kingdom—in the Messiah, in Christ. And it is open to all who will receive him, Jew and Greek. In Christ, God's kingdom is realized as he comes to rule in the hearts of his people.[16]

The expectation is that although the life of Jesus' followers *now* is filled with difficulty, once God's rule has been fully manifested, things *then* will become much better. (At the same time, despite persecution and suffering, the gospel keeps triumphing at the present time.) Thus, believers have truly experienced the "already but not yet" reality of the kingdom. They may not have named themselves (in their *present* experience as the persecuted church) "the kingdom." This term apparently belonged to their *future* hope of experiencing God's victory in all its fullness.

The People [of God] (Laos)

The noun *laos*, referencing the "people [of God]" or "My people," has a strong connection with the OT. Beginning in Exodus, the Israelites were

---

[16] Polhill, *Acts*, 546–47.

designated as a people belonging to God.[17] Redemption and covenant often were implicit in the phrase "My people" (for example, Lev 26:12; Ps 50:7; Isa 1:3). Especially noteworthy is the new covenant passage in Jer 31:33.[18]

Of the forty-eight instances of *laos* in Acts,[19] two reflect the theological conviction that God's work in building the church extended his covenant people from the OT.[20] The first is James's observation that in Peter's preaching to Cornelius, "God first intervened to take from the Gentiles a people for His name" (15:14).[21] The second is Jesus' pledge of personal safety to Paul while he was in Corinth, "because I have many people in this city" (18:10). Both texts convey that Christians are as much God's special possession as Israel.[22]

The Flock (Poimnion)

One final collective noun should be noted: "flock" (*poimnion*), a figurative term occurring twice in Paul's counsel to the elders of Ephesus. He asked them to be "on guard for yourselves and for all the flock" (20:28). And in the next verse he predicted savage wolves that would come, "not sparing the flock" (v. 29).[23]

Summary

Based on the singular nouns used in Acts, Jesus' followers, wherever they lived, both Jew and Gentile, regarded themselves as belonging to "the Way" and to "the church" (understood mainly as a local congregation but with a trace of translocal implication). They likely would not have named

---

[17] For example, Exod 3:7, 10. God's word to Pharaoh, "Let My people go" (Exod 5:1; 7:16; 8:1, 20) strongly suggests that he considered Israel his own possession.

[18] See also Lev 26:12; Ezek 37:26–27. Both 2 Cor 6:16 and Heb 8:10 quote Jer 31:33 as having ongoing fulfillment in God's NT people, the church.

[19] Most are secular instances, using *laos* much the same as today's English speakers use "people."

[20] The explicit language of "covenant" as applied to Jesus' followers is missing from Acts. The only instances of *diathēkē* (covenant) are 3:25; 7:8, and these are clearly Israelite references. Nevertheless, the language of *laos* as applied in Acts to Gentile followers of Jesus shows that a local, mixed-race congregation could have thought of itself as a "covenant community."

[21] James quoted Amos 9:11–12 in support of his conclusion.

[22] See the chapter by Paul House in this book.

[23] First Peter 5:2–3 is the only other NT reference to a congregation as a flock. This usage follows the OT concept of Israel as Yahweh's sheep (for example, Jer 23:2; Ezek 34:22) and Jesus' calling his followers a "little flock" (Luke 12:32).

their group "the company," "the kingdom," "God's people," or "God's flock," although they would have understood these as accurate descriptions of who they were. This terminology both builds on OT concepts and looks forward to eschatological fulfillment.

Jesus' Covenant Community in Acts: Plural Nouns

We move now to consider plural nouns that Luke used to refer to those committed to Jesus (that is, those of the church or the Way). These terms are especially important in determining how individuals who were part of this movement referred to themselves.

Brothers (Adelphoi)

Luke's favorite designation for Jesus' followers in Acts is "brothers." (This is noticeably different from his use of *adelphoi* in the Third Gospel.[24]) Of the fifty-seven instances of *adelphos* in Acts, thirty-two are in a plural form and refer to followers of Jesus in the sense of persons who are part of the same spiritual family.[25] "There are both Jewish and Gentile parallels to this use of *adelphoi* to denote members of the same religious community."[26] Luke uses *adelphoi* as essentially synonymous with "fellow believers" or "fellow Christians."[27]

"Peter stood up among the brothers" (1:15).

"Brothers, the Scripture had to be fulfilled" (1:16).

"Therefore, brothers, select from among you seven men" (6:3).

"When the brothers found out, they took him down to Caesarea" (9:30).

"Some of the brothers from Joppa . . ." (10:23).

---

[24] In Luke 6:41–42; 17:3 *adelphos* means "fellow human being." In 22:32, it implies "fellow apostles." Usually in Luke it refers to a male biological sibling.

[25] Brother in its literal sense of "male biological sibling" occurs in Acts 1:14; 7:13; 12:2.

[26] Bruce, *Acts,* 75.

[27] That by *adelphoi* (plural) Luke included female believers is clear from Acts 1:14–15, in which the women, including Jesus' mother, were called "brothers."

"The apostles and the brothers who were throughout Judea heard" (11:1).

"These six brothers accompanied me" (11:12).

". . . determined to send relief to the brothers who lived in Judea" (11:29).

"Report these things to James and the brothers" (12:17).

". . . poisoned the minds of the Gentiles against the brothers" (14:2).

"Men came down from Judea and began to teach the brothers" (15:1).

"They created great joy among all the brothers" (15:3).

"Brothers, you are aware that in the early days . . ." (15:7).

"James responded: 'Brothers, listen to me'" (15:13).

". . . Barsabbas, and Silas, both leading men among the brothers" (15:22).

"From the apostles and elders, your brothers . . ." (15:23).

"To the brothers from among the Gentiles . . ." (15:23).

". . . encouraged the brothers and strengthened them" (15:32).

"They were sent back in peace by the brothers" (15:33).

"Let's go back and visit the brothers in every town" (15:36).

". . . being commended to the grace of the Lord by the brothers" (15:40)

"The brothers at Lystra and Iconium spoke highly of him" (16:2).

"They saw and encouraged the brothers" (16:40).

"They dragged Jason and some of the brothers" (17:6).

"The brothers sent Paul and Silas off" (17:10).

"Then the brothers immediately sent Paul away" (17:14).

"Paul, having stayed on for many days, said good-bye to the brothers" (18:18).

"The brothers wrote to the disciples" (18:27).

". . . where we greeted the brothers and stayed with them" (21:7).

"The brothers welcomed us gladly" (21:17).

"There we found believers and were invited to stay with them" (28:14).

"Now the believers from there had heard the news" (28:15).

In Acts, Luke also used *adelphoi* in the sense of "fellow Jews," generally when one Jew (whether a follower of Jesus or not) spoke to another Jew (whether a Jesus follower or not).[28] Among followers of Jesus, Jews and Gentiles were equally recognized as siblings in God's new family (compare 6:3 with 15:36).

Disciples (Mathētai)

After "brothers," "disciples" was Luke's second-favorite term for Jesus' followers. This replicates the way all the Gospels, including Luke, use this term to refer to the students/followers of a particular religious teacher.[29] In Acts, of the twenty-eight instances of this word, twenty-two are in the plural, referring to persons committed to living according to Jesus' teachings.[30] As in the case of "brothers," the group comprising "disciples" is identical with the group of believers/Christians:

"As the number of disciples was multiplying" (6:1).

". . . summoned the whole company of the disciples" (6:2).

"The number of disciples in Jerusalem multiplied greatly" (6:7).

". . . threats and murder against the disciples of the Lord" (9:1).

"Saul was with the disciples in Damascus for some days" (9:19).

---

[28] For example, 2:29, 37; 3:17; 13:15, 26, 38; 22:1, 5; 23:1, 5, 6. Acts can also use "brothers" in historical references to mean "Israelites," for example, 3:22, 25, 26, 37.

[29] Usually the reference is to Jesus' disciples, but it may refer to John the Baptist's followers (Luke 5:33; 7:18) or disciples of the Pharisees (Luke 5:33). In the Gospels disciples could physically and literally follow after Jesus as he traveled. In Acts and the rest of the NT, following Jesus became figurative. In the Gospels, "disciples" could refer either to the Twelve or to the larger group who followed Jesus. In the Third Gospel, "apostles" was used sparingly and meant only the Twelve collectively. In Acts "apostles" continued to be used (but only in the plural form) to refer to the apostolic leadership group, while "disciples" included every Christian.

[30] Two instances in Acts refer to disciples of someone other than Jesus: disciples of Saul/Paul (9:25) and disciples of John the Baptist (19:1).

"The disciples heard that Peter was there" (9:38).

"The disciples were first called Christians in Antioch" (11:26).

"Each of the disciples, according to his ability, determined to send" (11:29).

"And the disciples were filled with joy and the Holy Spirit" (13:52).

"After the disciples surrounded him, he got up" (14:20).

". . . strengthening the hearts of the disciples" (14:22).

"They spent a considerable time with the disciples" (14:28).

". . . by putting on the disciples' necks a yoke" (15:10).

". . . strengthening all the disciples" (18:23).

"The brothers wrote to the disciples" (18:27).

"He found some disciples" (19:1).

". . . met separately with the disciples" (19:9).

"The disciples did not let him" (19:30).

"Paul sent for the disciples" (20:1).

". . . with deviant doctrines to lure the disciples into following them" (20:30).

"So we found some disciples and stayed there" (21:4).

"Some of the disciples from Caesarea also went with us" (21:16).

Only four individuals in Acts are called a disciple (singular): Ananias (9:10), Saul/Paul (v. 26), Tabitha/Dorcas (v. 36), and Timothy (16:1). Each, of course, could as easily have been called a "believer" or a "Christian."

Saints/Holy Ones (Hagioi)

No mere human[31] (or group of persons) was ever called "saint/holy one" (*hagios*) in Luke's Gospel. In Acts, the usage is different. Most instances

---

[31] Jesus was called "the holy One [*hagios*] to be born" to Mary (Luke 1:35; see also Acts 2:27), but this is manifestly different from the use of "holy one [*hagios*]" in reference to devout human beings. Is it possible that in Acts, Luke considered persons who had been transformed by "the holy One" to be "holy ones"?

of "holy" are in the combination "Holy Spirit," but four times ordinary followers of Jesus are called saints:

"How much harm he has done to your saints in Jerusalem" (9:13).

"He also came down to the saints who lived in Lydda" (9:32).

"Then he called the saints and widows and presented her alive" (9:41).

"I locked up many of the saints in prison" (26:10).

Where Luke derived this usage is unknown, although the same usage is prominent in Paul's letters. Nowhere in Acts (or the rest of Scripture, for that matter) is the singular form, "saint," applied to an individual believer. Thus, no "Saint Peter" or "Saint Mary Magdalene" or the like is anywhere in Scripture.

Servants/Slaves (Douloi)

Literal slaves were owned by earthly masters, and this was not a desirable social or economic condition. Yet as Christians thought through their relationship to the Lord Jesus, they came to think of themselves in a positive sense as his slaves.[32] In the Third Gospel, literal slaves are mentioned with some frequency, but in Acts the only instances of *douloi* refer to God's servants:

"Pour out My Spirit on My male and female[33] slaves" (2:18).

"Grant that Your slaves may speak Your message" (4:29).

"These men are slaves of the Most High God" (16:17 NRSV).

The first is Peter's quotation of Joel 2:29 on Pentecost, possibly the basis on which Christians considered themselves God's slaves. Note that Acts 4:29 is in a context of persecution: apostles had been threatened, so the believers were asking God to take care of his property. It seems

---

[32] The Israelites were the slaves/servants of Yahweh, owned by him: "They are My slaves I brought out of the land of Egypt" (Lev 25:42, 55). Moses was especially the Lord's slave (Rev 15:3).

[33] "Female slaves" translates *doulē*, the feminine of *doulos*. It is part of the quotation from Joel 2:29. The term *doulē* is never elsewhere used in the NT to refer to female followers of Jesus.

unlikely that the early followers of Jesus thought of "slave" as a primary name for themselves, yet they would not have rejected this designation (and Paul featured slave language prominently in his letters).

Christians (Christianoi)

"The disciples were first called Christians at Antioch" (Acts 11:26). This text indicates the historical origin of the name by which Jesus' followers have most often been known through the ages. It also shows the strong connection between "disciples" (*mathētai*) and "Christians"[34] (*Christianoi*). "Christians" is synonymous with "brothers." Originally, "Christian" was a term used by outsiders; "the first extensive usage by a Christian writer to designate fellow believers was by Ignatius, bishop of Antioch, around the turn of the second century."[35]

Jesus' Covenant Community in Acts: Participles

One more set of data will be considered: participle forms.[36] Two verbs are used in Acts to give Christians a designation. These are "believers" (ones who believe or ones who have believed) and "sanctified ones" (ones who have been sanctified).

Believers: Participle of Pisteuō

Fourteen participle forms of "believe" (*pisteuō*) occur. Sometimes these can be rendered into English as "believers" but not always. The following material separates usage by verb tense without calling attention to distinctions between singular and plural.

---

[34] The only other occurrences are in the singular. First is Agrippa's infamous question, "Are you going to persuade me to become a Christian so easily?" (Acts 26:28). Second is Peter's acknowledgment that being a follower of Jesus may include being persecuted: "If (anyone suffers) as a Christian, he should not be ashamed" (1 Pet 4:16). Both imply that bearing the name "Christian" likely will lead to scorn.

[35] Polhill, *Acts*, 273.

[36] Participles in Greek were flexible. They originated as verbs (such as "believe") but could be used as adverbs or adjectives (such as "after believing" or "_____ who believed"). In turn, adjectival participles (like other Greek adjectives) could be used as nouns (such as "believers"). The data in this section includes only participle forms of *pisteuo* in Acts referring to faith in Jesus. Thus, Acts 9:26; 24:14 have been excluded.

In five instances, Luke called Jesus' followers "believers" (or "those who believe") using a *present* participle of the verb *pisteuō*, "believe" or "have faith":

"Now all the believers were together and had everything in common" (2:44).

"Believers were added to the Lord in increasing numbers" (5:14).

"Everyone who believes in Him will receive forgiveness" (10:43).

"Everyone who believes in Him is justified" (13:39).

"I had those who believed in You imprisoned" (22:19).

In three instances, Luke called Jesus' followers "believers" (or "those who believed") using an *aorist* participle of *pisteuō*:

"Now the multitude of those who believed were of one heart" (4:32).

"A large number who believed turned to the Lord" (11:21).

"Did you receive the Holy Spirit when you believed?" (19:2).

In six cases, Luke called Jesus' followers "believers" (or "those who believed") using a *perfect* participle of *pisteuō*:

"Some of the believers from the party of the Pharisees . . ." (15:5).

". . . rejoiced because he had believed in God" (16:34).

"He greatly helped those who had believed through grace" (18:27).

"And many who had become believers came confessing" (19:18).

"How many thousands of Jews there are who have believed" (21:20).

"With regard to the Gentiles who have believed . . ." (21:25).

Two things are clear from this variety. First, Luke meant no distinction by changing from one verb tense to another. Second, when

Acts was written, there was no standard Greek way to refer to "believers"; present, aorist, and perfect participles of *pisteuō* were used alike.[37] Yet there is no question that the brothers/disciples/Christians would have agreed that they were indeed believers in Jesus.[38]

Sanctified Ones: Participle of Hagiazō

Only twice does the book of Acts use a form of the verb *hagiazō* ("sanctify, make holy"), closely related to the adjective *hagios* ("holy," see earlier discussion of "saints"). These are both perfect passive participles. In Acts 20:32, Paul commended the Ephesian elders to God and the message of his grace, "which is able to build you up and to give you an inheritance among all who are sanctified." And in 26:18, Jesus says the result of Paul's ministry will be that Gentiles "receive forgiveness of sins and a share among those who are sanctified by faith in Me [Jesus]."

The Church and Those Associated with It in the Book of Acts

We may now draw together the vocabulary of Acts regarding the church and its members.[39]

1. "Church" was the preferred name for the association of Jesus' followers in a particular city. There is no indication whether any of these cities had multiple house churches. The "church in _____" refers to the association of Jesus' followers in that city, wherever they met and however they were organized. These churches were led by elders. A congregation could think of itself as "the church of God." When they met together for a particular matter, a church

---

[37] This is against Patzia, *Emergence of the Church*, 249, who is wrong in noting, "In Acts, Luke primarily refers to individuals as 'disciples' (of Jesus) and 'believers.'"

[38] Only rarely did Paul refer to "believers." When he did so, he tended to prefer the present participle form (1 Cor 14:22; 1 Thess 1:7). Note also that Acts never uses the participle of *sōzō* ("save") to refer to Jesus' followers as "the saved." The only participle of *sōzō* in Acts is in 2:47, "those who were being saved" (present passive participle).

[39] "Members" should not be understood as implying that a formal roster existed for the congregations. Here it means those individuals who were generally accepted as belonging to the group. This study intentionally skims over verbal actions (such as being baptized, being filled with the Spirit, or proclaiming the word) of individual believers or of congregations as a whole, although such actions are mentioned later in the study. The principal focus here is noun vocabulary.

could be designated "the company." Considered as separate entities, these congregations were "the churches."

2. "Church" was also the name for the geographically widespread body of Jesus' followers. This anticipates the later concept of the worldwide or universal church. Yet in Acts, the preferred name for this group was "the Way." Also, "God's people" was an occasional description of the church in this broader sense that looked back to the Old Testament. A prominent topic of proclamation, looking ahead to the future victory, was "God's kingdom."

3. "Brothers" was the most frequent name by which Jesus' followers referred to themselves, indicating that they participated in the same spiritual family. The other important self-designation was "disciples," which continued usage established in the Gospels as a name for those who learned from and followed Jesus. The name "Christians" later came into usage as a synonym for these other terms.[40]

4. "Saints/holy ones" and "slaves/servants" were other ways that Christians described themselves. The first term indicated separation to God and from sin—a righteous quality of living expected of all Christians. The second term pointed to willing submission to God's sovereign ownership, again, a normative attitude for all.

5. "Believers" was far from a settled name for followers of Jesus in Acts. Yet Luke used this designation as a synonym for brothers/ disciples/Christians. These same persons could also be called the "sanctified."

6. All these names and designations included Jews and Gentiles. The same terminology was used wherever Christians were found and whatever their ethnic background.

---

[40] Graham H. Twelftree concludes: "Perhaps, above all else, Luke would say that the Church is the present and ongoing embodiment of Jesus and his mission. It is not that the Church is simply Christ-like or is to mirror and maintain the ministry of Jesus through emulating his activities and message. Rather, through receiving the empowerment and direction of the Spirit, the Church embodies and expresses the same powerful presence of God apparent in Jesus and his ministry" (*People of the Spirit: Exploring Luke's View of the Church* [Grand Rapids: Baker, 2009], 205–6).

Church and Churches in Revelation: *Ekklēsia* Vocabulary

We now shift from Acts, with its account of the beginning of the church, to Revelation, the other biblical bookend for the church.[41]

Ekklēsia *as an Intentional, Regularly Meeting, Local Association of Jesus' Followers*

Ekklēsia is used in Revelation twenty times. In every case it means either an association of Christians in a particular city or multiple such congregations, the famous seven churches of Asia. The singular form of *ekklēsia* is found in the address line for each of the seven short letters Jesus dictated to John. The formula is identical each time: "To the angel of the church in _____ write" (2:1, 8, 12, 18; 3:1, 7, 14). Of the thirteen plural forms of *ekklēsia*, seven are identical, expressing the concluding exhortation of each letter: "Listen to what the Spirit says to the churches" (2:7, 11, 17, 29; 3:6, 13, 22). This leaves six other instances of "churches" in Revelation:

"John: To the seven churches in the province of Asia" (1:4).

"Write on a scroll what you see and send it to the seven churches" (1:11).

"The seven stars are the angels of the seven churches" (1:20).

"The seven lampstands are the seven churches" (1:20).

"Then all the churches will know that I am the One who examines minds" (2:23).

---

[41] See my commentary on Revelation for the argument that Revelation may be structured around the four visions that John received from the risen Lord and that he faithfully recorded. Three of the four visions are church centered: vision 1 ("Jesus and His People Between His Two Comings," Rev 1:9–3:22); vision 3 ("Jesus and the Two Rival Cities," 17:1–21:8); and vision 4 ("Jesus and His Bride Throughout Eternity, 21:9–22:5). Kendell H. Easley, *Holman New Testament Commentary: Revelation* (Nashville: B&H, 1998). The literature on the book of Revelation follows a different trajectory than that on the book of Acts. The following commentaries are highly recommended: David E. Aune, *Revelation 1–5; Revelation 6–16; Revelation 17–22*, WBC (Nashville: Thomas Nelson, 1997, 1998, 1999); Gregory K. Beale, *The Book of Revelation*, NIGTC (Grand Rapids: Eerdmans, 1998); George Eldon Ladd, *A Commentary on the Revelation of John* (Grand Rapids: Eerdmans, 1972); Grant R. Osborne, *Revelation*, BECNT (Grand Rapids: Baker, 2002); Paige Patterson, *Revelation*, NAC (Nashville: B&H, 2012).

". . . sent My angel to attest these things to you for the churches" (22:16).

Thus, if we limited ourselves to the instances of *ekklēsia* in Revelation, we would think the word referred only to individual assemblies. These assemblies were, however, aware of one another (since the recipients were to be careful to hear what the Spirit said to *all* the churches). There is no indication whether each city had multiple house-churches, although all members of the congregation in each city could gather to hear Revelation read aloud (1:3). Leadership structure, beyond the reference to the "angel" of each church, is unknown. "Some interpreters see these [angels] as meaning a guardian angel for each congregation, an idea found nowhere else in the New Testament. . . . Other interpreters see these in the sense of human *messengers*. . . . These would almost certainly have been the pastors of the churches. . . . I prefer this interpretation."[42]

Jesus' Covenant Community in Revelation: Singular Nouns

We will now follow the same pattern of inquiry in Revelation that we followed in Acts (by moving from *ekklēsia* language to other key terms used to refer to Jesus' followers). We begin with collective (singular) nouns.

*The Kingdom (*Basileia*)*

Four times John noted that believers were identified with God's rule/kingdom:

> ". . . made us a kingdom, priests to His God and Father" (1:6).

> ". . . your brother and partner in the tribulation, kingdom, and perseverance" (1:9).

> "You made them a kingdom and priests to our God" (5:10).

> "The power and the kingdom of our God . . . have now come" (12:10).

The emphasis here differs slightly from the (eschatological) kingdom emphasis in Acts. In Revelation, followers of Jesus already *are* the

---

[42] Easley, *Revelation,* 19.

kingdom (just as we might say we *are* the church). This kingdom is expressed as believers overcome the persecutions inflicted by the Devil/dragon/serpent through the Lamb's blood (12:7–12).[43] As Gregory Beale notes, "Therefore, [Rev. 12] v. 10 does not merely anticipate the future kingdom, but celebrates the fact that the kingdom has begun immediately following Christ's death and resurrection."[44]

*Wife (*Gunē*) and Bride (*Numphē*)*

Isaiah 54:5–8 describes Israel as the wife of Yahweh, foreseeing her future restoration in purity and glory to her divine husband (so also Hos 2:19–20). The same imagery occurs in Revelation but specifically as the *Lamb's* bride (*numphē*) or wife (*gunē*).[45] As George Eldon Ladd reminds us, however, "No real distinction can be made between Israel as the wife of Jahweh [*sic*.] and the church as the bride of Christ."[46] The metaphor is striking and beautiful:

"His wife has prepared herself" (19:7).

". . . prepared like a bride adorned for her husband" (21:2).

". . . the bride, the wife of the Lamb" (21:9).

"Both the Spirit and the bride say, 'Come!'" (22:17).

These are the only NT passages that name the church as Christ's wife/bride, although Paul famously alluded to this figure in Eph 5:22–33.[47] In the Gospels Jesus referred to himself as the bridegroom,[48] but he

---

[43] The *basileia* (kingdom/rule) of those opposed to God is also named in Revelation: the kingdom of the world (11:15), of the beast (16:10), of ten kings (17:12, 17), and of the empire (17:18).

[44] Beale, *Revelation*, 658.

[45] Revelation 18:23 is the only additional use of *numphē* and refers to a human bride. *Gunē* is found a number of times in Revelation in its customary sense of "adult human female (woman)." That it means "wife" in 19:7 and 21:9 is understood from the wedding context of these verses.

[46] Ladd, *Revelation*, 248.

[47] Nowhere outside Revelation is wife/bride vocabulary for the church explicitly used in the NT. Contrary to popular preaching, the phrase "bride of Christ" is never found in the NT. When Paul reached the climax of his teaching that Christ's sacrificial love for the church is the model for a Christian husband's love for his wife, he said, "We are members of His body" (Eph 5:30), rather than "we are His bride (or wife)."

[48] In Revelation, Jesus is called the husband (*anēr*) of his wife (21:2) but not the bridegroom (*numphios*) of his bride.

left the identity of the bride unspecified (Matt 9:15; see also John 3:29; Rom 7:4).[49]

These instances of wife/bride language in Revelation occur only near the end. Therefore it appears unlikely that the churches addressed in Revelation would have seen themselves as already being the wife of the Lamb. Perhaps it is better to say that they considered themselves betrothed to him and destined to become his wife[50] in the glorious consummation of all things.

The People [of God] (Laos)

In Revelation, *laos* is used two times to refer to Christian people.[51] This carries the same sense of the OT "people of God" as the language found in Acts. The first occurrence is Rev 18:4: "Come out of her, My people." This implies God's ownership of those he redeemed and the importance of their not becoming entangled with the prostitute city Babylon. It parallels Isa 48:20 ("Leave Babylon, flee from the Chaldeans") and 52:11 ("Leave, leave, go out from there! Do not touch anything unclean").[52]

The second instance in Revelation of *laos* referring to God's people is in 21:3 ("They will be His people, and God Himself will be with them"). The OT foundation for understanding this promise is Lev 26:12 ("I will walk among you and be your God, and you will be My people") and Ezek 37:27 ("My dwelling place will be with them; I will be their God, and they will

---

[49] Paul in 2 Cor 11:2 spoke of the congregation as one that he had promised "in marriage to one husband—to present a pure virgin to Christ." However, he feared that the betrothed had already been unfaithful. In this context, Paul used the virgin-pledged-in-marriage-to-Christ metaphor to urge the Corinthians to give up false teaching. He was not thinking of the church as Christ's wife as he later did in Ephesians 5 or as this is developed in Revelation.

[50] The "marriage of the Lamb" and the "marriage feast of the Lamb" were still in the future when Revelation was written (19:7–9).

[51] *Laos* (singular and plural) also occurs seven times in the secular sense of people (5:9; 7:9; 10:11; 11:9; 13:7; 14:6; 17:15). In the first six of these, "people" is found in conjunction with "tribe" and "language" and "nation;" therefore, it might be understood as we currently use the phrase "people group." In particular, note 7:9, which speaks of the "vast multitude from every nation, tribe, people, and language, which no one could number, standing before the throne and before the Lamb." This speaks of the multi-national, global nature of the church, clearly an advance from the thinking that the people of God was limited to ethnic Israel.

[52] Paul cited Isa 52:11 in 2 Cor 6:17 ("Therefore, come out from among them and be separate").

be My people").[53] Note that the Leviticus text spoke of *present* enjoyment of God, while in Ezekiel the promise concerned the *future*. Perhaps the first readers of Rev 21:3 considered both realities as they interpreted the text: They were *already* God's people, and he was *already* walking among them (1:13; 2:1). Yet there was to be an even more glorious fulfillment of this promise after tears and death and pain had been banished (21:4). One striking note in Rev 21:3 is that the word translated "people," while often singular in Revelation (for example 18:4), here is plural, literally "peoples." This points to the great ethnic diversity of those in heaven.[54]

It may be noted that, as in Acts, the explicit language of "covenant" (*diathēkē*) is not applied to Jesus' followers, the church, in Revelation. The only covenant reference is to the mysterious heavenly "ark of His covenant" in 11:19. Presumably, however, the believers in Revelation, who had been freed from their sins by the blood of the Lamb (1:5; 5:9; 7:14; 12:11), believed they were in a covenant relationship with him and with others who had also been so redeemed. Parallels to the OT imagery of blood establishing a covenant are too strong to miss (for example, Exod 24:8).

[Holy] City (Polis)

"Then one of the seven angels . . . came and spoke with me: 'Come, I will show you the bride, the wife of the Lamb.' He then carried me away in the Spirit . . . and showed me the holy city, Jerusalem, coming down out of heaven from God" (Rev 21:9–10). This text provides adequate basis for making a connection between the "church" and the "holy city" of Revelation.[55] This is all the more evident when the "holy city" is set in contrast to the evil "great city."[56] The thirteen instances in which "city" (*polis*) appears to symbolize the church in future glory are:

---

[53] See also Jer 31:33; 32:38; 2 Cor 6:16.

[54] Easley, *Revelation*, 395.

[55] The magnificent contribution of Augustine in *The City of God* was to see all history as an ongoing conflict between the city of God and the city of man, with no doubt that the city of God would ultimately emerge victorious. We need not conclude, as Augustine did, that the church is the earthly, visible manifestation of the heavenly, invisible city in order to recognize the strong connection implied in Revelation between the "church" and the "holy city."

[56] The evil "great city" is noted eight times: 11:8; 17:18; 18:10, 16, 18, 19, 21. She is "Babylon," although the equivalent "great city" of the OT was Nineveh (Jonah 1:2; 3:2; 4:11).

"Write on him the name of My God, and the name of the city of My God" (3:12).

". . . the encampment of the saints, the beloved city" (20:9).

"I also saw the Holy City,[57] new Jerusalem, coming down out of heaven" (21:2).

"He . . . showed me the holy city, Jerusalem, coming down" (21:10).

"The city wall had 12 foundations" (21:14).

". . . a gold measuring rod to measure the city" (21:15).

"The city is laid out in a square" (21:16).

"The city was pure gold like clear glass" (21:18).

"The foundations of the city wall were adorned" (21:19).

"The broad street of the city was pure gold, like transparent glass" (21:21).

"The city does not need the sun or the moon to shine on it" (21:23).

"They may have the right to the tree of life and may enter the city by the gates" (22:14).

"God will take away his share of the tree of life and the holy city" (22:19).

Except for the first reference, all these occur in the final section of Revelation. They focus on the future, victorious, magnificent manifestation of the Lamb's wife. As with the references to the wife/bride, they appear to be "not yet." This is the church glorified, not the church presently being sanctified. The Revelation language is conceptually close to the heavenly

---

[57] "Holy city" language is based on OT texts referring to earthly Jerusalem, such as Neh 11:1; Isa 52:1. In the NT, only Matthew (4:5; 27:53) and Revelation refer to the "holy city." See Rev 11:2; 21:2, 10; 22:19 for the instances in Revelation. These are included in the *polis* list for Revelation above except for 11:2, which speaks of the "holy city" being trampled for 42 months. This study is not the place to debate the interpretation of the 42 months and the identity of that "holy city."

use of *polis* in Heb 12:22–23:[58] "You have come to Mount Zion, to the city [*polis*] of the living God (the heavenly Jerusalem) . . . to the assembly [*ekklēsia*] of the firstborn."

We may summarize what we have observed concerning the ways that Jesus' followers in Revelation thought of themselves collectively. On one hand, they belonged to "the church," thought of as a local congregation. Yet they had already been made "a kingdom" in opposition to rival evil kingdoms, and they understood that they were "God's people." They anticipated that their collective status as "the wife (bride) of the Lamb" would be gloriously manifested. One prominent image of their future glorious condition was as the stunning "holy city."

Jesus' Covenant Community in Revelation: Plural Nouns

We move now to consider plural nouns that John used to reference those who made up God's kingdom. There is considerable overlap with the terminology of Acts.

Saints/Holy Ones (Hagioi)

The most frequently used term for Jesus' followers in Revelation is "saints," occurring 13 times:

> ". . . bowls filled with incense, which are the prayers of the saints" (5:8).[59]

> ". . . incense to offer with the prayers of all the saints on the gold altar" (8:3).

> "The smoke of the incense, with the prayers of the saints, went up" (8:4).

> ". . . to the saints, and to those who fear Your name, both small and great" (11:18).

> ". . . permitted to wage war against the saints and to conquer them" (13:7).

---

[58] The other three instances of *polis* in Hebrews are all heavenly: 11:10, 16; 13:14.

[59] Beale (*Revelation*, 357) suggests that "saints" here and elsewhere in Revelation may be connected with the "saints" of Daniel 7 (NKJV).

"Here is the endurance and the faith of the saints" (13:10).

"Here is the endurance of the saints, who keep the commandments" (14:12).

"They poured out the blood of the saints and the prophets" (16:6).

"The woman was drunk on the blood of the saints" (17:6).

"Rejoice over her, heaven, and you saints, apostles, and prophets" (18:20).

". . . the blood of prophets and saints, and all those slaughtered on earth" (18:24).

"The fine linen represents the righteous acts of the saints" (19:8).

". . . surrounded the encampment of the saints, the beloved city" (20:9).

Revelation uses "saints" more frequently than Acts. The meaning has narrowed to focus on prayer and endurance in persecution. (Note also that the two-word name "Holy Spirit," so prevalent in Acts, is missing in Revelation.) As in Acts, so in Revelation the "saints" are identical with "believers/Christians."

Servants/Slaves (Douloi)

The use of *douloi* to refer to Christ's followers, as seen in Acts, also occurs in Revelation. Of the fourteen instances of *doulos*, seven are in the plural, referring to believers/Christians:

". . . to show His slaves what must quickly take place" (1:1).[60]

". . . teaches and deceives My slaves to commit sexual immorality" (2:20).

". . . until we seal the slaves of our God on their foreheads" (7:3).

"He has avenged the blood of His servants that was on her hands" (19:2).

---

[60] Beale notes that "His slaves" in 1:1 refers to "the community of faith" (*Revelation*, 183).

"Praise our God, all you His servants, you who fear Him" (19:5).

"His servants will serve Him" (22:3).

". . . to show His servants what must quickly take place" (22:6).

Two named individuals are also called God's slaves (John in 1:1 and Moses in 15:3); also, God's prophets are called his slaves in two instances (10:7 and 11:18).[61] In all these instances, God's ownership (and his commitment to care for his property) is vivid.

Brothers (Adelphoi)

"Brothers" was not John's preferred way to refer to believers (as it was for Luke in Acts). Yet he did use the term in this way three times:

". . . their fellow slaves and their brothers, who were going to be killed" (6:11).

"The accuser of our brothers has been thrown out" (12:10).

". . . a fellow slave with you and your brothers who have the testimony" (19:10).

These show that "brothers" and "slaves" were the same group. Further, it could be dangerous to be one of the brothers because they would be accused (by the Devil) and might face martyrdom.[62] Presumably these "brothers" included "sisters" (also as in Acts).

Priests (Hiereis)

Although the concept of the priesthood of all Christians is well developed in 1 Pet 2:5–9, Revelation is the only NT book that actually calls believers "priests" (*hiereis*):

". . . made us a kingdom, priests to His God and Father" (1:6).

"You made them a kingdom and priests to our God" (5:10).

---

[61] The remaining three instances of *doulos* (singular or plural) in Revelation reference human institutionalized slavery (where there was a human slave owner): 6:15; 13:16; 19:18.

[62] The only other instances of *adelphoi* in Revelation refer to John (1:1) or to the prophets (22:9).

"They will be priests of God and the Messiah, and they will reign" (20:6).

These are the only instances of priest vocabulary in Revelation, and all three are connected with "kingdom/rule" (*basileia* [noun]) or "ruling/reigning" (*basileuo* [verb]).[63] As with the reference to believers as "kingdom," so with priests: this identity has already been established in the present even though there are future implications.

Jesus' Covenant Community in Revelation: Participles

One more set of data needs to be considered: participles. Unlike Acts, participles of *pisteuō* ("believers") are not found in Revelation; in fact, *pisteuō* is altogether absent in verbal forms.[64]

Victors/Ones Who Are Victorious (Nikōn, Present Participle of Nikaō)

The theme of believers as victors is evident throughout Revelation. Such overcomers may face death because of opposition, but the rewards will be well worth the struggle. There are nine instances of the present participle of *nikaō*; only one (15:2) is plural:

"I will give the victor the right to eat from the tree of life" (2:7).

"The victor will never be harmed by the second death" (2:11).

"I will give the victor some of the hidden manna" (2:17).

"The victor and the one who keeps My works to the end . . ." (2:26).

"The victor will be dressed in white clothes" (3:5).

"The victor: I will make him a pillar in the sanctuary of My God" (3:12).

"The victor: I will give him the right to sit with Me on My throne" (3:21).

---

[63] Although one might have expected that prayers, rising like smoking incense, would be offered by "priests," in fact they were offered by "saints."

[64] "Faith" (*pistis* [noun]) is found four times: 2:13, 19; 13:10; 14:12. "Faithful" (*pistos* [adjective]) eight times: 1:5; 2:10, 13; 3:14; 17:14; 19:11; 21:5, 6; three of these refer to Jesus himself as faithful.

"Those who had won the victory . . . were standing on the sea of glass" (15:2).

"The victor will inherit these things" (21:7).

The larger context for understanding that believers are victors is threefold. First, Jesus is the supreme victor (3:21; see also 5:5).[65] Second, evil powers are permitted by God to gain temporary victory over God's people (11:7; 13:7). Finally, Rev 12:11 provides the key to victory: "They conquered [*nikaō*] him [Satan] by the blood of the Lamb and by the word of their testimony, for they did not love their lives in the face of death." As George Ladd has noted, "The victory is not a physical or worldly one; it is a victory analogous to the victory won by Christ himself. . . . The conqueror, then, is the victim of persecution whose death is not loss but is in reality his victory."[66]

Keepers [of God's Commands]/Ones Who Keep [God's Commands] (Tērountes, Present Participle of Tēreō)

In Acts, believers are not referenced explicitly as keepers of God's words/ commands. (The verb *tēreō* can mean either "obey" or "keep" or "guard.") In the NT, however, this sense of the verb is found in 1 John (2:3–5; 3:22, 24; 5:3), and the participle form is used in 1 John 3:24 ("The one who keeps His commands remains in Him, and He in him"). In Revelation, six participles of *tēreō* refer to Christians who keep/obey/guard God's commands:

". . . those who hear the words of this prophecy and keep what is written" (1:3).

"The victor and the one who keeps My works to the end . . ." (2:26).

"Those who keep the commandments of God . . ." (12:17).

"Here is the endurance of the saints, who keep the commandments" (14:12).

---

[65] John's Gospel speaks of Jesus' victory over the world (16:33). First John is the only NT book other than Revelation to speak of believers as victors, either over the evil one (2:13, 14) or over the world (4:4; 5:4, 5).

[66] Ladd, *Revelation*, 40–41.

"Blessed is the one who keeps the prophetic words of this book" (22:7).

". . . those who keep the words of this book" (22:9).

Israel of old was frequently exhorted by God to obey/keep his commands (Exod 20:6; Deut 4:2; Ps 78:7). In Revelation, the saints/slaves/brothers are also identified as keepers of God's words. Note that what is to be "kept" is expressed variously. It may be God's commands (12:17; 14:12) or his works. Or it may be the words of Revelation itself (1:3; 22:7, 9).

Sealed Ones (Esphragismenoi, Perfect Participle of Sphragizō)

The identity of the 144,000 sealed slaves of God from Israel's tribes is one of the hotly debated questions surrounding Revelation. For the sake of completeness in this study, the four participles of *sphragizō* are included. All are in the perfect tense:

"And I heard the number of those who were sealed" (7:4).

". . . 144,000 sealed from every tribe of the sons of Israel" (7:4).

". . . 12,000 sealed from the tribe of Judah" (7:5).

". . . 12,000 sealed from the tribe of Benjamin" (7:8).

Of the other four instances of *sphragizō* in Revelation, one refers to the sealed 144,000 as "the slaves of our God" (7:3), which elsewhere in Revelation means Christians generally. The OT foundation for this is Ezek 9:4: "Put a mark on the foreheads of the men who sigh and groan over all the abominations committed in [Jerusalem]." The connection with Paul's emphasis that all Christians have been sealed with the Spirit is striking (2 Cor 1:22; Eph 1:13; 4:30).

Fearers [of God]/Ones Who Fear [God] (Phoboumenoi, Present Participle of Phobeomai)

Two participles of *phobeomai* referring to God's people as they fear/respect him are found in Revelation.[67] First is 11:18 ("To give the reward to Your

---

[67] This participle form is found in Acts, but there it is used as a technical term for monotheistic Gentiles who revered the God of Israel (Acts 10:2, 22, 35; 13:16, 26).

servants the prophets, to the saints, and to those who fear Your name"). Second is 19:5 ("Praise our God, all you His servants, you who fear Him, both small and great"). This is surely based on the OT truth that the fear of God is fundamental to being in right relationship with him (Exod 20:20; Deut 6:2; Prov 2:5).

The Church and Those Associated with It in Revelation

We may now draw together the vocabulary of Revelation regarding the church and its members. This is all summarized below in table 1.

1. "Church" was the name for the association of Jesus' followers in a particular city. As in Acts, there is no indication of whether there were multiple meeting places within a city. The term "church" is used absolutely, without adjective or genitive modifiers. Further (also as in Acts), these congregations considered together were "the churches" (Rev 2:23; 22:16).
2. "Church" (singular) does not occur in Revelation referring to the widespread or worldwide church. Occasionally John uses "kingdom" and (God's) "people" for this purpose. Both represent a present reality.
3. There are two figurative names for the church as a whole, both of which look toward the future consummation. First is "wife/bride of the Lamb" and second is "holy city" (21:9–10). The wife/bride vocabulary is unique to Revelation in the NT.
4. "Saints" is the most common designation for Jesus' followers in Revelation. They are also called "brothers" and God's "slaves." All three of these terms are found in Acts as well. Although God's people are not called "disciples" (as in Acts), they are occasionally called "priests."
5. Unlike in Acts, where the most common participle form referring to Christians is "believers," the most common participle used in Revelation is "victors" (or overcomers). Other participles used occasionally are "keepers" (of God's commands) and "fearers" (of God). The "sealed" ones may also be mentioned here.

	Acts	Both Books	Revelation
Singular Nouns[68]	Church (17/23/114) The Way (6/20/101) Company (5/16/31) Kingdom (8/8/162) People (2/48/142) Flock (2/2/5)	Church Kingdom People	Church (20/20/114) Kingdom (4/9/162) Bride (3/4/8) Wife (2/19/215) People (2/9/142) City (13/27/163)
Plural Nouns[69]	Brothers (32/3/57/343) Disciples (22/4/28/261) Saints (4/0/53/233) Slaves (3/0/3/124) Christians (1/1/2/3)	Brothers Saints Slaves	Saints (13/0/25/233) Slaves (7/0/14/233) Brothers (3/1/5/343) Priests (3/0/3/31)
Participles[70]	Believers (14/37/241) Sanctified (2/2/28)		Victors (9/17/28) Keepers (6/11/70) Sealed (4/8/15) Fearers (2/6/95)

TABLE 1: COMPARATIVE SUMMARY OF NOUNS AND PARTICIPLES IN ACTS AND REVELATION REFERRING TO CHRIST'S COMMUNITY

Normative Activities of Jesus' Covenant Communities

This study has focused on nouns and participles used to describe Jesus' church. Before we move to the implications for today's Christians, we will

---

[68] In this first row of the table, read the parenthetical numbers as follows: The *first* number is the number of instances in which the *singular* form is used to refer to God's people collectively; the *second* number is the total number of times the Greek term is used in the Bible book cited; and the *third* number is the total number of times the Greek term is used in the Greek NT.

[69] In this second row of the table, read the parenthetical numbers as follows: The *first* number tells how many times the *plural* form is used to refer to God's people; the *second* number is the number of times the *singular* form is used to refer to an individual Christian; the *third* number refers to the total instances of the Greek term in the Bible book; and the *fourth* number is the total Greek NT usage.

[70] In this last row of the table, read the parenthetical numbers as follows: The *first* number tells how many times (singular and plural combined) the participle is used to refer to God's people; the *second* number refers to the total instances of the verb in the book cited; and the *third* number is the total Greek NT occurrence of the verb.

briefly review the most frequent actions (verb forms) used in these books to tell what the believers were doing.

Actions Centering on God

1. *Believing.* This is the most frequently referenced activity of Jesus' people in Acts.[71] Although this is sometimes expressed as "believing in the Lord," the object of faith is not always specified. In Acts being baptized was often closely connected with believing.[72]

2. *Praying.* Corporate or private prayer is also a frequently referenced activity of Christians in Acts.[73] Revelation likewise notes the importance of prayer.[74] In Acts, being filled with (or full of) the Spirit is linked with praying.[75]

3. *Worshipping.* Two verbs for worship are found in Acts and Revelation. *Proskuneō* emphasizes revering God.[76] *Latreuō* focuses on serving him.[77] If the Lord's Supper is understood as an act of worship, and if the "breaking of bread" in Acts means the Lord's Supper, then those instances should be included here.[78] Actions such as praising or glorifying God (and singing in worship) also may be noted.[79]

4. *Hearing and obeying.* It is normative for both individuals and congregations in Acts and Revelation to hear from God and to obey what he has said. This includes following his guidance when such obedience is costly.

---

[71] The verb *pisteuō* occurs thirty-seven times in Acts (including the participle forms noted earlier in this study). Although *pisteuo* is not found in Revelation, the noun *pistis* (faith) occurs four times (and fifteen times in Acts).

[72] The verb *baptizō* occurs sixteen times in Acts as a reference to the Christian ritual. (There are three references to John's baptizing and two to being baptized in the Spirit.) *Baptizō* is not found in Revelation.

[73] The verb *proseuchomai* occurs sixteen times in Acts. The noun *proseuche* is found nine times.

[74] In Revelation the noun *proseuche* occurs three times.

[75] Ten times Acts notes that a group or individuals were filled with or full of the Spirit.

[76] Four times in Acts; twenty-four times in Revelation.

[77] Five times in Acts; twice in Revelation.

[78] Five times in Acts. In Revelation, the heavenly "marriage feast of the Lamb" (19:9) has evidently replaced the breaking of simple bread found in Acts.

[79] "Glorifying" (*doxazō*) God is saints' activity in Acts (11:18; 13:48; 21:20) and Revelation (15:4). One of the words for "praising" God (*aineō*) is found in the first description of believers meeting together after Pentecost (Acts 2:47) and is in one of the last exhortations of Revelation (19:5). "Singing" in Acts is noted only in Paul and Barnabas's midnight experience in the Philippian jail. In Revelation, singing pervades the heavenly scenes, but singing by redeemed persons is found in 14:3; 15:3.

The Antioch congregation's sending out of Paul is a wonderful example. All seven churches of Revelation are exhorted to listen to the Spirit.

Actions Centering on the Members

1. *Teaching and building up believers.* "Teach" (*didaskō*) is used of the apostles' Jerusalem ministry (Acts 5:42) and Paul's ministry in Antioch and Ephesus (11:26; 15:35; 18:11; 20:20; but contrast Rev 2:20). "Build up" (*oikodomeō*) related to Christians is found only in Acts 20:32.

2. *Deliberating and deciding.* The Acts 15 council is the great example of a congregation meeting to deliberate and decide an important issue. In Revelation, the most obvious reference to collective deliberation is the implication that five of the seven churches need to assemble and repent of the sins pointed out to them in their letters from the risen Lord (2:5, 16, 22; 3:3, 19).

3. *Sharing material resources.* The description of believers in Jerusalem selling their capital assets to meet the needs of the congregation is well known (Acts 2:45; 4:32–35). This pattern continued with the generous support offered to widows (6:1–6), the famine relief that the Antioch Christians sent to Jerusalem (11:29–30), and the later collection that Paul gathered from the Gentile churches for Jerusalem (24:17; 2 Corinthians 8).

Actions Centering on Outsiders

1. *Evangelizing.* Sharing of the good news about Jesus with those who are not his followers occurs frequently in Acts and Revelation. Because this generally takes place outside a Christian congregational setting, it is Christian individuals who are identified as sharing the good news. A variety of verbs occur.[80]

2. *Facing hostility.* The historical record of Acts and the prophetic vision of Revelation show that persecution was normative for Jesus' followers.[81] Acts is replete with beatings and imprisonments. In Revelation, the hostility escalates. The ordinary term for "witness" (*martus*) came to

---

[80] "Tell the gospel" (*euangelizō*) is found frequently (for example, Acts 5:42; 8:4; 17:18; Rev 14:6). "Preach" (*kerusso*) is also used (for example, Acts 8:5; 9:20 KJV; 20:25). "Proclaim" (*katangellō*) is found only in Acts (for example, 4:2; 13:5; 17:3).

[81] For "persecute" (*diōkō*) see examples such as Acts 9:4–5; Rev 12:13. For "persecution" (*diogmos*) see Acts 8:1; 13:50. For "tribulation" (*thlipsis*), see Acts 11:19 ASV; 14:22 ASV; Rev 2:9–10; 7:14.

be used for those who died because of their witness and loyalty to Jesus. Martyrdom—beginning with Stephen and ending with those killed by the beast of Revelation—is held up as something Jesus prizes and rewards.[82]

An Ecclesiology of Acts and Revelation: From "Was" to "Ought"

Acts is descriptive, not prescriptive, yet its portrait of the first churches has instructive value for us. Revelation offers strong words of advice and promises of blessing for following its counsel. In the final section of this study, we move from analysis to synthesis, from what the churches and their people *were* and *did* in Acts and Revelation to the implications for churches today. If we were limited to Acts and Revelation for our knowledge of the church, what ought we to believe about ourselves and the church? What does the ecclesiology of Acts and Revelation mean for the twenty-first century? Table 2 summarizes this material.

We Are the People of God: Worshippers of the Lord Jesus

We are *the people of God*. This name reminds us that we belong to God. He has called us his own, and the primary reality of our lives is our relationship with him. We are his people so that he may have true worshippers. Because the name *the people of God* is rooted in the OT, we stand in continuity with the faithful Israelites to whom God made his covenant promises. And we are his people now and forever.

As the people of God, we are his *saints*, set apart for him; this name is also taken from the OT. In this regard, we are to be constantly *praying*—prayer is to permeate all Christian experience. We are also the *sanctified ones* and *priests* to our God.

Our *worshipping* includes many actions done by God's OT people (*praising, glorifying,* and *singing*). The people of God now, however, are identified by *believing* in Jesus as Lord and Savior and by *being baptized* in his name. A distinctive element of our worship as Christians is the regular *breaking of bread* (the Lord's Supper).

---

[82] Acts 22:20; Rev 2:13; 17:6.

We Are the People of God: Worshippers of the Lord Jesus	We Are the Kingdom of God: Wife of the Lamb Forever
People[A/R]	Kingdom [A/R]
Saints [A/R]	Wife of the Lamb[R]
Priests[R]	Bride[R]
Believing Ones [A]	City[R]
Sanctified Ones [A]	Sealed Ones[R]
(Baptized)	
(Praying)	
(Worshipping)	
(Hearing and Obeying)	
(Praising, Glorifying, Singing)	
(Breaking Bread = Lord's Supper)	
We Are the Church of God: Brothers in the Company of Disciples	**We Are the Servants of God: Faithful Victors over Evil**
Church(es)/Congregation(s) [A/R]	Slaves[A/R]
Brothers and Sisters [A/R]	The Way [A]
Flock [A]	Christians [A]
Company [A]	Victorious Ones[R]
Disciples [A]	God-Fearing Ones[R]
(Teaching and Building Up)	Keeping Ones [of His Word] [R]
(Deliberating and Deciding)	(Spirit-Filled)
(Sharing Material Resources)	(Facing Hostility)
(Repenting as Necessary)	(Martyred as Required)

TABLE 2: A SUMMARY OF THE ECCLESIOLOGY OF ACTS AND REVELATION[83]

We Are the Church of God: Brothers in the Company of Disciples

Second, we are *the church of God*. We exist in relationship to God more as congregations than as individuals. We must never forget that churches by definition assemble regularly, giving believers a way to relate to one

---

[83] The bold headings in table 2 are identical to the subheadings for the concluding section of this study. Terms ending in "ones" represent participles discussed. Terms in parentheses are based on the "normative activities" noted in the preceding section of the study. Superscript A = found in Acts; Superscript R = found in Revelation; superscript A/R = found in both Acts and Revelation.

another. Other community designations include *the flock* and *the company*. None of these is foreign to OT thinking, although now it is specifically *Christ's* church that we belong to.

As the church of God, we are *brothers* (borrowed from the way Jews referred to each other). This includes women disciples as *sisters*. We all belong to the same spiritual family, and the members of that family are *disciples* of Jesus, following after his teachings.

Church members should be *building up* each other, especially through the *teaching* of the Word. Disciples in congregations are to be taught by recognized spiritual leaders (teachers and elders). Sometimes churches meet for *deliberating and deciding* matters. And during the earthly pilgrimage, *repenting* is sometimes a necessary church activity. Another indispensable activity of a congregation is *sharing material resources* generously, both among its own members as well as from one church to another.

We Are the Servants of God: Faithful Victors over Evil

Third, we are—like the Israelites of old—*servants of God*. Because he is the Master and we are the slaves, we must do his bidding, even when this is uncomfortable or life threatening. He has called us to belong to *the Way*, which is narrow and leads to opposition from outsiders. We are *God-fearers* and put respect for him above our own agendas.

Because Christ has come, we bear the name *Christians*. We are *keepers* of the words Christ has given. God challenges us to be *victors* over the world and the forces of evil. Being *filled with the Spirit* is a provision of God (and the normative experience for Christians), for in this way we have the power both to be holy and to do the service God expects.

As God's servants we are to be *hearing* and *obeying* his Word. We are expected to be *proclaiming* the good news to outsiders (including *preaching* and *evangelizing*). And further, we should be found joyfully *facing hostility* when it comes, whether persecution or tribulation or martyrdom.

We Are the Kingdom of God: Wife of the Lamb Forever

Finally, we move from "the church militant" to "the church victorious." We belong to *the kingdom of God* because the rule of God though his Messiah is already established. As God's people we have been *sealed* and are guaranteed participation in the heavenly, everlasting fulfillment of all his promises. In Revelation, this fulfillment is expressed in the terminology of being the *wife (or bride) of the Lamb*. It is also expressed in the magnificent portrayal of God's people as *the holy city*, New Jerusalem, which will be revealed in glory.

May we never forget that these realities are already ours. We are indeed: (1) the people of God (worshippers of the Lord Jesus), (2) the church of God (brothers in the company of disciples), (3) the servants of God (faithful victors over evil), and (4) the kingdom of God (wife of the Lamb forever).

CHAPTER 4

The Church in the Pauline Epistles

David S. Dockery

T he doctrine of the church, so often neglected in the history of Christian thought, has moved to the forefront of exploration over the past few decades. Yet expansive discussions seem not to have resulted in any consensus regarding the identity, mission, ministry, nature, purpose, order, or organization of the church. Contributing to this lack of consensus is the flux in denominational life—now called postdenominational life by some—and the important role of the parachurch movement as well as the rise of ministry networks. Innovation and experimentation are hardly the exception; in fact, they are the norm. Thus, the essays in this volume on the church are not only informative but timely.

This chapter is one perspective in this broader ecclesiological discussion and will be limited to the teaching of the apostle Paul on this important subject. We will explore the background of Paul's thought, the relationship of the coming of the Spirit to the formation of the church, the nature of community, its leaders, its worship and practice, and the discipline of its members. We will conclude by looking at Paul's images of the church and the implications of his thought for developing a theology of the church for our day.

The Apostle Paul, the Holy Spirit, and Rabbinic Judaism

"When the completion of the time came, God sent His Son," wrote the apostle Paul to the believers in Galatia (Gal 4:4). Included within God's providential timetable was not only the fulfillment of the OT promises concerning the Messiah but also God's calling of one who would take the gospel to the Gentile world (Matt 28:19–20; Rom 1:16; Gal 1:15–16). That person was Saul of Tarsus (Acts 21:39; 22:28; Phil 3:5–8).[1]

Our purpose in this chapter is not to explore the full theology of Paul.[2] The scope of this chapter is limited to Paul's teaching concerning the church with a look at the significance of this teaching for today. Our approach will explore the development of themes and key topics in the thought of the apostle, though any attempt to approach Paul's writings in the traditional fashion of a fully-developed systematic theologian would seem to be inappropriate.[3]

While Paul nowhere in his letters gives us a systematic accounting of his central convictions (although his letter to the Romans comes close to such), the various letters represent Paul's responses to distinct occasions. Paul did not provide a systematic theology for us, but he was no doubt a systematic thinker.[4] Paul's understanding of the church was closely connected to and grew out of his teaching regarding the work of the Holy Spirit. Key aspects of the background to Paul's thought lie within Palestinian Judaism.[5] With this connection to the work of the

---

[1] See John McRay, *Paul: His Life and Teaching* (Grand Rapids: Baker, 2003), 21–59.

[2] See Frank Thielman, *A Theology of the New Testament: A Canonical and Synthetic Approach* (Grand Rapids: Zondervan, 2005), 219–33; F. F. Bruce, *Paul: Apostle of the Heart Set Free* (Grand Rapids: Eerdmans, 1977); W. D. Davies, *Paul and Rabbinic Judaism* (Philadelphia: Fortress, 1980); Donald Guthrie, *New Testament Theology* (Downers Grove: InterVarsity, 1981); Seymour Kim, *The Origin of Paul's Gospel* (Grand Rapids: Eerdmans, 1982); John B. Polhill, *Paul and His Letters* (Nashville: B&H, 1999); E. P. Sanders, *Paul and Palestinian Judaism* (Philadelphia: Fortress, 1977).

[3] See J. Christian Beker, *Paul the Apostle: The Triumph of God in Life and Thought* (Philadelphia: Fortress, 1980); Richard B. Hays, *Echoes of Scripture in the Letters of Paul* (New Haven: Yale, 1989).

[4] See Robert B. Sloan, "Images of the Church in Paul," in *The People of God: Essays on the Believers' Church*, ed. Paul A. Basden and David S. Dockery (Nashville: B&H, 1990), 148–65.

[5] Davies, *Paul and Rabbinic Judaism*, 215; also, see Sanders, *Paul and Palestinian Judaism*. Rudolf Bultmann attempted to frame Paul's thought within the mystical influences of the Graeco-Roman world (*Theology of the New Testament*, ed. K. Grobel [New York: Scribners, 1951–55]). Our approach rejects the Bultmannian model.

Spirit and this background setting in mind, we turn our thoughts to the development of Paul's understanding of the church.

The Holy Spirit's activity was basically regarded as a past phenomenon in Israel's history. The Spirit's work had indeed given to Israel its Torah, its prophets, and the rest of its Scriptures but seemed to have ceased when the prophetic office ended. Yet, there were individuals who were still conscious of the Holy Spirit's activity in their lives. W. D. Davies has suggested that Paul was reared within a Judaism that tended to relegate the Spirit's activities to the past. It was, however, a Judaism that cherished a strong expectation of the coming of the Holy Spirit once again in the future. The apostle Paul was a Jew who, through his dramatic and transformational conversion, now believed that the Messiah had come in Jesus of Nazareth and thus regarded the Messianic Age as the promised age of the Spirit.

This being the case, the apostle maintained certain expectations about this pneumatically-shaped time. In becoming a follower of Christ, he entered a new community and the pneumatic power that characterized it, observing evidence of the advent of the age to come. The active presence of the Spirit was a mark of the last days; the ministry of the Spirit authenticated the claims of Jesus as Messiah. Paul's eschatological expectations regarding the age of the Spirit were confirmed through observation and experience.[6]

The Formation of the Believing Community

One of the most important passages in Paul's writings pointing to the corporate initiation of Christ-followers into the shared new life is 1 Cor 12:13. Donald Guthrie has written that Paul's understanding of baptism in the Spirit is "another way of expressing the Spirit dominated life."[7] The concept that "we were all made to drink of one Spirit" shows the basic solidarity of all Christians in and with the Holy Spirit.[8]

---

[6] Davies, *Paul and Rabbinic Judaism*, 216–17.
[7] Guthrie, *New Testament Theology*, 563.
[8] See Anthony A. Hoekema, *Holy Spirit Baptism* (Grand Rapids: Eerdmans, 1972), 21.

The Holy Spirit and Entrance into the New Community

Although James D. G. Dunn and George E. Ladd have argued that "baptism" in 1 Corinthians 12 means "Spirit baptism" and not water baptism, many scholars believe that baptism refers to water baptism as the sign pointing to the reality that the Spirit has been imparted to believers.[9] We do not believe that there has to be an either/or answer to this issue. Rather, we believe a both/and answer is most satisfactory. "Baptism" in this passage is the work of the Spirit to form the church, while water baptism is the outward sphere where this work is demonstrated. When men and women believe and are baptized, they become members of the body of Christ. The Spirit has been given by the exalted Christ to form a new people, to join believers together in the baptism of the Spirit to constitute the body of Christ.

Paul viewed the Holy Spirit as the basis for true unity in the body of Christ. Fellowship in the Johannine epistles seems to be "with the Father and with His Son" (1 John 1:3), but Paul stresses "fellowship with the Spirit" (2 Cor 13:13; Phil 2:1–4). The passage in Philippians enlarges on the theme of unity and suggests a mutual participation of believers through the common bond of the Holy Spirit. The Spirit binds believers together and enables them to be of the same mind, which is the "mind of Christ" (1 Cor 2:16). The community of faith maintains the unity of the Spirit as expounded in 1 Corinthians 12.

Spiritual Gifts, Ministry, and Community Formation

While Paul contends that the Holy Spirit was given to all believers (Rom 8:9, 14), some received special gifts so that they did unusual things such as speaking in tongues. For many at Corinth though, this activity was the hallmark of community identity. By comparison, they downplayed the importance of Christian virtues for those in the church. Paul's discussion shows that the issue was primarily one of lordship (1 Cor 12:3), not

---

[9] See James D. G. Dunn, *Baptism in the Holy Spirit* (Philadelphia: WJK, 1970), 116–38; George E. Ladd, *New Testament Theology* (Grand Rapids: Eerdmans, 1974), 479–80; G. R. Beasley-Murray, *Baptism in the New Testament* (London: MacMillan, 1962), 167; John R. W. Stott, *Baptism and Fullness* (Downers Grove: InterVarsity, 1971), 48. For a nice explanation of these differences, see Frederick D. Brunner, *A Theology of the Holy Spirit* (Grand Rapids: Eerdmans, 1970). Also, see David S. Dockery, "Paul's View of the Spiritual Life," in *Exploring Christian Spirituality*, ed. K. J. Collins (Grand Rapids: Baker, 2000), 339–52.

libertinism. All spiritual gifts, if they were to edify the church, must be exercised under Christ's headship. If the exercise of the gifts is in any way inimical to Christ, they cannot be of God.

The apostle listed examples of spiritual gifts but proceeded to the more excellent way of love (1 Cor 12:31–13:13). He did not deny the function or place of the gifts; however, for the sake of community formation, the important thing was the manifestation of ethical qualities, especially love. For the sake of public worship, the exercise of the gifts, insisted Paul, must be done "decently and in order" (14:40).[10]

Paul claimed that the gifts that have been given to the community have been sovereignly distributed by the Spirit of God to produce spiritual results (1 Cor 12:11). The gifts were not distributed indiscriminately but were given to meet the needs of the community through its members. For this reason no one should despise another's gifts, for each gift has been given for the good of all (v. 7). The Spirit who has been given to the church is sovereign over the church, granting gifts according to his will. He is also personal, bringing together all these gifts for the life of the community. In typical Pauline form, sovereignty was balanced with human responsibility (v. 31).[11]

Three lists of gifts can be found in 1 Corinthians 12, and these gifts played a significant role in Paul's understanding of the life and ministry of the church. James D. G. Dunn has suggested that the concept of giftedness (*charismata*) was almost entirely a Pauline concept.[12] Paul assumed that all believers shared in the gifts of the Holy Spirit (12:4) and that all gifts were granted for the common good and the building up of the community (v. 7; 14:12). The apostle helps us see that the community had speaking gifts, leadership gifts, sign gifts, and helping gifts. While some gifts may have seemed less significant, it is often the unheralded gifts that advanced and strengthened the believing community.[13] The

---

[10] See Leon Morris, *The First Epistle of Paul to the Corinthians* (Grand Rapids: Eerdmans, 1958), 166.

[11] See D. A. Carson, *Divine Sovereignty and Human Responsibility* (Atlanta: John Knox, 1981).

[12] James D. G. Dunn, *Jesus and the Spirit* (Philadelphia: Westminster, 1975), 205; also David S. Dockery, "Life in the Spirit in Pauline Thought," *Scribes and Scriptures*, ed. D. A. Black (Winona Lake: Eisenbrauns, 1993), 142–50.

[13] See James D. G. Dunn, *Unity and Diversity in the New Testament* (Philadelphia: Westminster, 1977), 109–10; William Baird, *1 Corinthians/2 Corinthians* (Atlanta: John Knox, 1980), 53.

gifts were sovereignly given for the edification of the community; thus, it was impossible to predict when and where they might be manifested. Since some of the supernatural gifts were associated with apostles and prophets for the foundation of the church (see Eph 2:20), it is possible that some of the gifts were primarily and particularly for the apostles.[14]

In 1 Corinthians 13, Paul proclaimed the superiority and necessity of love. The exercise of the spiritual gifts within the community meant nothing without love (12:31–13:3). The essential character of Christian love and its enduring nature were amplified by Paul's discussion in 13:4–12, for love was greater than faith and hope. Paul developed guidelines in 1 Corinthians 14 to give shape to his view of the community. Because God is not a God of disorder, but of peace (v. 33), all things, as we have noted, should be done in an orderly manner (v. 40).

Paul's principles emphasized order and peace, often creating a sense of tension with the Spirit's gift of freedom (2 Corinthians 3).[15] Nevertheless, even in the exercise of such principles, there was an absence of legalism in Paul's vision for the community. The Corinthian letters emphasized the edification of the community and the correcting of triumphalism and ecstatic experiences that appeared to be out of control in Corinth. The community was given shape and formation through the guiding gifts of the apostles and prophets (1 Corinthians 12; 14; Eph 4:11–16). True spirituality was evidenced by love (1 Cor 13:1–13) and unity (12:13), under Christ's lordship (v. 3).

Leadership

We have seen that the church was instructed to do everything decently and in order (1 Cor 14:40). For the church to function in a faithful and orderly way, leadership was needed (Eph 4:11–16; 1 Tim 3:1; Titus 1:5). Paul's understanding of the kind of leadership needed in the church was

---

[14] See Ladd, *New Testament Theology*, 536; Wayne Grudem, *The Gift of Prophecy in 1 Corinthians* (Washington, DC: University of America Press, 1982); E. Earle Ellis, *Prophecy and Hermeneutic* (Grand Rapids: Eerdmans, 1978).

[15] See F. F. Bruce, "All Things to All Men: Diversity and Unity and Other Pauline Tensions," in *Unity and Diversity in New Testament Theology*, ed. R. Guelich (Grand Rapids: Eerdmans, 1978), 82–90; also, I. Howard Marshall, *New Testament Theology: Many Witnesses, One Gospel* (Downers Grove: InterVarsity, 2004), 707–31.

shaped both by his rabbinic background and his missionary endeavors (Acts 13–14).

Order, Organization, and Leadership

In Ephesians 4 Paul discussed church leadership within the broader context of the church's unity. The spiritual blessings (1:3) that God graciously gave to the church included the distribution of gifted persons for the building up of the body of Christ. The discussion of gifted people focused on apostles, prophets, evangelists, pastors, and teachers (4:11).

Apostles and prophets were foundational for the church's work (Eph 2:20; 3:5). Apostles served as spokespersons for God, bringing new revelation and understanding to the church. All apostles were prophets, but not all prophets were apostles. Prophets provided exhortation, edification, and comfort to the church (see 1 Cor 14:3). They had authority while speaking under the Spirit's inspiration. Prophets primarily revealed God's will for the present (forthtelling) and occasionally predicted the future (foretelling).

Evangelists were gifted to spread the gospel and to plant churches, patterns that continue to this day. Pastors provided oversight, comfort, and guidance as the church's shepherds (Acts 20:28; 1 Pet 5:2–4). Teachers instructed and helped apply God's Word to the life of the church. Teachers now, as then, must be more concerned with passing on the church's revealed teachings (see 1 Cor 15:3–4) than with bringing new inspirational insights like the prophets. The teaching gift remains indispensable in building up the church and is necessary to enable believers to distinguish false doctrine from true teaching.[16]

Overseers and Deacons

Apparently in the development of the church in the first century, function preceded form. As the church moved more and more in the direction of order and organization, two offices, elder/overseer and deacon, emerged

---

[16] See John R. W. Stott, *God's New Society: The Message of Ephesians* (Downers Grove: InterVarsity, 1979), 148–50; Leon Morris, *Expository Reflections on the Letter to the Ephesians* (Grand Rapids: Baker, 1994), 117–20; F. F. Bruce, *The Epistle to the Ephesians* (Old Tappan, NJ: Revell, 1961), 83–84.

where the various leadership gifts could be carried out to serve the entire congregation. The main duty of these offices was to care for God's people.

For elders/overseers (1 Tim 3:1; Titus 1:5), this care was primarily given through teaching and shepherding. The elder/overseer was called a steward in the household, one entrusted with God's work. The congregation seemingly approved these leaders. The reference to public care, and the practice initiated by Paul in Acts 14, indicates that the congregation at least participated in affirming those who were appointed. These leadership offices had developed by the time of Paul's later writings to the Philippians (1:1), to Timothy, and to Titus. Elders/overseers had the responsibility for leading, providing oversight, teaching, preaching, shepherding, and offering pastoral care.

The list of qualities for these leaders indicates that they were to be people of unquestioned integrity or irreproachable character, marred by no disgrace. J. N. D. Kelley said they should offer no loophole for criticism. Thus these leaders should be blameless in the home, blameless in character, blameless in conduct, and blameless in doctrine and orthodoxy. The connection of the "household" (one of Paul's favorite images for the church, see 1 Tim 3:15) to the home is important in both 1 Timothy and Titus.[17]

Paul's two lists in 1 Timothy and Titus included twenty character qualities and only one requirement concerning ability ("an able teacher," 1 Tim 3:2). By way of contemporary application, this stands in contrast to the modern emphasis upon personality and ability in the calling of leaders and the little concern given to spirituality and character in many congregations. The practices in our twenty-first century churches often seem backward from the guidelines presented in Scripture.

The list of requirements for deacons (1 Tim 3:8–13; see Phil 1:1) called for similar characteristics although not with the same degree of detail. Two obvious differences were present. Deacons were not required to be able to teach. This should not be taken to mean that deacons were unable to teach nor that they should not teach but merely that it was not a requirement for the diaconal office.

---

[17] See Ray Van Neste, "The Meaning of Titus: An Overview," *SBJT* 7, no. 3 (Fall 2003): 18–30; J. N. D. Kelly, *The Pastoral Epistles* (Peabody, MA: Hendrickson, 1993), 230–31; Donald Guthrie, *Pastoral Epistles*, 2nd ed. (Grand Rapids: Eerdmans, 1990), 195; and David S. Dockery, "Overseers and Bishops," *BI* (Spring 2004).

The second difference is the statement that deacons should not be double tongued. Historically, the Pauline teaching has been applied in ways so that deacons have been responsible for the offering, for visitation and counseling, for the care of the sick, for the poor and the needy, and for the distribution of the Lord's Supper. Such ministry demands personal involvement; thus, deacons should not be gossips or those who distort the truth.[18] While leadership and giftedness were quite important for providing shape and direction for the believing community, it was the practice of corporate worship that was ultimately prioritized in Paul's vision for the church.

Worship Practices in the Pauline Churches

Worship was central for the existence and continuation of the church. Paul maintained that the ultimate purpose of the church is the worship and praise of the One who called it into being (Eph 1:4–6). Worship, which is desired by God, is made possible by the gift of God's grace in, to, and among the believing community. To worship God the Father involves the expression of awe, as well as Spirit-enabled service expressed in prayer, giving, or the ministry of the gospel (Rom 14:6–23). Worship in the community of believers (then and now) produces a life that is pleasing to God (12:1–2). Thus, a close and obvious relationship exists between the community at worship and the dedication of believers to a life of service to God.[19]

The Trinitarian Shape of Worship
The elements of Christian worship had connections to those of OT worship, yet two new ideas at the heart of Paul's thought brought about a decisive reorientation. First, Paul recognized that Christian worship at its core emphasized the worship of God the Father through Jesus Christ the

---

[18] See the discussions in John R. W. Stott, *Guard the Truth: The Message of 1 Timothy and Titus* (Downers Grove: InterVarsity, 1996), 173–79; George W. Knight, *The Pastoral Epistles* (Grand Rapids: Eerdmans, 1992); Thomas D. Lea and Hayne P. Griffin, *1, 2 Timothy, Titus* (Nashville: B&H, 1992).

[19] See John R. W. Stott, *Romans* (Downers Grove: InterVarsity, 1994); Thomas Schreiner, *Romans* (Grand Rapids: Baker, 1998); Douglas J. Moo, *Romans* (Grand Rapids: Zondervan, 2000); C. E. B. Cranfield, *A Critical and Exegetical Commentary on the Epistle to the Romans*, 2 vols. (Edinburgh: T&T Clark, 1975–79).

Son. Second, he recognized the work of the Holy Spirit in the life and worship of the church.

Paul portrayed the worshipping community as standing in relation to God on the basis of adoption in Christ. Prayers were made in the name of Jesus Christ. The work of God in the Son became the theme and focus of the church's praise. The church's confession was grounded in the affirmation that Jesus Christ is Lord (Rom 10:9; 1 Cor 12:3). Preaching focused on proclaiming the work of Christ (2 Cor 4:5), and the Lord's Supper represented the celebration of Christ's sacrifice for sin (1 Cor 11:26). Financial gifts were offered on the basis of God's gift of his Son (2 Cor 9:15). The centrality of the risen and exalted Christ in the church's worship gave new depth and content to the worshipping community.[20]

The worship of God the Father through the Son was enabled and energized by God the Holy Spirit. Prayers were offered with the divine help of the Holy Spirit (Rom 8:26). Praise involved rejoicing in the Spirit (Eph 5:18–20). Confession of sin took place under the conviction of the Holy Spirit (1 Cor 12:3; 1 Thess 5:19). Holy Scripture, which was inspired by the Holy Spirit at the time of inscripturation, was also brought to life by the illumination of the Holy Spirit (1 Cor 2:14; 2 Tim 3:16). Preaching took place through the power of the Holy Spirit (1 Cor 2:14). The church's worship flowed from believers walking in the power of the Spirit (Gal 5:16, 22–23).[21] Fitting and acceptable worship can only be offered by and through the Holy Spirit, the life giver.

Worship and the Marks of Community

The worship and practice of the early church was carried forth in recognition of and submission to the lordship of Jesus Christ. Members of these Christ-centered communities offered worship, praise, and thanksgiving to the Lord while dedicating themselves for ministry (Rom 12:1). Worship practices led to lives of obedience, resulting in the edification and expansion of the churches through evangelism, teaching, and service.

These ministry practices soon became the visible marks of believing communities that had been transformed by the renewing work of God's Spirit (Rom 12:2). Paul's vision for these reconciled communities as

---

[20] See David Peterson, *Engaging with God: A Biblical Theology of Worship* (Downers Grove: InterVarsity, 1992).

[21] See David S. Dockery, "Fruit of the Spirit," in *DPL*, 316–19.

instruments of encouragement, strength, grace, and peace created a dynamic sense of belonging (vv. 3–8; Eph 2:11–21).

Paul encouraged the believers in areas of love, discernment, and devotion to and honor for one another. These marks of authentic community were augmented by patience, humility, generosity, and genuine care for one another.

From observing these marks, we can learn much that applies to the struggles and challenges faced by congregations in our day. For where these worship practices and marks of authenticity are present, communication will be encouraged, intimacy and fellowship will be developed, mutual burden bearing will be found, prayer will become a frequent practice, and a sense of belonging will be created. Belonging creates identity for the people of God. The primary markers of identity are baptism and the Lord's Supper. Jesus commanded that both of these practices be continued in the churches as symbols of the Lord's ongoing presence. It is to these two powerful symbols that we now turn our attention.

Baptism

Christian baptism has its background in the OT act of ritual purification, proselyte baptism, and the baptism of John. The church was commanded by the resurrected Christ to continue the practice of Christian baptism as an aspect of discipling the nations (Matt 28:18–20).[22]

For Paul, baptism was primarily an act of identification with the death, burial, and resurrection of Christ (Rom 6:1–4). Baptism also served as a sign of covenant relationship with Christ and his people (Col 2:9–13). That Paul did not conceive of baptism as an essential saving ordinance or salvific sacrament is clearly indicated in 1 Cor 1:10–18. For the worshipping community, baptism became the initiation act whereby one was made a member of the community, the body of Christ, identifying with Christ and his people. The act of baptism was not restricted to any class of people (Gal 3:27–28); no distinction of ethnicity (Jew or Greek), gender (male or female), or social status (slave or free) was made. All were regarded as having been baptized into Christ as a result of having put on Christ (Eph 4:2–6; Col 3:10).

---

[22] See David S. Dockery, "Baptism," in *DJG*; David S. Dockery, "A Theology of Baptism," *SwJT* 43 (Spring 2001): 4–16.

Baptism essentially connected the believing community with the death and resurrection of Christ. Not to be associated with cleansing, baptism symbolized burial with Christ in his death. Baptism also meant new life, signifying that believers share Christ's risen life. Baptism, for Paul, symbolized the transition that had occurred in and among believers as they moved from death to life. It involved the believer in the dying and rising of Christ through a kind of reenactment. Baptism also symbolized that death had taken place in the life of the believer, recognizing that a new life had begun. New life in the community of faith required a whole new set of values. The act of baptism served as a teaching medium for new believers, and the entire church was helped to understand the theological meaning reflected in the symbolism.[23]

The Lord's Supper

The Lord's Supper was instituted by the command of Christ and by his example as well. Paul's teaching regarding the Lord's Supper was both the earliest and fullest treatment of the subject in the NT. When the church celebrated the Supper, it did so to remember Jesus' broken body and shed blood and the love that motivated his bearing the cross. The Supper visibly represented the body and blood of Christ in the partaking of the bread and the cup. That this practice was connected with the concept of remembrance in the Passover meal is indicated in the phrase "after supper" (1 Cor 11:25), most likely pointing to the Passover meal.

The Supper was identified in a variety of ways in the teaching and practice of Paul: (1) Lord's Supper (1 Cor 11:20), (2) Lord's Table (10:21), (3) Communion (v. 16), (4) Eucharist (11:24), and the breaking of bread (see Acts 20:7). The Supper's initial focus was table fellowship around a shared meal. As the bread and cup were taken, the Lord's presence was to be recalled in the words "in remembrance of Me" (1 Cor 11:24). To recall means to transport an action buried in the past in such a way that its original potency and vitality are not lost but are carried over into the present. Paul emphasized the remembrance of the life and death of the Lord.[24]

---

[23] See Beasley-Murray, *Baptism in the New Testament*; Stanley J. Grenz, *Theology for the Community of God* (Grand Rapids: Eerdmans, 1994), 529–31; Dale Moody, "Baptism in Theology and Practice," in Basden and Dockery, *The People of God*, 41–50.

[24] See David S. Dockery, "The Church, Worship and the Lord's Supper," in *The Mission of Today's Church*, ed. Stan Norman (Nashville: B&H, 2006).

Paul was certainly aware that the Passover allowed the Jews to relive the experience of their forebears in the land of Egypt. Similarly, the Lord's Supper took believers back to the Lord's redemption, leading them again to receive the blessings of his passion.

For the church, the bread symbolized the sinless life of Jesus Christ that qualified him to be a perfect sacrifice for sin. The bread represented his body, in which he bore our sin on the cross (2 Cor 5:18–21). The cup similarly represented his shed blood. The participation of the believing community in the Supper represented their response to the substitutionary love that bore the cross.[25]

In the teaching of the apostle Paul, the Lord's Supper served as an announcement of the gospel (1 Cor 11:26), a sermon in silence by the entire church. The Supper quickened anticipation of the Second Coming, pointing beyond itself to a future hope in the kingdom of God. As believers participated in the Supper, they were reminded of the oneness within the body of Christ and of the fellowship among believers and with the exalted Christ (10:16). The church has been exhorted to continue the practice of the Supper in order to help focus congregational life on the death and resurrection of the Lord that established the new covenant (11:24–25). The practice was intended to be observed regularly on the first day of the week (see v. 20; Acts 20:7).

Past, present, and future are thus gathered up in one sacred and joyful festival of the Lord's Supper in Pauline practice and teaching. In this Supper, the essence of the Christian faith is powerfully expressed: one Lord, incarnate, atoning, resurrected, and exalted. The symbolic observance portrays a dramatic interrelationship with God. The essence of the experience includes fellowship and worship, eating and rejoicing together, while at the same time remembering the death of the Lord Jesus Christ on our behalf.[26]

---

[25] See C. K. Barrett, *Ministry and Sacraments in the New Testament* (Grand Rapids: Eerdmans, 1985).

[26] See Gordon D. Fee, *The First Epistle to the Corinthians*, NICNT (Grand Rapids: Eerdmans, 1987); Donald G. Bloesch, *The Church: Sacraments, Worship, Ministry, Mission* (Downers Grove: InterVarsity, 2002); Ralph P. Martin, *Worship in the Early Church* (Grand Rapids: Eerdmans, 1975).

Church Discipline

While not an identity marker like baptism and the Lord's Supper, the practice of church discipline was nonetheless an important element of Paul's teaching concerning the church. The apostle spoke frequently about church discipline, highlighting a significant disconnect between the Pauline churches and the contemporary Christian community, in which church discipline is generally a neglected practice. The apostle deemed church discipline a fitting response to various sins, and it took various forms (Rom 16:17–18; 2 Thess 3:14–15; 1 Tim 1:20).

Public rebuke was a common practice for Paul (Rom 16:17; 1 Cor 5:4–5; 1 Tim 1:20). Other forms of discipline included warning and admonition (1 Thess 5:12–14), withholding of fellowship (2 Thess 3:6), and abstaining from association, particularly during the church's gathering around the Lord's Supper (1 Cor 5:11–15). All discipline reflected the holy love and loving holiness of God and the command of Jesus Christ (see Matt 18:17–18; Heb 12:6, 11).

The purpose of discipline, in that regard, was redemptive (2 Cor 2:4; Gal 6:1). Excommunication was only the final option in the process (1 Tim 1:20). Thus, the act of discipline was intended to be carried out in love and humility in order to restore the wayward back to fellowship. Sometimes moving toward repentance included shame (2 Thess 3:14) and sorrow (2 Cor 2:7). Yet Paul warned against excessive punishment that might bring about excessive grief (v. 7). Discipline protected the church from decay (1 Cor 5:6). Paul understood that discipline served as an important reminder of the propensity toward sin and also produced a zeal for holiness in the believing community (2 Cor 7:11).

Images of the Church

It seems wise before we move to our concluding thoughts to examine the overall purpose of the believing community, as expressed by Paul through images. Paul Minear's often quoted study, *Images of the Church in the New Testament*, contains a seemingly unending list of pictures, images, and metaphors related to the NT presentation of the church.[27] Of the nearly

---

[27] Paul Minear, *Images of the Church in the New Testament* (Philadelphia: Westminster, 1960).

one hundred pictures identified by Minear, we will limit our survey to four of the more prominent ones for the purposes of this chapter.

The People of God

The first image to be considered is the church as the people of God. The church's beginning, history, and glorious destiny all depend on God's gracious initiative among his people. The church is a people called forth by God, incorporated into Christ, and indwelt by the Holy Spirit. Having been chosen and elected by God, the church belongs to God and is thus "My [God's] People" (Rom 9:25). The title, which God previously applied to Israel, is now applied to the church, showing historical continuity in his redemptive program, but not necessarily a revocation of the term's original application. The people of God are enabled and indwelt by the Spirit of God. The church is therefore the assembly of those united together in the reality and fellowship of the indwelling Spirit (Phil 2:1).

As we saw earlier, the Holy Spirit energized the church for ministry through the distribution of gifts. The presence of the Spirit continues to give the church a supernatural dynamic and therefore makes it unique among all human bodies. The life and ministry of the true church can be carried forward only where the holy presence and the work of the Spirit are known.[28]

Body of Christ

A second important image in the writings of Paul is the body of Christ. The apostle's favorite description of the church is the metaphor of the head and body. Christ is the head of the body, which is his church (Rom 12:5; 1 Cor 12:12–31; Eph 1:22–23; Col 1:18). The body of Christ is composed of all of those who are united to Christ through baptism of the Spirit. This metaphor pictures the one true church under the headship of the exalted Jesus Christ.

Paul's description of the body of Christ is figurative. He did not mean for the church to be understood as an equal to Christ or as a physical extension of his incarnation. The picture of the church as Christ's body

---

[28] See Sloan, "Images of the Church in Paul," in Basden and Dockery, *The People of God*, 148–65; N. T. Wright, *The New Testament and the People of God* (Minneapolis: Fortress, 1992).

points to its unity, its variety, and its mutuality. The idea of the body of Christ living under its head also points to Christ's lordship.[29]

Temple of God/Building of God

A third picture worthy of consideration is the church as the temple of God/building of God (1 Cor 6:19; Eph 2:14–15). This image is linked to that of the church as the body of Christ. For example, the gifts can be said to build up the church, as either a building or a body is built up. In the first century, the body was portrayed as both a building and a house (see 2 Cor 5:1–10).[30]

Paul spoke of our bodies as a temple or earthly house, calling the resurrection bodies of believers a building from God not made with hands. The temple and building metaphors focused on the church's foundation, the person and work of Jesus Christ. Without Christ, the church would be only a human construction and not a building of God. While Christ is the ultimate foundation, the teachings of the apostles and prophets are also pictured as a foundation for believers (Eph 2:20). Therefore, the church is built upon the true foundation of Christ, even as it stands upon the apostolic teaching found in inspired Scripture.

Household of God

The household image is paramount in the Pastoral Epistles (1 Tim 3:15). It suggests that the church's structure of responsibility and authority bears some resemblance to the structure of responsibility and authority in a home. Thus, the guidelines for leadership noted in both 1 Timothy and Titus must be understood within the context of this portrayal of the church, over which Jesus Christ is Lord.[31]

---

[29] See James D. G. Dunn, "The Body of Christ in Paul," in *Worship, Theology and Ministry in the Early Church*, ed. Michael J. Wilkins and Terence Paige (Sheffield: JSOT, 1992), 146–62; also A. J. M. Wedderburn, "The Body of Christ and Related Concepts in 1 Corinthians," *SJT* 24 (1971): 74–96.

[30] See J. Coppins, "The Spiritual Temple in the Pauline Letters and Its Background," *SE* 6 (1973): 53–66; also, Robert Saucy, *The Church in God's Program* (Chicago: Moody, 1974), 24–32.

[31] See Malcolm Yarnell, "*Oikos Theou*: A Theologically Neglected but Important Ecclesiological Metaphor," *MJT* 2, no. 1 (Fall 2003): 53–65. Helpful discussion of all of these images can be found in *DPL*.

Jesus Christ as Lord of the Church

Each of these Pauline metaphors emphasizes the lordship of Christ, one of the central Christological and redemptive themes of Holy Scripture. Jesus Christ is Lord of the church; everything that the church is and does is rooted in Christ and in his redemptive work on behalf of his people. The church is his; Christ is the church's foundation, builder, and head. The church's overarching purpose includes making known "God's multi-faceted wisdom" (Eph 3:10). The term "multi-faceted," traditionally translated "manifold," means multicolored or wonderfully complex, like a beautiful jewel. The history of the Christian church and the unfolding drama of redemption is a graduate school for the rulers and authorities in the heavenly realm regarding God's multi-faceted wisdom. Paul's vision of the church is central to his understanding of God's working in history. John Stott has suggested that the church is not only central to history but to the gospel and Christian living as well. If the church is central to God's plan, then we cannot push it to the periphery.[32]

In Ephesians, Paul apparently expanded the meaning of "church" beyond a local body of believers to include all the people of God on earth at any one time, plus all believers in heaven—the invisible, universal church. In origin and in purpose, the church is God's church. God created it, not human efforts. Constituted by him and for him, membership in the church is by divine initiative. God created a fellowship of people indwelt by the Holy Spirit. Paul presents the church not only as the people of God, the household of faith, the body of Christ, and the building or temple of the Holy Spirit, but also as the fellowship of the Spirit (Phil 2:1), the family of God (1 Thess 4:10), the pillar of truth (1 Tim 3:15), the new creation (Eph 2:15), and the Israel of God (Gal 6:16; Eph 2:12).[33]

The church is thus more than a human organization. It is the people who are reconciled to Christ and to one another. The church must live in recognition of the headship of the exalted and cosmic Christ (Col 1:15–20), seeking to remain in continuity with the past, primarily the

---

[32] See Stott, *God's New Society*; also, Thomas R. Schreiner, *Paul, Apostle of God's Glory in Christ: A Pauline Theology* (Downers Grove: InterVarsity, 2006).

[33] See P. T. O'Brien, "The Church as a Heavenly and Eschatological Entity," in *The Church and the Bible in the World*, ed. D. A. Carson (Grand Rapids: Baker, 1987), 88–119; also, James D. G. Dunn, *The Theology of Paul the Apostle* (Grand Rapids: Eerdmans, 2006).

apostolic doctrine and practice made known in Holy Scripture (Eph 2:20; 3:2–13).[34]

Conclusion

God has called the church into being for fellowship with himself and with other believers. The church has not only been called to build up its members (Eph 4:11–16) but also to demonstrate and proclaim the gospel to a fallen world (Gal 1:4; Eph 2:1–10). Paul's teaching on the church includes such themes as worship, service, ministry, fellowship, and celebration. Moreover, the church has a missionary task that is not optional. Thus the church exists not merely for itself but as a manifestation of God's grace in and for the world.

Paul's theology of the church provides a foundation for our theology of the church today.[35] We sometimes hear voices suggesting that theology should be de-emphasized, but that would be contrary to the Pauline practice. Without good theology, the church cannot and will not mature in the faith. The people of God will be tossed back and forth by waves, being blown here and there by every wind of teaching (Eph 4:14).

The depths of Paul's inspired teaching about the church will never be fully grasped this side of heaven. Nevertheless, we have learned much from him, not only about his understanding of the church but also about how we can glorify God by applying his words to our twenty-first-century context.[36] In doing so, we will no doubt find ourselves echoing Paul's doxology of Rom 11:33–36:

> Oh, the depth of the riches
> both of the wisdom and the knowledge of God!
> How unsearchable His judgments

---

[34] See David S. Dockery, "A Theology for the Church," *MJT* 1 (2003): 10–20.

[35] Ibid.

[36] Helpful attempts to do so include: Veli-Matti Kärkkäinen, "Ecclesiology," in *Mapping Modern Theology*, ed. Kelly Kapic and Bruce L. McCormack (Grand Rapids: Baker, 2012), 345–76. Bloesch, *The Church*; Millard J. Erickson, *Christian Theology*, vol. 3 (Grand Rapids: Baker, 1995); George R. Hunsberger and Craig Van Gelder, *The Church between Gospel and Culture* (Grand Rapids: Eerdmans, 1996); David Smith, *All God's People: A Theology of the Church* (Wheaton: Bridgepoint, 1996); Miroslav Volf, *After Our Likeness: The Church as the Image of the Trinity* (Grand Rapids: Eerdmans, 1988).

and untraceable His ways!
For who has known the mind of the Lord?
Or who has been His counselor?
Or who has ever first given to Him,
and has to be repaid?
For from Him and through Him
and to Him are all things.
To Him be the glory forever. Amen.

CHAPTER 5

The Church in the General Epistles

Ray F. Van Neste

The General Epistles have much to say about the church—what it is (or should be) and what it is to do.[1] The churches addressed are often struggling. They struggle with false teaching but should be orthodox. They face temptation but must be holy. They face the pressures and persecutions of a hostile world but must remain faithful, living in light of the return of Christ.

This study examines each letter (or group of letters) individually for teaching concerning the church. To present the material in an orderly manner, two main headings are used in the treatment of each letter: (1) identity and ethic and (2) function and structure.

The Church in Hebrews: Identity and Ethic

Renewed Israel

As the author of Hebrews reminds his readers that Jesus fulfills (and thus is superior to) the old covenant, he also points out that the new

---

[1] I do not assume the posture of a disinterested observer (of the text or of the church about which it speaks). I am a committed, interested member of this church and thus write from this perspective. When referring to the church in a specific location, I will use third person, but when speaking of the church in general, I will use first person.

covenant community fulfills the old covenant community. The church is the restored Israel. This is evident in Heb 12:22–24, where Christians are described as coming to "Mount Zion, to the city of the living God (the heavenly Jerusalem), . . . to the assembly [*ekklēsia*] of the firstborn whose names have been written in heaven, and to God, who is the judge of all, to the spirits of righteous people made perfect, to Jesus (mediator of a new covenant)." The privileges, blessings, and promises of Israel under the old covenant are given to the church because of the new covenant mediated by Jesus and his "sprinkled blood." "Mount Zion," "city of the living God," and "assembly of the firstborn" all refer to God's people, the communion of saints.[2] To this community believers have come, "not merely into its presence . . . but into its membership."[3] The church is now part of this assembly in heaven, even while it labors on earth.

On several occasions the author of Hebrews applies to the church language that the OT uses to reference Israel. In Heb 2:12 he cites Ps 22:22 as an instance of Jesus announcing his spiritual kinship with the "congregation." In Psalm 22 "congregation" (LXX, *ekklēsia*) referred to Israel. Now it refers to the church. In Heb 2:13 (citing Isa 8:18) Christians are called God's children, a term typically used of Israel in the OT.[4] Likewise in Heb 2:16 Jesus lays hold (redemptively) of Abraham's offspring. Because this is addressed to Jewish Christians, this could be understood merely as referring to biological descendants of Abraham. However, given the emphasis of the book on the transition to a new covenant, we may also see here the application of Israel terminology to the church.

Hebrews 3 frequently mentions God's "house" (vv. 2–6). Moses was faithful in God's house (vv. 2, 5), God built the house (v. 4), and Jesus is over it (v. 6). Because Moses served in this "house," it includes OT Israel. Hebrews 3:6 declares that we (new covenant believers) are God's house. Thus, continuity is in God's people across the testaments because believers in both covenants are part of God's house.[5] The term "house" is picked up from OT texts (e.g., Num 12:7; 1 Chr 17:14 [LXX]) where

---

[2] See Peter T. O'Brien, *The Letter to the Hebrews* (Grand Rapids: Eerdmans, 2010), 486.

[3] F. F. Bruce, *The Epistle to the Hebrews* (Grand Rapids: Eerdmans, 1990), 359.

[4] For example, Isa 1:2, 4; 30:1, 9; 41:8–10 (LXX); 63:8; Jer 3:14; Ezek 16:20–21; Hos 1:10.

[5] Harold Attridge, *The Epistle to the Hebrews* (Philadelphia: Fortress, 1989), 111.

it refers to God's people.[6] Similarly, in Heb 8:8–10 "house of Israel" and "house of Judah" mean essentially "family, tribe, specific community." Thus, designating the church the "house" of God identifies it with God's OT people.[7]

"People of God" (4:9 NASB; 10:30) has a similar connotation.[8] Hebrews 10:30 notes that as his people, believers are subject to his judgment. In 4:9 the phrase explicitly links the people of God in the OT with those in the New; the Sabbath rest that was promised for God's people in the OT remains for us now in the new covenant. Craig Koester agrees that "people of God" is essentially synonymous with "house" and stresses the continuity of the people of God across the covenants.[9] "His people" in 10:30 is also drawn from OT contexts and reflects continuity across the covenants.[10] Jeremiah 31:33 ("they will be My people") is cited in Heb 8:10 in reference to the church.

The point is clear. In Hebrews, the church stands in continuity with God's OT people. The church is the restored Israel, the heir of the old covenant promises, and the true people of God.

Family

Family imagery is first used in Heb 2:10, where God is said to be at work "bringing many sons to glory" (see also "children" in 2:13–14). God is Father to believers. The Father accomplishes this work through the Son, and the Son is not ashamed to call believers his brothers (2:11–12; see also v. 17). Thus, salvation creates a familial setting in which Christians receive the amazing privilege of regarding God as their Father and Jesus as their brother. As Father, God disciplines his sons (12:7–11). This family

---

[6] Though at times "house" language refers to the temple, this does not seem to be the case in these instances.

[7] Craig Koester, *Hebrews* (New York: Doubleday, 2001), 252–53.

[8] The reference to "the people" (*ho laos*) in Heb 13:12 should probably also be included here.

[9] "He does not speak of an old and new Israel . . . or contrast Israel and the church . . . but perceives the continuity in the people of God under old and new covenants" (Koester, *Hebrews*, 272). Paul Ellingworth also writes, "Continuity is maintained between the people of God in the old and new dispensations: there is for the writer of Hebrews only one *laos tou theou*" (*The Epistle to the Hebrews* [Grand Rapids: Eerdmans, 1993], 255).

[10] See Koester, *Hebrews*, 453.

connection, like all other aspects of the church's identity, arises from its connection to Christ.

A family connection also is between believers. The author calls the Hebrew Christians "brothers" (3:1). This use of "brother" continues throughout the book (3:12; 10:19; 13:22–23), and Christians are exhorted to continue in brotherly love (13:1). The exhortation to care for one another (discussed below) makes particular sense in a family context.

Spirit-Empowered

The church in Hebrews has received and been empowered by the Holy Spirit.[11] The gospel had been confirmed among them, since they received the Holy Spirit and witnessed signs and wonders (2:4). They had been enlightened (6:4; 10:32), "tasted the heavenly gift," "became companions with the Holy Spirit," and "tasted God's good word and the powers of the coming age" (6:4–5). Although the precise meaning of these phrases is debated, they obviously point to the work of the Spirit in the church.[12]

Holiness

The church is to be holy. This is seen readily in the use of "saints" to refer to the church (6:10; 13:24; see also "holy brothers" in 3:1),[13] as well as in the various ethical commands (concentrated in chap. 13). Believers are "those who are sanctified" (10:14), whose consciences have been cleansed (9:14). Therefore, the church is to struggle against sin and to strive for holiness (12:4, 14), and to allow no immorality (v. 16; 13:4). As a loving Father, God disciplines his children so that they might "share His holiness" (12:10).

---

[11] Some argue that baptism is in view in 6:2, 4 and 10:22. I am not convinced and thus do not deal with baptism in this section (see O'Brien, *Hebrews*, 367–68; George H. Guthrie, *Hebrews* [Grand Rapids: Zondervan, 1998], 344).

[12] That some with this experience in 6:4 turn away does not negate this point. The problem is that certain people have experiences that suggest they are believers even though they are not actually believers. Still, the author assumes that all believers have had these experiences. For a good explanation of these phrases, see O'Brien, *Hebrews*, 219–23.

[13] It is unfortunate that the TNIV and NIV1984 render *hagios* in 6:10 and 13:24 as "God's people" and the NLT renders it as "believers." These renderings leave out any reference to holiness, which is the main point of this term.

Distinct

In Hebrews the church is seen as a gathered community distinct from worldly society and often marginalized by society. The believing community has pilgrim status. It is outside the camp (13:13) in this world but awaiting the city made by God (11:10), the kingdom that cannot be shaken (12:28). Because society disdains believers, their status as a family is all the more important.

Eschatological

The writer to the Hebrews understood that the church had come into being by the proclamation of the gospel and was confirmed by the Spirit's powerful manifestation. However, difficult current circumstances seemed to contradict the reality of God's present rule. So the writer turns the church's attention to the ultimate goal: by living in light of the future, they will live properly in the present. The church is essentially an eschatological community, living in light of the certain hope of the culmination of God's plan, including the vindication of Christ and his people.

Christ's work involves bringing many sons to glory, and because he is still leading us there, we have not yet reached this glory (2:10).[14] Because Jesus has gone ahead as our forerunner into God's presence, we have "a sure and firm anchor of the soul," knowing he will also take us there (6:19–20). Believers are "companions in a heavenly calling" (3:1), called by Christ *from* heaven and *to* heaven, awaiting the heavenly rest (3:7–4:13) and our promised eternal inheritance (9:15). Like Abraham, we are "looking forward to the city that has foundations, whose architect and builder is God" (11:10). As such, the church is made up of "those who are waiting for Him" (9:28) and gathers to encourage one another because the final day is drawing near (10:25). This reality is captured by Augustine in the closing lines of *The City of God*: "There we shall rest and see, see and love, love and praise. This is what shall be in the end without end. For what other end do we propose to ourselves than to attain to the kingdom of which there is no end?"[15]

---

[14] O'Brien notes the connotation of "leader" in *archēgos* and states, "By calling Jesus the 'pioneer' of *their salvation* the author encourages his hearers to press on towards their final destination" (*Hebrews*, 107).

[15] Augustine, *The City of God*, trans. Marcus Dods (22.30).

This future hope does not lead to passive withdrawal from the world but rather forms the basis for endurance and continuing witness in the world. This is the point of the examples in Hebrews 11 and the exhortations in Hebrews 12. In Peter O'Brien's words, the church in Hebrews is "the eschatological congregation of God, which from one perspective is already assembled around the exalted Christ (12:22–24) but is still very much part of the world (2:14–18), and which meets in Christ's name and under his authority here on earth."[16]

The Church in Hebrews: Function and Structure

Worship

The church is a worshipping community. As "the first covenant also had regulations for ministry" (9:1), regulations for worship are significant in the new covenant. This theme arises in the discussion of Jesus as the ultimate priest and sacrifice. Because of his work, believers are cleansed more thoroughly than before. They can now draw near to God (4:16; 7:25; 10:22; 11:6; 12:22).[17] This theme culminates at the end of the letter. The church draws near to "the heavenly Jerusalem" (12:22) and therefore is to "serve God acceptably, with reverence and awe" (v. 28). New covenant worship is not an occasional activity either, but we are called to offer up a sacrifice of praise to God "continually" (13:15). This sacrifice includes not only praise from the lips but also doing good and sharing one's possessions (v. 16). Thus, the church worships God with lives reverent toward him and loving toward others.

Oversight of Souls

The necessity of perseverance is a key theme in Hebrews.[18] The church is defined as a persevering people in 3:6, 14; 10:39. As a good pastor, the author desires that the readers have "the final realization of [their] hope" (6:11) and points them to the example of Abraham (vv. 14–15). He calls

---

[16] O'Brien, *Hebrews*, 111.

[17] Ellingworth, commenting on the verb translated "draw near" in these passages, notes that "*proserchomai* in Hebrews is always used in a cultic sense, of worshippers approaching God" (*Hebrews*, 269).

[18] "That believers should 'hold fast' (*kataschōmen*) to what they have is one of the major paraenetic emphases of Hebrews" (Attridge, *Hebrews*, 111).

on the people to "seize the hope set before us" (v. 18) and to "hold on to the confession of our hope without wavering" (10:23; see also vv. 35–36). As the church, they have suffered scorn and affliction and have stood with others enduring similar hardship (vv. 32–34).[19]

Perseverance is not only a church characteristic but also a church responsibility. At this point Hebrews makes one of its great contributions to ecclesiology. The church is one of the primary means given by God to help people persevere in the faith. This is accomplished as both the congregation and church leaders watch over one another's souls.

Responsibility of the Congregation

Hebrews 3:7–4:13 discusses the duty of church members to watch over one another, holding each other accountable. Hebrews 3:1–6 closes with the statement that we are God's house "if we hold on" (v. 6). Because some may turn away, the author points them to Ps 95:7–11 and the Israelite rebellion in the wilderness. The point is that just as the Israelites failed to enter rest, so people who turn away today will not enter the rest.[20] So the author exhorts, "Watch out, brothers, so that there won't be in any of you an evil, unbelieving heart that departs from the living God" (Heb 3:12).

Significantly, it is church members ("brothers") who are called to beware on behalf of one another. Church leaders are discussed elsewhere (13:7, 17), but the emphasis here is on the duty of the congregation in helping one another to persevere. Christians must "encourage each other daily . . . so that none of you is hardened by sin's deception" (3:13). This assumes regular, substantive interaction among church members concerning the state of our souls. The author adds that we should fear lest any of us seem to be turning away from God (4:1). This is not a casual relationship. This is a group of people deeply committed to one another's spiritual welfare, ready and willing to ask probing questions, to rebuke when necessary, and to encourage when possible. They fear for the welfare of one another the way parents fear for the well-being of their children.

---

[19] "Holding fast to their confession and receiving the glory God has promised entails the kind of perseverance that disregards the shame associated with Jesus' cross" (Koester, *Hebrews*, 253).

[20] The NT envisions people who profess faith and appear to be Christians for some time only to abandon the faith later (e.g., Mark 4:1–20; 1 John 2:19). By their failure to persevere, they show they have never been converted.

After an exposition of the theme of rest, the author returns to his exhortation, calling on the congregation to strive to enter this rest "so that no one will fall" (4:11). Earnestness in this effort is again underscored.[21] And again, corporate effort on behalf of every individual is required. Similarly, in 10:24–25 the congregation is commanded to "be concerned about one another in order to promote love and good works," to be faithful in meeting together, and to encourage one another. The verb translated "be concerned" (*katanoeō*) is difficult to capture with one English word. It involves a call for the people to direct their minds toward one another so that they will be aware enough to help.[22] The same verb is used in 3:1 calling them to "consider" Jesus. Just as we fix our gaze on Jesus as our chief priest, so we also fix our gaze on our brothers and sisters, intent on aiding them.

This help is described as provocation (*paroxusmos*) of love and good works.[23] Thus, we must look for ways to provoke one another to love and good deeds. This requires intentional involvement in the lives of others, with serious effort from the congregation on behalf of each individual member. Together, all are concerned for each one individually.

This theme occurs again in Heb 12:15–17. In the context of a call to perseverance, the entire congregation is exhorted to "see to it that no one falls short of the grace of God," to make sure no root of bitterness springs up, and that no one is sexually immoral or unholy. The verb translated "see to it" (*episkopeō*) is also used of pastoral oversight in 1 Pet 5:2 and has the sense of taking care, watching out for danger.[24] It is used in the Septuagint to describe the work of a good shepherd.[25] The congregation is expected to help shepherd each other, taking responsibility for keeping one another out of spiritual trouble, caring for and preserving one another. The picture is of people linking arms, purposing to make it together to the

---

[21] *Spoudazō* ("make every effort") typically connotes eagerness, effort, diligence (BDAG, 939).

[22] O'Brien, *Hebrews*, 369–70; J. A. Lee, *A History of New Testament Lexicography* (New York: Lang, 2003), 18–25.

[23] This word is "used to convey intense emotion, often of a negative kind, such as anger (Deut 29:28 [LXX 27] or strong disagreement (Acts 15:39)" (O'Brien, *Hebrews*, 370). It appears the author is intentionally using a negative word to emphasize his point.

[24] Ellingworth, *Hebrews*, 603. J. Rhode says this verb refers to the work of pastors here in Hebrews and in 1 Peter 5 ("*episkeptomai, episkopeō*") in *EDNT* 2:34). This misses the context of Hebrews 12, however.

[25] *TDNT* 2:604.

promised land, saying, "We do not intend to get there without you." Some will turn away, but none will slip through the cracks. They will have to leave intentionally because we will not let them go.

Responsibility of Leaders

Hebrews also emphasizes the role of leaders in watching over members of the congregation (13:7, 17). In v. 7 the recipients are called upon to "remember" their leaders and to imitate their faith. These leaders are those who taught them God's Word. Under the ultimate rule of Christ there is an authority structure in which certain members exercise authority over other members.[26] This is not a pure democracy.

The task of the leaders is made more explicit in 13:17, where the congregation is called upon to "obey" (*peithō*) and "submit to" (*hupeikō*) their church leaders. These leaders clearly exercise significant authority. The verb translated "obey" is often used with the sense of "be persuaded," so some have sought to downplay the authority represented here for leaders. However, the sense of "obey" is found both in the NT and in Jewish writings.[27] *Hupekeite*, which occurs only here in the NT, is a strong term and means "to give way, yield or submit to someone."[28] Certainly despotic authority is not in view, and these leaders will seek to persuade; but the picture here is of a congregation following the godly direction of its leaders.

Leaders are granted this authority in order to "keep watch" (*agrupneō*) over the souls of the people. The wording suggests diligent care flowing from deep concern for the spiritual well-being of the people. These leaders labor to guide their people safely home to "the city" (11:10) and the "rest" (4:11).[29] Such diligent pastors engage deeply in the life of each member. Here, as elsewhere in Scripture, authority is linked to love and care.

---

[26] "In Hebrews, the sole priesthood of Christ does not obviate the need for pastoral leadership in the community; but it is exercised by a group (see Phil 1:1), not by a single individual" (Ellingworth, *Hebrews*, 723).

[27] Romans 2:8; Gal 5:7; Jas 3:3. See 4 Maccabees 6:4; 8:17, 26; 10:13; 12:4, 5; 15:10; 18:1.

[28] BDAG, 1030; see O'Brien, *Hebrews*, 329.

[29] "The leaders had imposed upon them by God nothing less than the care for the eschatological salvation of the individual participants in the community. . . . Their service was directed toward the community's attainment of eschatological salvation" (William L. Lane, *Hebrews* [Dallas: Word, 1991], 2:555).

The requirement of oversight by both leaders and congregational members is evident in Hebrews. Too often this work of oversight has been seen as the responsibility only of leaders. However, this is a post-NT error, not a NT teaching.

The Church in Hebrews: Summary

In Hebrews the church is the renewed Israel, heir of the promises of God rooted in Christ, set apart to him and holy, persevering in this world with an eschatological hope as it draws near to God. Members and leaders diligently care for one another. The church is a tight-knit community where people know and care for each other and leaders are involved in the lives of members. Shallow relationships do not allow for striving together for perseverance (4:11) and guarding one another from sin (3:12–13; 12:15–16). The leaders are not simply speakers from a distance but shepherds tending to the spiritual health of the members, laboring to see each one make it safely home.

The Church in James: Identity and Ethic

Continuity with Israel

The ethnic makeup of the church addressed in James is much debated.[30] Certainly Jewish Christians are involved; some Gentile Christians may be included. What is certain, however, is that this community is considered the true Israel, in continuity with the people of God under the old covenant. James refers to them as "the 12 tribes" (Jas 1:1), i.e., God's restored people.[31] They are "firstfruits" of God's creatures (1:18), a term used of historical Israel and the new Israel (Rom 11:16; Rev 14:4). These believers are also "heirs of the kingdom" (Jas 2:5). God's kingdom is no longer associated particularly with national Israel but with the church, which in

---

[30] See Scot McKnight, *The Letter of James* (Grand Rapids: Eerdmans, 2011), 65–68; Craig L. Blomberg and Mariam J. Kamell, *James* (Grand Rapids: Zondervan, 2008), 28–29; and Dan McCartney, *James* (Grand Rapids: Baker, 2009), 32–36.

[31] "The sum-total of Jewish believers in Jesus, considered as the new Israel" (F. F. Bruce, *New Testament History*, 353n7 [cited by R. P. Martin, *James* (Waco: Word, 1988), 8]). See also McKnight, *James*, 66–68; Blomberg and Kamell, *James*, 28–29.

this passage is defined as those who love God, and is particularly identified with the poor.

Like OT Israel, the church has been chosen by God (Jas 2:5), and by God's will it has been brought into being (1:18). As the "firstfruits" (v. 18), the church is compared to "the first ripe fruit which promises the coming full harvest and . . . the special possession of God" in the sacrificial system of the OT.[32] The church, not Israel, is this especially-devoted-to-God portion. As the representative of further harvest (see also Rom 16:5; 2 Thess 2:13; Rev 14:4),[33] the church advances the work of gathering people to God.[34] The discussion of salvation in Jas 2:20–26 assumes unity in the way of salvation for people on both sides of Jesus' coming. This is the only way an appeal to Abraham and Rahab makes sense. This congregation stands in continuity with God's redeeming work under the old covenant.

Terms for Church

In James the church is called "assembly" (*sunagōgē*, 2:2 ESV) and "church" (*ekklēsia*, 5:14). Both terms have significant background in Jewish usage. *Ekklēsia* is commonly used in the LXX to refer to the congregation of Israel. *Sunagōgē* is typically used to refer to Jewish synagogues (e.g., Matt 23:6; Mark 12:39). The use of *ekklēsia* is in keeping with the rest of the NT and links the NT church with the OT people of God. The use of *sunagōgē* is more surprising, as this is the only place in the NT where this word is used to refer to a Christian gathering. Some debate the precise meaning of the word here, but most likely it refers to the gathering of the church.[35]

---

[32] Peter H. Davids, *James* (Peabody, MA: Hendrickson, 1989), 90.

[33] McKnight, *James*, 131. McKnight states, "God's intent is to restore individuals in the context of a community that has a missional focus on the rest of the world" (131).

[34] Ibid.; McCartney, *James*, 111. McCartney writes, "A further implication of this is that the 'firstfruits' are the exemplars who reflect God's character to the world" (*James*, 111).

[35] Some suggest the use of the term here means that the church is meeting in a synagogue. This is possible, but this word can also mean "assembly" without the technical connotation of a Jewish synagogue (see Davids, *James*, 108). There is also debate as to whether the meeting in view is for worship or for church discipline, like what is envisioned in 1 Corinthians 6. Most important for this study is to note that James refers to a meeting of the church (see the commentaries, Davids, *James*, 108–9; McKnight, *James*, 181–86; McCartney, *James*, 138; Blomberg and Kamell, *James*, 110–11).

Family

James repeatedly refers to his readers as "brothers" (1:2, 9, 16, 19; 2:1, 5, 14–15; 3:1, 10; 4:11 [3x]; 5:7, 9–10, 12, 19).[36] This is common of early Christianity, but the frequency of the term in James suggests more than casual usage. Rather, James envisions a "brotherhood community,"[37] a tight-knit familial community. This brotherly connection is foundational to the ethic that James teaches.[38] The address "(my) brothers" often introduces exhortations in the letter. As brothers, James calls the recipients to listen to one another and to be slow to anger (1:19). As brothers, he charges them not to show partiality (2:1, 5). Their faith should compel them to meet the needs of any "brother or sister" (v. 15). Brothers ought not to speak evil against one another (4:11; see 3:10) or complain about one another (5:9). And James closes with an admonition to them as brothers to watch out for one another, to bring back an erring brother and "save his life from death" (vv. 19–20).

This "brotherly" ethic is based on the reality that God is the common Father of believers (note the image of God birthing the community in 1:18). Thus, we are brothers and sisters. James refers to God as our Father when he rebukes those who curse people made in God's image (3:9). In Jas 1:27 God is identified as Father; then we are called upon to care for widows and orphans. The fatherhood of God creates a familial setting for the church and provides a model of care for imitation.

Eschatological

The church in James is focused on the future in-breaking of God's reign.[39] The ethics of the letter often grow out of a call not to pursue the values of this age but to await the vindication to come. Riches in this life are fading (1:9–11), but the one who remains steadfast will, one day, receive the crown of life (v. 12). We are not to pursue earthly fame but to let God exalt

---

[36] "Neighbor" in 4:12 probably also refers to the community because the previous sentences refer to one's "brother." James shifts to "neighbor" to allude to Lev 19:18 and Jesus' teaching in Matt 22:39 (see McCartney, *James*, 221).

[37] This term comes from McKnight, *James*, 71.

[38] "Throughout the letter we find a community-shaped ethic" (McKnight, *James*, 45).

[39] "The great task of the Church, according to James, is to live in the hope of the coming of the Lord that has now drawn near " (Mark Seifrid, "The Waiting Church and Its Duty: James 5:13–18," *SBJT* 4, no. 3 [Fall 2000]: 32).

us (4:10). We are to be patient, waiting for "the Lord's coming" (5:7) and strengthening our hearts "because the Lord's coming is near" (v. 8). The church is an eschatological community shaped by the certainty of Christ's return and the reckoning that day will bring.

The Church in James: Function and Structure

Worship

In James, worship is central to church life. Prayer and praise, public and private, are mentioned often. James urges the people to pray for wisdom (1:5–6), rebukes selfish prayer (4:2–3), and calls for prayer for the sick in the context of repentance and restoration (5:13–18). The mention of receiving "the implanted word" (1:21) seems to refer to preaching—a conclusion supported by the reference to hearing the word in the verses that follow. The church blesses "our Lord and Father" (3:9) and sings praise (or psalms; 5:13)[40] to God.

Leadership

In James, recognized leaders are in the congregation. The warning in Jas 3:1 that "not many should become teachers" shows that teaching is a recognized role, exercised only by certain people. This teaching entails responsibility and, presumably, leadership. Further, Jas 5:14 refers to "elders of the church." Again, these are clearly identified leaders who can be called on for spiritual help, and there is more than one elder in the congregation.[41] From these two texts deductions can be drawn. First, teaching is not open to anyone. There is some guarding of the teaching function. Secondly, a recognized body of leaders exists. This is not the amorphous, leaderless community that some suggest was the norm for

---

[40] Ralph P. Martin, *Worship in the Early Church* (Grand Rapids: Eerdmans, 1964), 43, argues that this refers to singing psalms. For a treatment of the place of psalm-singing in the NT, see Ray Van Neste, "Ancient Songs and Apostolic Preaching: How the New Testament Laid Claim to the Psalms," in *Forgotten Songs: Reclaiming the Psalms for Christian Worship*, ed. Richard Wells and Ray Van Neste (Nashville: B&H, 2012).

[41] There is some debate whether "elders" here refers to an actual office in the church or simply to mature men who have the respect of the people (McKnight, *James*, 435–37, says it probably does not refer to an office; Davids, *James*, 192–93, and Martin, *James*, 206–7, say it does). Acts 21:18 notes the office of elder in the Jerusalem church; thus, the office was present from the early days of the church, and I see no need to understand the term "elder" any differently in this text.

early churches. Third, multiple leaders are in a single church. Fourth, these leaders provide spiritual and physical care for the congregation. They are men of prayer and spiritual vitality (else why call them when ill?). They are not only managers but caregivers.

Oversight and Congregational Care

As Dan McCartney has stated, "The concept of 'brotherhood' entails a mutual responsibility of believers."[42] This ethic goes beyond "do no harm" to "care for one another." When James lists caring for widows and the fatherless as a defining mark of true religion (1:27), he implies such needy people were within the church.

James 5:16 shows that the community exercises mutual care by confessing sins to one another and praying for one another. This prayer will lead to healing from both physical and spiritual ailments. In v. 14 the elders are called to pray for the sick person. Here, in contrast, James describes the responsibility of the members for one another.[43]

Scot McKnight is correct in stating about the confession of sins, "Church praxis has evolved out of this command by James."[44] We need to recover this practice. Yet, this command does not require a place in the weekly liturgy (although such a practice can be helpful). The verse does not specify that an individual must confess his sin to the congregation as a whole (though that is necessary in certain instances). Because the reference to prayer for one another implies private interaction between individuals, it is reasonable to understand confession to one another in the same manner.[45] This requires a community where the members are close enough to one another that they can confess their sins to each other. By doing so, they receive the forgiveness, help, encouragement, and prayer they need.

---

[42] McCartney, *James*, 71.

[43] "The text here widens to make prayer and confession, and so pastoral responsibility, the 'privilege and responsibility' of all in the congregation" (Martin, *James*, 211). "It is the *ordinary* member in good standing, not just the elders or prophets, whose prayer is powerful" (Davids, *James*, 196).

[44] McKnight, *James*, 446.

[45] John Calvin argued for this corporate idea (against the idea of confessing to a priest): "We should lay our infirmities on one another's breasts, to receive among ourselves mutual counsel, mutual compassion, and mutual consolation" (*Institutes of the Christian Religion*, ed. John T. McNeill, trans. Ford Lewis Battles, vol. 1 [Louisville: Westminster John Knox, 1960], 630).

James 5:19–20 takes this a step further. A situation is introduced where someone in the community turns away from the gospel (whether by practice or profession) and another turns him back. James lists the benefits of turning a wandering brother back (the salvation of his soul and the covering of his sin) and commands the congregation to turn back erring brothers. The task of turning back such ones is open to anyone (Gk., *tis*) in the congregation, not only leaders. Congregational care for one another is a matter of life and death.

The Church in James: Summary

The church in James is the renewed Israel, a worshipping family created by God to care for one another and to help one another to persevere. The church lives in light of Christ's return.[46] Elders are the lead, but not sole, caregivers in the community.

The Church in 1 Peter: Identity and Ethic

First Peter is rich in teaching related to the church,[47] and that teaching is similar to what we have seen in Hebrews and James. The church is first of all the new people of God, a close-knit familial group distinguished from the society around it.

---

[46] See Christopher W. Morgan, *A Theology of James: Wisdom for God's People*, Explorations in Biblical Theology (Phillipsburg: P&R, 2010), 160–68, 184–85.

[47] "The letter speaks of the recipients as members of a clearly defined, divinely prescribed community: the elect and holy people of God (1:3–2:10) brought into being by the activity of God the Father, the Holy Spirit and Jesus Christ (1:1–2). To the public they were known as the 'Christians' (4:16). Separated from the rest of society through a voluntary termination of, and conversion from, past familial, social and religious ties (1:3–5, 10–12, 18–21; 2:4–10; etc.), theirs was a familial-like community or brotherhood (1:22; 2:5, 17; 5:9) defined by a unique faith in Jesus as the Christ, as the agent of the salvation for which they hope (1:2, 3, 6–8, 13, 18–21; 2:3, 4–10) and an ethic which prescribes religious allegiance, 'fear' (1:17; 2:17; see 3:6, 14) and 'obedience' (see 2:8; 3:20; 4:17) to the will of God alone (2:15; 3:17; 4:2, 19). The salvation (1:5, 9, 10; 2:2; 3:21; 4:18) or divine grace (1:2, 10, 13) in which all members share equally (3:7; 4:10; 5:5, 10, 12) is anticipated in full measure at the final advent of Jesus Christ soon to take place (1:5, 7, 13; 4:13; 5:1). Until this time the sect is to maintain strict internal discipline (1:22; 2:1; 3:8; 4:7–11; 5:1–5) and to contend vigorously [*sic*] against any encroachment from, or assimilation to, outside pressures (1:14–16, 18–21; 2:11; 3:9, 13–17; 4:1–6, 12–19; 5:8–9)" (John H. Elliott, *A Home for the Homeless: A Sociological Exegesis of 1 Peter, Its Situation and Strategy* [Philadelphia: Fortress, 1981], 75.

New People of God

Peter applies to the church language and promises that refer to Israel in the OT, understanding "the Christian community as having assumed the mantle of God's people from the Jews."[48] He opens by addressing his readers as "temporary residents of the Dispersion . . . chosen" (1:1). In the first century, *diaspora* (translated "temporary residents" or "exiles") was used to refer to Jews scattered from their historic land. Thus, Peter took a phrase referring to the Jewish people and applied it to the church.[49] The church is now God's people. A few verses later, he regards the church as heir to the OT promises, a reality indicated by his statement that the OT prophets were serving the church (vv. 10–12). Their prophecies find fulfillment in Christ and his church.

First Peter 2:11 calls the church "aliens and temporary residents," terms also used together in Gen 23:4 and Ps 39:12 (LXX, 38:13); these are the only occurrences in the LXX of the word translated "temporary residents." These terms are here used of the church. Like Abraham (Gen 23:4) these believers are exiles, belonging to God's family and looking ahead to their eternal home.

By citing Ps 34:12–16 in 1 Pet 3:10–12, Peter equates "the righteous" in the psalm with these Christians. The church is also "God's flock" (1 Pet 5:2) in need of good shepherds, a common OT picture of Israel (Jer 13:17, "the LORD's flock"; 38:10 [LXX]; Zech 10:3). As Paul Achtemeier stated, "Language from the OT seems naturally to apply to the new community of faith for our author."[50]

This comes out especially in 1 Pet 2:4–10. The primary metaphor for the church in this text is "spiritual house" (v. 5). The word translated

---

[48] Paul J. Achtemeier, *A Commentary on First Peter*, Hermeneia Series (Philadelphia: Fortress Press, 1996), 269. How this is understood depends significantly on whether the recipient churches were Jewish or largely Gentile. While there has been some debate on this, the majority view today is that the churches were predominately Gentile. The description of their preconversion life in 1:18 and 4:3–4 fits Gentiles very well but would be hard to identify with Jews. See also Thomas R. Schreiner, *1, 2 Peter, Jude*, NAC (Nashville: B&H, 2003), 38–41.

[49] "The Jews of the Diaspora considered themselves to be the elect people of God. The author of 1 Peter takes this prevalent Diaspora theme and applies this designation to his readers" (Troy W. Martin, *Metaphor and Composition in 1 Peter* [Atlanta: Scholars Press, 1992], 163–64). Elliott (*A Home for the Homeless*, 37–49) argues that "exiles" refers to political status. However, several have critiqued Elliott's reading. See Schreiner, *1, 2 Peter, Jude*, 39–41.

[50] Achtemeier, *1 Peter*, 148.

"house" (*oikos*) is commonly used for the temple in the OT (e.g., 2 Sam 7:13; 1 Kgs 3:2) and NT (Matt 21:13; John 2:16–17; Acts 7:47, 49). This, along with Peter's references to priesthood and sacrifices, makes it clear that he equates the church (the people, not a building) with the temple of the old covenant.[51]

The church is likewise "God's household" (1 Pet 4:17; "the house of God," KJV; *ho oikos tou theou*). In the LXX this phrase refers often to the temple (e.g., 1 Kgs 5:14, 17, 19; 7:31, 34, 37).[52] Additionally, echoes of Ezekiel 9 (judgment beginning at the temple) and Malachi 3 (the Lord coming to refine the temple) show that the church is portrayed as God's temple. As Thomas Schreiner states, "We see here that Peter, in concert with the other New Testament writers (1 Cor 3:16; 2 Cor 6:16; Eph 2:19; 1 Tim 3:15; Heb 3:6), now conceives of the church, God's people, as his temple."[53] So the church is the new covenant equivalent of the old covenant temple. This use of temple imagery fits with what has been stated above: the church is the locus of God's people. In the church, God manifests his presence in a special way. Humanity now meets with God in the church, the people of God.

First Peter 2:9 continues describing the church with four phrases full of OT significance: "Chosen race," "royal priesthood," "holy nation," and "people for His possession."[54] Israel was known as God's chosen people, but now this chosen group is the church, composed of both Jews and Gentiles. The next two phrases were used of Israel at her national birth at Sinai. The church, rather than Israel, is now the one set apart to God ("holy nation") and given the task of showing to the world the supremacy of Yahweh ("royal priesthood"). The church is God's prized possession, the apple of his eye ("people for His possession"). Alluding to Hos 2:23, Peter tells these primarily Gentile Christians that although they had once

---

[51] "Despite the hesitation of some scholars, Peter clearly here identified the church as God's new temple" (Schreiner, *1, 2 Peter, Jude*, 105). So also Achtemeier, *1 Peter*, 156; Davids, *James*, 86–87.

[52] Schreiner, *1, 2 Peter, Jude*, 227, gives a long list of references. Furthermore, "Used with God's name, *oikos*, as in secular Greek, means the temple, the sanctuary" (J. Goetzmann, "House," in *NIDNTT*, vol. 2, ed. Colin Brown [Grand Rapids: Zondervan, 1971], 247). See Martin, *Metaphor*, 164.

[53] Schreiner, *1, 2 Peter, Jude*, 227. See Achtemeier, *1 Peter*, 316.

[54] The Greek phrase translated "chosen race" appears in Isa 43:20–21. "Royal priesthood" and "holy nation" are taken from Exod 19:6. "People for His possession" alludes to Mal 3:17 and Isa 43:21.

not been "a people,"[55] they are now the people of God; though previously they had not known God's mercy, now they have received mercy. This is a startling claim. As John H. Elliott has noted, "All that had been anticipated aforetime under the Old Dispensation has now reached its culmination in the union between the Elect Stone and the Elect Race [the church]."[56]

Family

The church is a loving family. God is the Father (1 Pet 1:17) who caused Christians to be born again (v. 3) by the seed of his word (v. 23). Believers are to be "obedient children" (v. 14) who love one another. Silvanus is a "faithful brother" (5:12), and Mark is Peter's "son" (v. 13). That they have been born again by the "seed" of God's word is a reason for them to love each other from a pure heart (1:22).[57] Thus, Peter refers to the recipients as "dear friends" (2:11; 4:12). Brotherly love is basic to Christian life (1:22; 2:17; 3:8). "Love the brotherhood" in 1 Pet 2:17 is particularly striking. This brotherhood extends throughout the world (5:9), and the church in Rome (v. 13) is presented as a sister to the churches addressed. The church is, then, both local and universal.

The family setting grounds the emphasis on loving one another. Peter says, "Above all, keep your love for one another at full strength" (4:8). Covering one another's sin, showing hospitality to one another, and being clothed with humility all fit within this family framework (4:8–9; 5:5). The charge in 3:8, "all of you should be like-minded and sympathetic, should love believers, and be compassionate and humble," is a call to healthy family life. The "kiss of love" (5:14) emphasizes "that all Christians were to regard themselves as members of the Christian family, and hence to treat each other with kindness and consideration."[58]

---

[55] The word for "people" (*laos*) in the LXX is "a specific term for a specific people, namely Israel, and it serves to emphasize the special and privileged religious position of this people as the people of God" (H. Strathmann, "*laos*," in *TDNT* 4:32).

[56] John H. Elliott, *The Elect and the Holy* (Eugene, OR: Wipf and Stock, 2005), 198. Similarly, L. Coenen writes, "What the author wishes to underline is the fact that the Christian community is nothing new; it is to be understood as the fulfillment of the promises and hopes given to Israel" ("Church," in Brown, *NIDNTT*, vol. 1 [1986], 305).

[57] The participle that opens 1 Pet 1:23 (*anagegennēmenoi*) is causal. Thus HCSB translates "since you have been born again" (similarly NASB, ESV, NLT, TNIV, NIV 1984; this is obscured in RSV and NRSV).

[58] Achtemeier, *1 Peter*, 356.

Distinct

This family is a countercultural entity, distinct from the society around it. Believers are regarded primarily neither as Jew nor Gentile but as "Christian[s]" (4:16). Peter refers to their conduct among the "Gentiles" (a term used here to refer to unbelievers), demonstrating that they are distinct from these Gentiles. While Gentiles "speak against you as those who do evil" (2:12), Christians no longer do what the Gentiles want to do. As a result, the Gentiles are surprised and malign them (4:3–5; see v. 14). Because they have been chosen and called by God to a new way of life (1:14–16, 22; 2:1; 4:2–5), they are in exile, alienated from the world around them.[59] The church is expected to stand out due to personal holiness and sole allegiance to Christ (3:15).

However, being countercultural does not mean being rebellious. The church submits to proper human authority (2:13–15) as both free people and "God's slaves" (v. 16). Thus, believers are not servile, and their submission is not absolute. They submit to human government as part of their service to their ultimate Master, God. "If they are God's slaves, then God, and not political powers, must be granted one's absolute subordination."[60]

Eschatological

The church's ethic (proper submission, resistance to sin, etc.) is rooted in eschatological hope (awareness that this world, with its standards and its glory, is not all there is). Those now despised will find "praise, glory, and honor at the revelation of Jesus Christ" (1:7). Those who rejoice in sin and appear to get away with it will give account one day (4:5). This awareness of Christ's coming and the resulting reversal of standards undergirds the letter (1:5, 7, 13; 2:12; 4:7; 5:1, 10). This community of faith makes sense only with the return of Christ in view. For the church, all of life is shaped by this reality, and from this reality Christians draw strength to persevere.

Rooted in Christ

Lastly, the church is radically Christocentric, rooted in Christ. Jesus is the cornerstone of the church (2:6); "the entire building (i.e., the

---

[59] "Believers are exiles because they suffer for their faith in a world that finds their faith off-putting and strange" (Schreiner, *1, 2 Peter, Jude,* 50).

[60] Achtemeier, *1 Peter,* 186.

church) takes its shape from him."[61] Members love Jesus and believe in him (1:8). Through Jesus they are believers in God (v. 21). They can be referred to as those who are in Christ (5:14) and are known by his name: "Christian" (4:16).[62]

The Church in 1 Peter: Function and Structure

The family theme already discussed suggests mutual care, as in Hebrews and James, but is addressed less explicitly in 1 Peter. Also, the church's ethic of holiness has been mentioned so it will not be repeated here.

Gifts and Service

First Peter 4:10–11 makes four basic points about service within the church: (1) each one has received a gift; (2) these gifts are for serving one another; (3) the gifts come from God; and (4) the ultimate purpose of the gifts is God's glory.[63] Each member is expected to be a good steward of his gift (v. 10). Some speak, some serve (v. 11), but all have a part to play in the work of the kingdom.

The believers minister to fellow church members. This corresponds to the vibrant member-to-member care in Hebrews and James. Members use their gifts for one another, and by implication members receive the ministry of others' gifts. The church glorifies God by caring for one another and serving one another according to God-given giftedness.

Baptism

This letter contains an important reference to baptism. First Peter 3:21 shows that baptism is important for the church, though many questions have been raised about this verse's meaning: "Baptism, which corresponds to this, now saves you (not the removal of the filth of the flesh, but the pledge of a good conscience toward God) through the resurrection of Jesus Christ."

---

[61] Schreiner, *1, 2 Peter, Jude,* 109.
[62] Acts 11:26 suggests this is a name first given to believers by outsiders. In the only other occurrence of the word in the NT (Acts 26:28), an outsider used it (see Achtemeier, *1 Peter,* 313).
[63] These points are similar to Paul's statements in 1 Corinthians 12–14.

"Baptism . . . saves you" is a strong statement. This is not baptismal regeneration, however. Peter qualifies that baptism is not the mere external act of being put under water (resulting in the removal of dirt) but involves an appeal to God for the cleansing of sins and thus a clean conscience.[64] This is based on the finished work of Christ's resurrection. Even though baptism does not have saving value in itself, Peter holds it up as valuable and important. In this context baptism pictures the believer going under the waters of judgment (like the flood) and being brought safely through (like Noah). Peter reminds his readers of their baptism in the context of calling them to trust God while suffering persecution. Baptism is important; it is even a basis for encouragement in the midst of suffering.

Furthermore, this verse suggests that immersion is the proper mode of baptism, for the deluge is said to prefigure Christian baptism. Additionally, baptism here (as elsewhere in the NT) is closely linked with conversion (the appeal for forgiveness of sin). Thus, in the NT, baptism was the public profession of faith, the way in which one identified as a follower of Jesus.[65]

Proclamation

Earlier we noticed how 1 Pet 2:4–10 clarifies the identity of the church. Now we return to that text to note a function of the church: proclamation. As noted above, v. 9 identifies the church as the new Israel. Then the apostle states the church's purpose: "that you may proclaim the praises of the One who called you out of darkness into His marvelous light."

To proclaim God's praises obviously includes worship, but here it also includes evangelism. True worship of the only true and living God necessarily involves rejecting other would-be gods and calling all to recognize Yahweh's kingship. Worship that is authentic and pleasing to God is missionary.[66]

---

[64] There is not space here to exegete this text fully. A full argument for this position can be found in Schreiner, *1, 2 Peter, Jude,* 193–97, and Achtemeier, *1 Peter,* 266–72.

[65] For sample texts and further argumentation, see Ray Van Neste, "Reinvigorating Baptist Practice of the Ordinances," *Theology for Ministry* 1 (2006): 78–91.

[66] Walter Brueggemann powerfully makes this point in his sermonic essay, "Psalm 100," *Int* 39 (1985): 65–69.

Thus, this text affirms worship and mission (proclamation) as key purposes of the church.[67] The church, like OT Israel, is to worship God aright and to be a light to the nations.[68] Evangelism is also seen in 1 Pet 3:15–16, where believers are called to be prepared to give a reason for the hope they have. This presumes interaction with outsiders who do not understand the hope shown by suffering believers. In that setting, the church is an evangelistic community as Christians are prepared to explain the gospel.

Leadership and Oversight

As noted earlier, 1 Pet 4:10–11 teaches that all believers are gifted. Ministry is not the task of only a select few. However, that does not mean there are no leaders. First Peter 5:1–4 is one of the most important texts on pastoral ministry in the NT. Note where this discussion of leadership occurs: flowing out of the discussion of suffering in 4:12–19.[69] Gracious, shepherding leaders are important for the preservation of the flock. As Paul Achtemeier has noted, "Leaders must function pastorally, not dictatorially, if those wounded by external social pressures are to remain within the community."[70]

As in James, elders function as leaders in the church. That these elders are called to pastor (i.e., shepherd) and exercise oversight suggests that elder, pastor, and overseer (KJV, "bishop") all refer to the same role.[71] If these elders were not expected to exercise authority in the congregation, there would be no need to exhort them not to domineer. They are supposed to lead and exercise authority but not oppressively.

Peter notes several important points about the role of elders. First, the congregations that elders lead belong to God and not to them. It is God's flock they are to shepherd. Note the statement of ownership. The flock belongs to God. Elders lead and serve, but they do not own. They serve under the chief Shepherd (1 Pet 5:4), a term that recalls the earlier

---

[67] So also Achtemeier, *1 Peter,* 156; Schreiner, *1, 2 Peter, Jude,* 116; Elliott, *The Elect and the Holy,* 185, 195.

[68] As Elliott (*The Elect and the Holy,* 195) states, the priesthood in view is "an *outer-directed mission* pertaining to the witness of the Church toward all that is non-Church."

[69] First Peter 5:1 begins with *oun,* a particle that marks a connection to previous material.

[70] Achtemeier, *1 Peter,* 322.

[71] For a defense of this view, see Benjamin L. Merkle, *The Elder and Overseer: One Office in the Early Church* (New York: Peter Lang, 2003).

description of Jesus as the "shepherd and guardian of your souls" (2:25). So leaders in the church function under Jesus' authority, following his example. He is *the* Shepherd. These leaders "are fundamentally servants, not autocrats."[72] The use of "shepherd" along with Jesus' example shapes the picture of pastoral ministry. Jesus, the good shepherd (John 10:11–16), contrasts with the false shepherds in the OT who treated God's people with force and harshness (Ezek 34:4). They scattered and destroyed God's flock (Jer 23:1–4), and God was angry with them (Zech 10:3). Jesus and his human undershepherds fulfill God's promise of good shepherds for his people (Jer 3:15; 23:4; Ezek 34:15).

This shepherding is further explained as "overseeing" (1 Pet 5:2). Often this oversight is thought of in terms of superintending or managing, more in a business sense. However, the OT background suggests a different emphasis. In Ezek 34:11 the Lord says he will search for the sheep and watch over them, using the related verb *episkeptomai* (LXX).[73] In Ezekiel shepherds are expected to strengthen the weak, heal the sick, bind up the injured, bring back strays, and seek the lost (34:4).[74] In Jer 23:2 the shepherds are rebuked for failing to attend (*episkeptomai*) the sheep. In Zech 10:3, because the human shepherds have failed, the prophet says God will care for (*episkeptomai*) the flock himself. In the context of shepherding, oversight means vigilant care for individuals in the flock. It goes beyond public proclamation to personal care, raising the fallen, bolstering the weak, rebuking the sinful, and bringing back the straying. While managing is entailed in leadership of any group, this is not the primary point of oversight here. Rather, Peter stresses watchful care. Managing can be done at a distance; pastoral oversight cannot.

The Church in 1 Peter: Summary

The church in 1 Peter is the new people of God, a loving family, rooted in Christ, distinct from the world, living in light of a future hope. This community operates under the lordship of Christ, guided by loving shep-

---

[72] Schreiner, *1, 2 Peter, Jude,* 236.

[73] *Episkopeō* and *episkeptomai* are treated as near synonyms in *TDNT, NIDNTT,* and *EDNT.*

[74] "So the office of a shepherd is represented to us as a very onerous and responsible vocation, requiring unwearying vigilance and readiness for sacrifice" (Walther Eichrodt, *Ezekiel* [Philadelphia: Westminster, 1970], 470).

herds, and with each member exercising his own gifts. Baptism marks the members of this community who proclaim the glory of their Savior in worship and evangelism.

The Church in 2 Peter and Jude: Identity and Ethic

Family

Several themes noted in the previous letters occur here as well. The church is again a loving family, with the recipients addressed as brothers (2 Pet 1:10). Brotherly love is considered a basic aspect of the Christian life (v. 7). This love and familial connection is rooted in God as believers are "loved by God the Father" (Jude 1). "Beloved" is a common form of address for fellow believers (2 Pet 3:1, 8, 14–15, 17; Jude 17, 20 NKJV), suggesting a love among believers that mirrors the Father's love for the Son (2 Pet 1:17). That false teachers are rebuked for caring only for themselves (Jude 12) suggests that the community standard is for members to care for one another.

Distinct and Holy

The church is distinct from the world. Its members are cleansed from their sin (2 Pet 1:9), have "escaped from those who live in error" (2:18), and have "escaped the world's impurity" (v. 20). They are saints (Jude 3), a holy people (2 Pet 1:9; 2:9, 21; 3:11).[75] Further, they are distinct from the heretics who do not have the Spirit (Jude 19). Gene Green aptly comments, "What explicitly marks the church is the possession of the Spirit and the communion with God through his agency."[76]

Continuity with Israel

These letters do not address directly the church's relationship to Israel, though references to believers as called and elected (2 Pet 1:10; Jude 1) and as recipients of God's love echo OT references to Israel. Some connection is in view, given the use of the OT in 2 Pet 2:4–10, but it is not spelled

---

[75] "The issue of holiness is intimately connected with the church community in this epistle" (Ruth Ann Reese, "Holiness and Ecclesiology in Jude and 2 Peter," in *Holiness and Ecclesiology in the New Testament*, ed. Kent E. Brower and Andy Johnson (Grand Rapids: Eerdmans, 2007), 327–28, 341.

[76] Gene L. Green, *Jude and 2 Peter* (Grand Rapids: Baker, 2008), 121.

out. Further, both letters assume the communities addressed consider the biblical narrative to be their own story.[77]

Eschatological

Anticipation of Christ's return is significant in the letters and shapes the ethos of the church.[78] Peter urges faithfulness in the midst of a sinful world, reminding believers about the day of judgment (2 Pet 2:9), when God will destroy the wicked and rescue his own. Peter demands holiness and godliness in anticipation of "the coming of the day of God" (3:12). Jude mentions that one means of perseverance is awaiting Christ's mercy at his coming (Jude 21). This waiting is not a "merely passive attitude, but an orientation of the whole life toward the eschatological hope."[79] The church is a community living in the present but radically shaped by the future.

The Church in 2 Peter and Jude: Function and Structure

Leadership

These letters contribute to our understanding of the role of church leaders by negative examples. Some people have "come in by stealth" (Jude 4). They appeal to dreams to support wicked lifestyles (Jude 8). This suggests they are teaching on the basis of supposed private revelation.[80] Jude's charge that they shepherd only themselves may allude to Ezek 34:2, where Israel's spiritual leaders are chided for tending to their own desires rather than feeding the flock.[81] Peter rebukes would-be leaders for their reliance on dreams, their immorality, and their rebellion. He says the presence of false teachers in the church is certain (2 Pet 2:1), but in contrast to them he highlights the certainty of Scripture (1:19–21).

---

[77] See Reese, "Holiness and Ecclesiology in Jude and 2 Peter," in Brower and Johnson, *Holiness and Ecclesiology*, 329.

[78] "A vigorous hope for the Lord's return animates the letter" (Schreiner, *1, 2 Peter, Jude*, 409).

[79] Richard Bauckham, *Jude, 2 Peter* (Waco, TX: Word, 1983), 114.

[80] See Douglas J. Moo, *2 Peter and Jude*, NIVAC (Grand Rapids: Zondervan, 1996), 244; Davids, *James*, 55; Schreiner, *1, 2 Peter, Jude*, 455; Green, *Jude and 2 Peter*, 74–75; Bauckham, *Jude, 2 Peter*, 55.

[81] "The use of this pastoral language suggests that these heretics had assumed some form of leadership position in the church" (Green, *Jude and 2 Peter*, 95). See Bauckham, *Jude, 2 Peter*, 87; Schreiner, *1, 2 Peter, Jude*, 466.

Proper leaders are marked by allegiance to God's revealed word, which includes exhibiting the holiness it enjoins. A claim to, or even possession of, a leadership role does not in itself invest authority. As we have seen elsewhere, pastors have significant authority; but this authority extends only so far as they conduct themselves in accord with Scripture. When leaders run counter to Scripture, church members must oppose them. Christ rules his church and does so by means of his Word taught and applied by church leaders.

Worship

Both letters refer to the church's celebration of the Lord's Supper, though in a negative context. Jude warns that false teachers are "like dangerous reefs at your love feasts [literally, "loves"]" (v. 12), and 2 Peter says they are "blots and blemishes . . . as they feast with you" (2:13). The feast in view in both texts is likely a meal that culminated in the Lord's Supper.[82] The Jude text is the first instance of the word "love" (*agapē*) to refer to the Lord's Supper, but this later became common.[83] The term highlights the centrality of love in the Christian life and shows that care for one another was a central issue in the Lord's Supper. One means of preserving and building the church is prayer in the Holy Spirit (Jude 20). As Green notes, "Prayer in the Holy Spirit defines the life of those who are the true people of God."[84]

Defense of the Faith

Significantly, Jude did not address church leaders but Christians in general (v. 1). So his exhortation to contend for the faith (v. 3) includes all believers, not only leaders. One duty of the Christian church is to fight "for the preservation of the received faith over against the theological/ moral novelty of the heretics."[85] "Contend" (*epagōnizesthai*), used in the context of athletics, warfare, debate, or the pursuit of virtue, envisions great effort. In the context of this letter, it refers to exposing error as well as speaking and living truth. And Jude writes of this with impassioned language: the church is to be zealous for the faith, i.e., the gospel.

---

[82] See Bauckham, *Jude, 2 Peter,* 84–85; Davids, *James,* 68–69; Green, *Jude and 2 Peter,* 94; Schreiner, *1, 2 Peter, Jude,* 352, 465.

[83] Bauckham, *Jude, 2 Peter,* 84, lists numerous early Christian sources.

[84] Green, *Jude and 2 Peter,* 121.

[85] The wording is Green's (*Jude and 2 Peter,* 56), but he is not making this point about the role of the church.

Member Care

Jude's closing exhortation offers insight into the role of members in the church. Again, the exhortation is addressed to the church collectively. Members keep themselves in the love of God by building one another up in the faith, praying in the Spirit, and eagerly anticipating Christ's return. All these verbs are plural. This is a call for members to pursue growth together as they pray with and for each other, anticipating Christ's return. In this way, they help one another persevere (remain in God's love) and resist being misled by false teachers.

In addition to sustaining one another, the church pursues those who have been led astray (Jude 22–23; similar to Jas 5:19–20). They are to "save" whom they can by "snatching" them from the fire of eternal judgment. This suggests a forceful, quick action (*harpasate*) in order to rescue those who are being led away from the true faith and thus toward eternal judgment.[86]

During this caring pursuit of the erring, the church must guard against being dragged into sin. All this pictures a community in which no one simply slips away or is forgotten. There is a point at which one must be turned out (like the heretics), but before that, the community acts in mercy to pursue any who stray.

The Church in 2 Peter and Jude: Summary

In 2 Peter and Jude the church is the set apart people of God, a family gathering regularly for a "love" meal and building one another up through prayer in the Holy Spirit and Scripture. It defends the faith, holding fast and awaiting the return of Christ.

---

[86] Green (*Jude and 2 Peter*, 125) cites a helpful parallel from *Joseph and Aseneth* 12:8, "For [just] as a little child who is afraid flees to his father, and the father, stretching out his hands, snatches him off the ground, . . . likewise you too, Lord, stretch out your hands upon me as a child-loving father, and snatch me off the earth." Green (*Jude and 2 Peter*, 126) notes: "Rapid and drastic measures must be taken to rescue those who have become wayward. Errant members are not to be simply dismissed but also sought out and delivered from the error into which they have fallen. This mutual care for errant members became a key theme in the corporate life of the church (Matt. 18:15–20; 1 Cor. 5:1–5; 1 Thess. 5:14; 2 Thess. 3:6–15) and was not simply the domain of the congregational leadership. . . . [T]o bring the whole church into the attempt to modify the behavior of the individual is a powerful means of persuasion and an effective plan of rescue."

The Church in John's Epistles: Identity and Ethic

Love and Family

These letters radiate with the theme of love. John[87] declares his love for his readers (1 John 3:2; 4:1, 7; 2 John 1; 3 John 1, 2, 5) and calls on them to love one another (1 John 3:11, 23; 4:7; 2 John 5). Indeed, love for fellow believers is a nonnegotiable mark of true conversion (1 John 2:9–11; 3:11–18; 4:7–12; 5:1).

This love marks the church because it reflects the character of God ("God is love," 1 John 4:8). God has given believers his love, thereby making them his children (3:1). Because believers are born of God (2:29; 3:9; 4:7; 5:4, 18) and have God's seed (3:9), we bear the family characteristic: love. Because God is Father to all believers, they are brothers. Repeatedly God is called Father (1 John 1:2, 3; 2:1, 13, 15, 16, 22–25; 3:1; 4:14; 5:1; 2 John 3, 4, 9); believers, God's children (1 John 3:1, 2, 10; 5:2); and fellow believers, brothers (2:9, 10, 11; 3:10, 13, 14, 15, 16; 4:20, 21; 5:16; 3 John 5). Thus God's children love him as Father (1 John 5:1, 2) and each other as siblings.

Although God is the ultimate Father, John also is fatherly toward his readers, referring to them as children (1 John 2:1, 12, 18, 28; 3:7, 18; 4:4; 5:21; 3 John 4). Within the church others can be referred to as fathers as well (1 John 2:13, 14).[88] So the church is a family where love abounds and where people love in deed and truth as they meet real needs.

Throughout these letters the identity of the church is rooted in the triune God. Believers abide in God (2:6, 24, 28; 3:6; 4:13, 15, 16; 5:20), and God abides in them (2:14; 3:24; 4:12, 13, 15, 16). They know God (4:6, 7, 8; see 3:6) and are endowed with his Spirit (2:27; 3:24; 4:13).[89] They believe in Jesus, that he is Messiah and Son of God (3:23; 5:1, 5, 10, 13). Indeed they "have" the Son (5:12; 2 John 9). This is reflected in the way prepositions are used to describe believers in relation to God. They are the ones who are "of" or "from" God (1 John 3:10; 4:4, 6; 5:19; 3 John

---

[87] Johannine authorship of these letters is assumed here.

[88] See Robert W. Yarbrough, *1–3 John* (Grand Rapids: Baker, 2008), 116–18.

[89] Similarly, Yarbrough states, "There is hardly a verse or even clause anywhere that does not name a person of the Godhead (Trinity), a divine attribute, or a divine work" (ibid., 27).

11),[90] who await Christ's coming (1 John 2:28–3:3). Thus, the church is God-centered, drawing its life, identity, and mission from him.

Truth

Truth is also central to the church's identity. John says we "know we belong to the truth" (1 John 3:19) and the truth remains in us (1:8; 2:4; 2 John 2). Christians are those who "have come to know the truth" (2 John 1; see 1 John 2:21), walk in the truth (2 John 4; 3 John 3, 4), and love in truth (1 John 3:18). If someone has fellowship with God, he practices the truth (1:6) because "the Spirit is the truth" (5:6) and can be called the Spirit of truth (4:6).

Holiness

Holiness or righteousness marks the church. Believers struggle with sin (1 John 1:10), but by the work of Christ they are cleansed from it (vv. 7–9; see 3:4–10; 5:18). The church is made up of those who do the will of God (2:17) and keep his word (v. 5).

Distinct

Because of the church's love, purity, and devotion to Jesus, it is distinct from "the world," from false teachers, and from those who follow them.[91] A key point of 1 John is to make clear the distinction between true believers and false ones. The church is not to "love the world or the things that belong to the world" (2:15) and should not be surprised that the world neither knows us (3:1) nor listens to us (4:4–6) but hates us (3:13). This animosity is because we are from God, but the world lies in the evil one's power (5:19). Believers are not to fear the world's hatred, however, because by God's power we will overcome the world (vv. 4–5).

Eschatological

The love and holiness that mark the church are rooted in an eschatological vision. This world and its allures are passing away, so there is no point

---

[90] Though different English prepositions are used, in each case the Greek preposition is *ek*.

[91] "Mankind is divided into two groups, those who belong to God through divine birth and faith in Jesus Christ and those who belong to the world" (I. Howard Marshall, *The Epistles of John* [Grand Rapids: Eerdmans, 1978], 53).

in chasing them. In contrast, the one who does God's will abides forever (1 John 2:15–17). The reality of the future informs life in the present. In the same way, awareness of Christ's return is the basis for John's call to holiness (2:28–3:3). We live in the last days (2:18) with confidence for "the day of judgment" (4:17). The church is oriented in light of Christ's return and all that entails.

The Church in John's Epistles: Function and Structure

Leadership

These letters contain little on the structure of the church. The author of 2 John and 3 John identifies himself as "the elder," a term denoting a specific church office (as we have seen in other letters). John, having identified himself as an elder, refers to his authority, which had been rejected by Diotrephes (3 John 9). The negative example of Diotrephes demonstrates that proper response to church leadership is not self-promotion or rebellion.

Because John identifies himself as an elder, we can deduce some things about proper pastoral ministry from his example.[92] In contrast to Diotrephes, John does not exalt himself. He is an apostle, one of the Twelve, but he only identifies himself as an elder. John regularly states his love for his people. His use of "children" or "my children" suggests a fatherly care, and he rejoices greatly when the children walk in truth. Both 2 John and 3 John close with comments on how he longs to see them face-to-face and not communicate from a distance. This is not a leader who cares primarily for the success of an institution. This is a shepherd who knows the sheep and is concerned about what comes into their homes (2 John 10). He gives of himself to see each one persevere in the faith.

Guarding Doctrine

These letters demonstrate concern for the church to guard proper doctrine in the face of antichrists, false prophets, and deceivers (1 John 2:18, 22; 4:1–3; 2 John 7–10). The church is to be alert, not believing everyone who claims to speak by the Spirit but testing what is said to see if it concurs with apostolic teaching. False teachers are to be rejected. The church must

---

[92] This paragraph was inspired by and follows significantly Yarbrough, *1–3 John*, 26–28.

refuse to give them aid or support (2 John 10–11). Eternal life is linked with proper doctrine (as well as proper living, which these teachers also abandon), so the discerning work of the church is crucial.

Support of Missions

An interesting glimpse into the church's role in supporting missions is found in 3 John 5–8. The recipients of this letter had labored to support those sent out to take the gospel to other regions, and John commends them for this support. The support of missionaries is a faithful work (v. 5), and we ought to join it (v. 8). Indeed, we do well to support them in a manner worthy of God (v. 6). Thus, the church should not only guard the gospel but also proclaim it to the nations, doing all it can to support missionaries.

Member-to-Member Care

The church must care for one another. The love that marks the church is not simply a benevolent feeling or mere talk but an action (1 John 3:18). This love is modeled on the love of the Father and the Son, the Son who laid down his life for us (v. 16) and the Father who sent the Son to bear his wrath for rebellious sinners (4:9–10). Thus, the church should be a place where members are ready to lay down their lives for one another (3:16), where we give our possessions to meet one another's needs (v. 17).

John calls all Christians, not only leaders, to intercede for sinning brothers (5:16), for such prayer will lead to life, i.e., the preservation of the brother's soul. Similarly, in 2 John 8 believers are exhorted to "watch [blepete] yourselves," lest anyone be led astray by false teachers.[93] Each person watches out for himself and for others.

The Church in John's Epistles: Summary

Wrestling with false teachers within and the world without, the church in John's letters, as in other letters, is struggling to be what it ought: a close-knit family bound together by the love of God that pursues holiness, and proclaims Christ until he comes.

---

[93] The same verb is used for member-to-member care in Heb 3:12.

Conclusion

While each of these letters has its own setting and distinctive emphases, striking commonalities arise in their teaching about the church. The church is consistently portrayed as the restored Israel, the new people of God. Believers are God's children and are thus brothers and sisters, making the church a family marked by love. This family connection is valuable since believers are distinct from the society around them, often despised and oppressed. Conflict with the world arises because of their new lifestyle (holiness) and their new allegiance (to Christ). The church's approach to life is oriented around the return of Christ, which will bring judgment, destruction of sinful ways, and the exaltation of Christ's people. This truth kindles the church's perseverance as the anticipation of seeing Christ spurs devotion, obedience, and worship.

In the meantime, believers hold fast to one another, gather together, and help one another to persevere. They meet practical needs, pray for one another, bring back the straying, and encourage one another on a regular basis. They are close knit, not busybodies, but intentional about caring for one another. The church plays a role in its members' perseverance. We help each other toward heaven, linking arms and heading toward the celestial city, crying, "No one left behind!"

In this family elders lead by teaching the Scriptures and helping those who are hurt or straying (morally or doctrinally). These elders do not own the church but serve the Great Shepherd by graciously tending the flock and fighting off wolves. They take the lead in watching over the souls of the congregation, in full awareness that they will give account for their work on judgment day.

The church guards the purity of the gospel, worships the triune God who has saved it, and proclaims his excellencies to the fallen world that despises and at times oppresses them. Believers have a new identity that sets them apart from the world as they submit to their Lord Jesus Christ. The church seeks to live in submission to the secular government and all proper authority, but loyalty to Jesus trumps all other allegiances. May close attention to these letters move us closer to this ideal, for our own good and for the glory of our Lord who has redeemed us.

CHAPTER 6

The Church in History:
Ecclesiological Ideals and
Institutional Realities

James A. Patterson

A brief survey of Christian history reveals a breathtaking diversity of views among the followers of Jesus Christ concerning the nature, structure, polity, and mission of their Lord's church. Furthermore, it is difficult to track the Christian movement through history apart from its corporate expression in the multitude of tangible congregations, assemblies, and denominations for which the New Testament term *ekklēsia* (church) has been employed. In addition, most Christian traditions have invoked a more elusive meaning of "church" by extending it to include such concepts as the mystical body of Christ, the company of the faithful through the ages, and the eschatological bride of Christ. In the process, Christianity has effectively compelled a meaningful and even obligatory relationship between its adherents and the church.

Nonetheless, careful thinking about the church has often taken a backseat to consideration of other weighty theological matters such as the Trinity, Christology, and soteriology. For example, early confessional statements such as the Apostles' Creed mentioned "the holy catholic church" and "the communion of saints" but put primary focus on the life, death, resurrection, ascension, and exaltation of the church's founder and not so much on a doctrine of the church. Likewise, the major ecumenical councils of the patristic age such as Nicaea and Chalcedon engaged in few ecclesiological debates, even if such gatherings implicitly raised the issue of the role and authority of ecclesiastical councils. Further, many notable theologians in Christian history—John of Damascus, Thomas Aquinas, Martin Luther, Karl Barth, and Carl Henry to name a few—were not known for their ecclesiological contributions. Ecclesiology was an afterthought that failed to engage some of the faith's best minds when other concerns were deemed more urgent.

All this is compounded by the reality that pragmatic considerations helped shape the church's thinking about its forms and practices. In church government, for instance, secular political models often have exercised as much influence as New Testament teaching. More so than with other areas of doctrine, ecclesiology has been vulnerable to subtle cultural and institutional pressures. As a result, churches in various eras have looked quite different from those in the book of Acts or Paul's letters. The New Testament does not purport to be a complete manual of church order, but the ecclesiological ethos found there was at times obscured in the ensuing centuries.

The Early and Medieval Churches: Growing Institutional, Sacerdotal, and Sacramental Impulses in the East and West

Movements and organizations typically develop more complicated structures in the context of growth and with the passing of their founding leaders. This inevitable institutionalization is not necessarily bad and may be essential to group identity and sustainability. At the same time, it can have considerable repercussions. Indeed, what unfolded in the postapostolic age did not always follow a natural or predictable trajectory from what was manifest in the New Testament church.

The Early Churches

In the transition from the apostolic period to the second-century church, authority fell increasingly to those holding church offices, and they came to be regarded as almost exclusive guardians of apostolic truth. The *Didachē*, an early second-century church manual, spoke briefly of designated or appointed bishops and deacons while simultaneously indicating a continuing role for prophets in church life. Shortly afterward, however, the letters of Ignatius of Antioch appeared to correlate genuine prophetic voices with those holding the office of bishop. Ignatius additionally set forth a threefold ministry of bishop, elders, and deacons in each congregation. Thus, he introduced a distinction between the first two offices— even though the New Testament implied that bishop, elder, and shepherd (pastor) were the same office (e.g., Acts 20:17–28; Phil 1:1; 1 Tim 3:1–7; Titus 1:5–9; 1 Pet 5:1–4).[1] Ignatius anticipated a second-century trend that saw the elevation of the role and authority of the ruling bishop, although his letters implied that bishops supervised one local congregation, not several churches in a region.

Three major factors help to explain the enhancement of episcopal power during the second century. First, with the death of the original apostles, the leadership void was filled by a new generation of church officers who—it was claimed—were placed in their positions by the apostles.[2] Bishops understood themselves to be at the top of a hierarchical structure with elders in a subordinate rank.

Second, bishops rallied the churches in the midst of persecution. Although opposition from the Roman state was sporadic and not empire-wide in the second century, it did flare up occasionally and disrupted church life. In that context, bishops offered courageous leadership that assisted their congregations in maintaining unity and stability.[3]

Finally, theological controversy gave bishops the opportunity to establish themselves as official defenders and interpreters of the faith. When Gnostics appealed to secret traditions or Montanists invoked a divine source for their prophetic utterances, orthodox bishops used the authority of their office to criticize and condemn those who deviated from the teachings of the apostles.[4] The conflict with Montanism in particular

---

[1] See *Didachē* 11–15; and Ignatius of Antioch, *To the Philadelphians* 7. The classic study of the tension between spiritual power and institutional authority in early Christianity remains Hans von Campenhausen, *Ecclesiastical Authority and Spiritual Power in the Church of the First Three Centuries*, trans. J. A. Baker (Stanford, CA: Stanford University Press, 1969).

[2] Late in the first century, Clement of Rome argued in his letter to the Corinthians, *1 Clement* 42.4–5 and 44.2–3, that the elders illegitimately deposed in Corinth had been granted their authority by the apostles themselves. This represented a primitive version of the concept of apostolic succession, which became a much more developed principle by the end of the second century.

[3] W. H. C. Frend, *Martyrdom and Persecution in the Early Church: A Study of a Conflict from the Maccabees to Donatus* (New York: New York University Press, 1967), 133–222.

[4] Von Campenhausen, *Ecclesiastical Authority*, 149–77.

highlighted a tension between those who emphasized the special work of the Holy Spirit and those who appealed to the authority of church officers. The former believed that some holders of church office were obstructing the spontaneous operation of *charismata* (spiritual gifts) in church life.

No one illustrated the emergent order in the late second century better than Irenaeus, who became bishop of Lyons in Gaul in 177 after the martyrdom of his predecessor, Pothinus. In addition to guiding his flock during a time of challenge, he also stood as the foremost opponent of various Gnostic sects. In that context, Irenaeus held up the authority of a bishop as the principal weapon in the battle against heresy. What was incipient in Clement of Rome about apostolic succession became explicit in Irenaeus's *Against Heresies* (c. 180–90), in which he stressed the role of the true, Catholic church—through its bishops and presbyters—as the primary bearer of apostolic tradition:

> True knowledge is the teaching of the Apostles, the order of the church as established from the earliest times throughout the world, and the distinctive stamp of the body of Christ, passed down through the succession of bishops in charge of the church in each place, which has come down to our own time, safeguarded without any spurious writings by the most complete exposition, received without addition or subtraction; the reading of the Scriptures without falsification; and their consistent and careful exposition, avoiding danger and blasphemy.[5]

Hence, Irenaeus linked the preservation of apostolic truth to the office of bishop.

Still, Irenaeus's concept of apostolic succession centered more on the transmitted faith of the church than the inherent power of ecclesiastical office. He did not discuss ordination, which later served as a guarantor of the unbroken chain of bishops. Furthermore, he focused the work of bishops mostly in local congregations, even though he apparently engaged in mission work beyond Lyons and probably exercised considerable regional influence. In addition, his citation of a succession of bishops

---

[5] Irenaeus, *Against Heresies* 4.33.8. "Complete exposition" probably referred to the Rule of Faith, a consensus of orthodox belief that eventually developed into the Apostles' Creed. Additional passages on the succession of bishops can be found in *Against Heresies* 3.2–5. On the inclusion of presbyters, see *Against Heresies* 3.2.2.

in Rome functioned mostly as a response to Gnostics who had set forth a succession of their own authoritative teachers. In the same context, Irenaeus's commendation of the Roman church for its faithfulness to apostolic teaching appears to be, in the words of J. N. D. Kelly, "an ideal illustration" and not an early version of Petrine dogma.[6] In short, Irenaeus portrayed the bishopric as a potent office, yet one whose authority resided mainly in its didactic function.

Developments in church order during the second century laid a foundation for continuing institutionalization of both Eastern and Western churches during the third, fourth, and fifth centuries. As part of that dynamic, distinctions between church leaders and the laity were drawn more sharply than in earlier stages of Christian history. Once again, the dual hazards of persecution and false doctrine meant that bishops were charged with navigating the church through dangerous and sometimes uncharted waters. Even after persecution ceased in the fourth century, strong leadership helped the church adjust to a new relationship with the Roman government. In the process, the power of clerical office—especially in the territorial bishoprics—expanded.

In mid-third century North Africa, Bishop Cyprian of Carthage (martyred during the Valerian persecution in 258) contributed to the growing complexity in ecclesiastical organization. Much of his thinking about the church surfaced during controversies. His major ecclesiological treatise, *On the Unity of the Church*, emphasized the visible, Catholic church. He included a condemnation of those who would divide it, as well as his oft-quoted dictum that "you cannot have God as your father unless you have the Church as mother."[7] His maternal imagery helped to establish "holy mother church" in the West as an important ecclesiastical symbol; as Christianity advanced in the Roman world, the use of "mother" nearly eclipsed that of "bride."

In many ways, Cyprian marked a historical transition to what may be termed a "high church" perspective. As a result of his teaching, Christians increasingly associated the work of the Holy Spirit with church office

---

[6] J. N. D. Kelly, *Early Christian Doctrines*, rev. ed. (San Francisco: Harper & Row, 1978), 193. The relevant passage is Irenaeus, *Against Heresies* 3.3.2. A short but helpful discussion of Irenaeus's ecclesiology is in Everett Ferguson, *Church History, Volume One: From Christ to Pre-Reformation* (Grand Rapids: Zondervan, 2005), 108–9.

[7] Cyprian, *On the Unity of the Church* 6. One key implication of this declaration was his statement in *Letter* 73.21 that "there is no salvation outside the Church."

and the sacraments. As church historian Everett Ferguson has correctly observed, Cyprian "was among the first extensively to speak of the bishop as a priest, the eucharist as a sacrifice, and the Lord's table as an altar."[8] In a similar vein, Hans von Campenhausen attributed to Cyprian a major influence on the Roman Church: "The image of Cyprian, the holy bishop and martyr, controls—despite some lapses in dogmatic taste—the ecclesiological thinking of Roman Catholicism to this day."[9] By about the middle of the third century, a priestly class had replaced the priesthood of all believers and a more complicated liturgy emphasized the mediatorial role of the clergy. As part of these trends, infant baptism became common by the end of the third century.[10]

Developments in the fourth century increased the power of the priestly hierarchy. As Constantine the Great gained military and political control of the West in 312 and then the entire empire in 324, Christianity derived certain benefits as a legal, recognized, and even favored religion. On one hand, persecution virtually ceased; on the other hand, the church faced for the first time the temptations that accompanied a cozy association with the state. Secular politics influenced the church through the fourth century, and the edicts of Emperor Theodosius established Christianity as the single official state religion by 392. As a result, triumphalist and theocratic impulses emerged in ecclesiastical life in stark contrast to the ethos of the earlier, embattled church.[11]

---

[8] Ferguson, *Church History, Volume One*, 165. *Didachē* 14.1–3 earlier referred to the Eucharist as *thusia* ("sacrifice") but probably in terms of an offering of thanksgiving rather than a literal resacrificing of Christ's body and blood. Ignatius of Antioch's *To the Smyrnaeans* 7.1 and *To the Romans* 7.3 appear to contain an incipient notion of what was later dubbed "Real Presence."

[9] Von Campenhausen, *Ecclesiastical Authority*, 266.

[10] Paul K. Jewett, *Infant Baptism and the Covenant of Grace* (Grand Rapids: Eerdmans, 1978), 16–45.

[11] For a qualified defense of Constantine, including the changed significance of the sacraments after the emperor's victories, see Peter J. Leithart, *Defending Constantine: The Twilight of an Empire and the Dawn of Christendom* (Downers Grove: IVP Academic, 2010). Leithart concludes: "In the end it all comes round to baptism, specifically to infant baptism. Rome was baptized in the fourth century. . . . Through Constantine, Rome was baptized into a world without animal sacrifice and officially recognized the true sacrificial city, the one community that *does* offer a foretaste of the final kingdom. Christian Rome was in its infancy, but that was hardly surprising. All baptisms are infant baptisms" (341, italics are original). In the Constantinian era, baptism and the Eucharist replaced pagan sacrifices; in the process, regeneration lost its status as a prerequisite to participation in the Christian ordinances.

In less than a century, the church had been profoundly transformed. In particular, Constantine's policies led to more formal worship at convenient hours, a more dramatic liturgy, and the adoption of the Roman basilica as the primary setting for worship on Sunday, which Constantine officially declared a day of rest in the empire.[12]

The church's new role in the state seemed to require further refinement in its hierarchical structures. Bishops who ruled all the churches in a given area or diocese possessed more power than bishops in local congregations. As pragmatic demands of church life stymied serious ecclesiological reflection, territorial bishops functioned more as administrators than pastors. Moreover, bishops in larger cities enjoyed at least practical advantages and more prestige than their counterparts in less-populated areas. During the fourth and fifth centuries, the bishops—or patriarchs as they were sometimes called—of Rome, Alexandria, Antioch, Jerusalem, and Constantinople exercised considerably more control than other bishops. This became evident at important theological councils such as Nicaea, Constantinople, and Chalcedon, where a ranking of bishops was formally recognized.[13] The dominance of bishops at these councils likely gave rise to the belief in the Catholic and Orthodox traditions that councils possessed an inherent authority. This was later rejected by Protestant theologians who affirmed that councils were authoritative only insofar as they conformed to Scripture.[14]

Church hierarchies in the East differed from those in the West. Eastern patriarchs essentially saw themselves as equals, a pattern still reflected in Orthodoxy today, with each national or ethnic branch of the church conducting its affairs in an autocephalous (self-governing and independent) mode. The Roman bishops, however, asserted primacy over other bishops in the West and eventually over all other bishops. Located in the original capital of the empire, the Roman Church was in a good position to assert primacy for several reasons: (1) it was less theologically

---

[12] Craig Harline, *Sunday: A History of the First Day from Babylonia to the Super Bowl* (New York: Doubleday Religion, 2007), 17–25.

[13] Ferguson, *Church History, Volume One*, 212; and Kelly, *Early Christian Doctrines*, 406. Emperors also participated regularly in church councils, beginning with Constantine at Nicaea in 325.

[14] For an insightful discussion of the relationship between Scripture, councils, and tradition, see Gerald Bray, *Creeds, Councils and Christ* (Downers Grove: InterVarsity, 1984), 32–65.

contentious; (2) it had no significant competition in the West; (3) when the Western Empire fell in 476, Roman bishops did not have to answer to any centralized political authority for more than 300 years; and (4) it justified its elevated standing by citing Matt 16:18–19, interpreted to support the concept of a Petrine succession exclusive to the bishopric of Rome.[15]

Roman claims to a universal jurisdiction met with resistance in the East. J. N. D. Kelly assessed the situation this way: "While showing it immense deference and setting great store by its pronouncements, the Eastern churches never treated Rome as the constitutional centre and head of the Church, much less as an infallible oracle of faith and morals, and on occasion had not the least compunction about resisting its express will."[16] Roman pontiffs from at least the fourth century promoted their unique station in the broader church, which they rooted in the authority of Peter. References to this succession theory surfaced before the middle of the fifth century, but Leo I (440–61) was the first to articulate this view definitively. He bluntly communicated his view of papal headship in correspondence with Constantinople:

> The Lord made St. Peter the head of them all [apostles], that from him as from their head his gifts should flow out into all the body. So that if anyone separates himself from St. Peter he should know that he has no share in the divine blessing. . . . For nothing will stand which is not built on the rock [Peter] which the Lord laid in the foundation. . . . I am the guardian of the catholic faith and of the decrees of the church fathers. . . . [T]he holy Roman church, through St. Peter, the prince of the apostles, is head of all the churches of the whole world.[17]

To this day, the Eastern churches have refused to accept papal primacy, and this conflict contributed heavily to the still unresolved Catholic-Orthodox schism of 1054.[18] Like Rome, Eastern Orthodoxy affirms the

---

[15] Ferguson, *Church History, Volume One,* 138–40, 301–3.

[16] Kelly, *Early Christian Doctrines,* 407.

[17] Leo I, "The Petrine Theory Stated," in *A History of Christianity: Readings in the History of the Early and Medieval Church,* ed. Ray C. Petry (Englewood Cliffs, NJ: Prentice-Hall, 1962), 189–90. Dates given for popes are the years of their papacies.

[18] For a concise overview of the Great Schism, see Mark A. Noll, *Turning Points: Decisive Moments in the History of Christianity* (Grand Rapids: Baker, 1997), 129–50.

apostolic succession of the episcopacy but does not couple that with a concept of Roman supremacy.

The Medieval Churches

In effect, Leo I launched the medieval papacy. Gregory VII (1073–85) enhanced papal authority with his claim that "the Roman church has never erred and will never err to all eternity, according to the testimony of the holy scriptures."[19] A century later, Innocent III (1198–1215) taught what some earlier popes had hinted at: the inferiority of the secular government to ecclesiastical government. As perhaps the most powerful pope ever, Innocent III not only elevated the pope's status from Vicar of Peter to Vicar of Christ, he also compared "pontifical authority" to the sun and "royal power" to the lesser light, the moon. The inference was clear: "The royal power derives the splendor of its dignity from the pontifical authority."[20] Not all popes succeeded as well as Innocent III in backing up such assertions, yet the medieval Catholic Church continued to emphasize papal power. Church government in that era was far removed from biblical ecclesiology. Medieval popes usually failed to comprehend the extent to which the hierarchical government of the Western church imitated secular imperial structures that had been around long before the rise of a strong papacy.

A different church-state dynamic in the East prevented the Orthodox patriarchs from regarding the secular political realm as subordinate. Until 1453, when Constantinople fell to the Turks, Eastern primates generally found themselves under the thumb of the Byzantine emperors in a system often dubbed "Caesaropapism." Emperors might occasionally be challenged, perhaps on a moral principle, but bishops usually toed the imperial line. There was no strong ecclesiastical figure, as in the West, to rally the church against interference by the state. Even though the

---

[19] Gregory VII, "Dictates," in Petry, *A History of Christianity*, 237. Papal infallibility was not explicitly proclaimed until Vatican I in 1870. See "The Dogmatic Decrees of the Vatican Council, Pius IX, 1870," in *A History of Christianity: Readings in the History of the Church from the Reformation to the Present*, ed. Clyde L. Manschreck (Englewood Cliffs, NJ: Prentice-Hall, 1964), 374–75. This decree also reaffirmed Petrine supremacy for the papacy.

[20] Innocent III, "Some Observations on Papal Power," in Brian Tierney, *The Crisis of Church and State, 1050–1300: With Selected Documents* (Englewood Cliffs, NJ: Prentice-Hall, 1964), 131–32. The documents from Innocent III include a sermon from his consecration and a letter to a prefect and nobles in Tuscany.

patriarch of Constantinople sometimes enjoyed practical primacy—a first among equals—holders of that office lacked the resources to contend effectively with emperors. A similar situation prevailed later in the relationship between the Orthodox patriarchs of Moscow and the Russian czars.[21]

Sacramental theology likewise changed in the transition from the late patristic period to the Middle Ages. These developments built on the pronounced sacerdotalism (priestly hierarchy and privileges) that Cyprian inspired in the mid-third century. In the fourth-century East, Cyril of Jerusalem tied the operation of the Holy Spirit to the waters of baptism. For him, baptism was a mysterious "divine and life-giving" plunge into "the waters of salvation."[22] Cyprian also proposed a eucharistic theory that suggested a conversion of the bread and wine into the body and blood of Christ. As with baptism, he emphasized the mysterious character of the Lord's Supper. Just as Jesus changed the water to wine at Cana of Galilee, Cyril argued, he can transform the wine into blood. Perhaps because it was a mystery, Cyril's language was ambiguous about the nature of Christ's presence in the Supper:

> For in the type of bread, his body is given to you, and in the type of wine, his blood is given to you, so that by partaking of the body and blood of Christ you may become of one body and blood with him. . . . So do not think of them as just bread and wine. As the Lord himself has declared, they are body and blood. And if your senses suggest otherwise, then let faith establish you, and be assured beyond doubt that you have received the body and blood of Christ.[23]

Cyril's formulation was distinctly Eastern. The mysteries of baptism and the Eucharist were to be experienced in the Holy Spirit, not logically explained. He stopped short of the Western doctrine of transubstantiation, which explained rationally how the change occurred in the Eucharist.

---

[21] On the situation in the East, see Ferguson, *Church History, Volume One*, 323–52, 396–99. On Caesaropapism, see Gilbert Dragon, *Emperor and Priest: The Imperial Office in Byzantium*, trans. Jean Birrell (Cambridge: Cambridge University Press, 2003). For a cautious approach to applying the term Caesaropapism to the Eastern Empire, see Deno J. Geanakoplos, "Church and State in the Byzantine Empire: A Reconsideration of the Problem of Caesaropapism," *Church History* 34 (December 1965): 381–403.

[22] Cyril of Jerusalem, *First Address on the Mysteries* 1–3. This was part of his *Catechetical Lectures*, dating to 348.

[23] Cyril of Jerusalem, *Fourth Address on the Mysteries* 2–6.

At the same time, the Eastern Orthodox tradition shared with Roman Catholicism a conviction that the sacraments had much more than a symbolic or commemorative significance.

In the West, Augustine of Hippo (354–430) was a primary shaper of sacramental doctrine. He challenged the Donatists (a North African schismatic movement that insisted on the purity of the officiant at baptism and communion) and argued that a suitably ordained person, regardless of moral character, could perform a baptism or preside at the Lord's Supper without hindering the impartation of divine grace: "When baptism is administered by the words of the gospel, however great the evil of either minister or recipient may be, the sacrament itself is holy on account of the one whose sacrament it is."[24]

Consequently, the Western church adopted the phrase *ex opere operato* ("it is worked by the work") to describe its sacramental doctrine, expressing that grace was imparted through the sacrament itself and not the minister officiating.[25] Augustine, indeed, advocated infant baptism because he believed that it literally washed away the stain of original sin; baptismal grace was regenerative and did not require the subject's professed faith in Christ prior to being baptized. He eventually balanced his sacerdotal and sacramental impulses, which tended to emphasize the visible church, with a predestinarian doctrine that directed more attention to the invisible church made up of a more limited number of the elect.[26]

In regard to the Eucharist, Augustine held some concept of Real Presence without overtly embracing a belief in the conversion of the elements into something other than bread and wine. When he spoke of "sacrifice," he included the offering of the church herself:

> The whole of that redeemed city, that is, the congregation or communion of saints, is offered as a universal sacrifice to God through the High Priest. . . . This is the sacrifice, as the faithful understand, which the Church continues to celebrate in the sacrament of the altar, in which it is clear to the Church that she herself is offered in the very offering she makes to God.[27]

---

[24] Augustine, *On Baptism* 4.16.18.
[25] See Kelly, *Early Christian Doctrines*, 427. He notes that this understanding could also be found in the East.
[26] Ferguson, *Church History, Volume One*, 276–79.
[27] Augustine, *City of God* 10.6.

In the long run, Augustine's baptismal views found a more central place in Roman Catholic teaching than did his eucharistic theory.

In both East and West, sacramental theology reinforced the sacerdotal features of Christendom during the Middle Ages. Despite substantial ecclesiological continuity between late patristic and medieval theologians, doctrinal development proceeded in notable ways, perhaps more in the West than in the East. For example, the conversion theory of the eucharistic bread and wine evolved into a full-fledged theory of transubstantiation. During the ninth century, debate broke out at a monastery in the Picardy region of France between Paschasius Radbertus and fellow monk Ratranmus over the nature of Real Presence. Radbertus did not use the term "transubstantiation," but he contended that the communion elements "are nothing but Christ's flesh and blood . . . nothing different from what was born of Mary, suffered on the cross, and rose again from the tomb." Appealing to the Incarnation and John 6, Radbertus explained the Eucharist as a divine miracle: "Just as through the Spirit true flesh was created without sexual union from the Virgin, so the same body and blood of Christ are created by mystical consecration out of the substance of bread and wine."[28] On the other hand, Ratranmus repudiated the notion that a tangible change occurred in the bread and wine, preferring to understand the presence of Christ in figurative or spiritual terms:

> After the mystical consecration, when they are no longer called bread and wine, but the body and blood of Christ, as far as the external appearance is concerned, the likeness of flesh cannot be discerned in that bread, just as the actual liquid of blood cannot be seen. . . . How then can they be called the body and blood of Christ when no change can be seen to have taken place?[29]

Apparently the precise nature and meaning of the Eucharist remained unsettled well into the medieval period.

Over the next centuries, the view of Radbertus triumphed over that of Ratranmus in the Western church. The Fourth Lateran Council,

---

[28] Paschasius Radbertus, *On the Flesh and Blood of Christ* 1.4 and 4.1.
[29] Ratranmus, *On the Flesh and Blood of Christ* 15–16. The two monks shared the same title for their treatises.

which met in 1215 under the leadership of Pope Innocent III, granted its authoritative imprimatur to the dogma of transubstantiation:

> There is one Universal Church of the faithful, outside of which there is absolutely no salvation. In which there is the same priest and sacrifice, Jesus Christ, whose body and blood are truly contained in the sacrament of the altar under the forms of bread and wine; the bread being changed (transubstantiatis) by divine power into the body, and the wine into the blood, so that to realize the mystery of unity we may receive of Him what He has received of us. And this sacrament no one can effect except the priest who has been duly ordained in accordance with the keys of the Church, which Jesus Christ Himself gave to the Apostles and their successors.[30]

Perhaps better than any other official document of the late Middle Ages, this canon illuminated the extent to which institutional, sacerdotal, and sacramental forces prevailed in that era.

Not long after the Fourth Lateran Council, the famous Dominican friar Thomas Aquinas (c. 1224–74) explained transubstantiation through the use of Aristotelian logic. He posited a distinction between the "accidents," or the outward forms of the bread and wine, and the "substance," or inward reality (i.e., the true body and blood of Christ).[31] While this approach enjoyed almost canonical status in later Roman Catholic theology, it had minimal impact in the Eastern churches, which probably thought it removed too much of the mystery from the sacrament. Thomas, however, maintained that the conversion of the elements was "wholly supernatural, brought about only by the power of God."[32]

The last significant development in medieval sacramentalism was the consensus in Eastern and Western churches that there were seven sacraments. In the twelfth century, Peter Lombard listed them as "baptism, confirmation, the bread of blessing (that is, the Eucharist), penance,

---

[30] Canon 1 of the Fourth Lateran Council, "The Creed, the Church, the Sacraments, and Transubstantiation," in Petry, *A History of Christianity*, 322–23.

[31] Thomas Aquinas, *Summa Theologiae* 3a q. 75. aa. 2–5.

[32] Aquinas, *Summa Theologiae*, aa. 4. His transubstantiation theory, which saw Christ as fully present in each element, gave support to the medieval Roman Catholic practice of denying the cup to the laity. See Ferguson, *Church History, Volume One*, 490.

extreme unction [last rites], ordination, and marriage."[33] These seven gained the official approval of the Council of Florence in 1439 in an attempt to heal the Catholic-Orthodox schism. Although the schism was not repaired, the Eastern churches broadly agreed with the Roman Church on the seven sacraments, even if they did not administer them in the same way.[34]

By the end of the fifteenth century, institutions and hierarchies dominated the Christian world. Church-state relationships in the East and the West made it difficult for dissenters to question the sacerdotal and sacramental trajectories that had developed. John Wycliffe (c. 1330–84) and John Hus (1374–1415) boldly raised questions in England and Bohemia respectively, particularly in reference to transubstantiation and abuses of church office. Their ideals clashed with institutional realities. For their efforts, Wycliffe was condemned as a heretic, and Hus was executed.

Within the Roman Church, the conciliar movement sought to bring structural changes by assigning more authority to church councils, especially in response to embarrassment caused by the Great Schism. But little changed. The Council of Constance (1414–18) posthumously attacked Wycliffe's orthodoxy and burned Hus. The same council reunited the papacy amid claims of rival popes, strengthening monarchical government in the Catholic Church and effectively subordinating councils to the authority of the pope. As it turned out, the widespread corruption that characterized the Renaissance papacy eventually contributed to the tumultuous events of the sixteenth century that rocked Western Europe, even if the Eastern Orthodox churches remained relatively immune from the waves of reform.[35]

---

[33] Peter Lombard, *Four Books of Sentences* 4.2.1.

[34] Council of Florence (1438–45), "The Doctrine of the Seven Sacraments," in *Creeds of the Churches: A Reader in Christian Doctrine from the Bible to the Present,* ed. John L. Leith, 3rd ed. (Louisville: John Knox, 1982), 60–61. For example, the Orthodox churches immersed babies (and adults), whereas the Roman Church sprinkled them. In Eastern Orthodoxy, an ordained priest—as long as he did not aspire to be a bishop—could be married; the Roman Church required celibacy of all those in holy orders. These divergent traditions have continued to the present.

[35] On late medieval reform efforts, see Steven Ozment, *The Age of Reform, 1250–1550: An Intellectual and Religious History of Late Medieval and Reformation Europe* (New Haven: Yale University Press, 1980); and *Advocates of Reform: From Wyclif to Erasmus,* vol. 14, Library of Christian Classics, ed. Matthew Spinka (Philadelphia: Westminster, 1953). A representative ecclesiological statement can be found in John Hus, *Tractate on the Church* 7.

The Reformation and Modern Churches: Mounting Ecclesiological Diversity

In its extraordinary challenge to Roman Catholicism, the Protestant Reformation brought forward various ecclesiological models that fractured Western Christendom into competing traditions, eventually spurring the emergence of denominations. Doctrines such as the supremacy of Scripture and salvation by grace through faith drove the Reformation and had profound implications for ecclesiology. Over against the inherited Roman Catholic ecclesiology, Protestant leaders moved in different directions. Some proposed more radical changes than others.

Reformation Churches

Martin Luther (1483–1546), the German monk who pioneered the Reformation with his *Ninety-Five Theses* in 1517, never presented a systematic ecclesiology. In fact, there is to this day no distinctive Lutheran church polity. Often Lutheran churches have been governed by bishops, but this is not a universal practice; further, the authority of their bishops is not grounded in apostolic succession. Pragmatism has dominated Lutheran church government, as in Luther's own time when he allowed secular rulers to serve as "emergency bishops" under certain circumstances.[36]

Most of Luther's ecclesiological contributions stemmed from his early battles with the papacy, which resulted in his excommunication in 1521. In his 1520 *Appeal to the German Nobility*, Luther vigorously propounded what became known as the doctrine of the priesthood of all believers. In opposition to the pronounced hierarchicalism of the medieval church, he took aim at the division between clergy and laity that the "Romanists" had constructed:

> All Christians are truly of the spiritual estate, and there is no difference among them, save of office alone. . . . We are all consecrated as priests by baptism, a higher consecration in us than Pope or bishop can give. . . . Since we are all priests, no man may

---

[36] See Eric W. Gritsch, "The Function and Structure of Gospelling: An Essay on 'Ministering' According to the Augsburg Confession," *Sixteenth Century Journal* 11 (June 25, 1980): 37–46 ; and Lewis W. Spitz, "Luther's Ecclesiology and His Concept of the Prince as *Notsbischoff*," *CH* 22 (June 1953): 113–41.

put himself forward or take upon himself, without our consent or election, to do that which we have all alike power to do.[37]

Luther introduced a revolutionary concept that challenged the ecclesiastical structures that had dominated the churches for centuries. He targeted Rome as the main culprit in the neutering of the laity.

Luther assaulted the sacramental system in another 1520 tract, *The Babylonian Captivity of the Church*. Using Scripture, he disparaged transubstantiation and the denial of the cup to lay people in the Eucharist. He also reduced the number of sacraments from seven to three: baptism, the Lord's Supper, and penance.[38] Luther eventually rejected penance as a sacrament.[39]

Although Luther emphasized the faithful preaching and hearing of God's Word as the first mark of a true church, he nevertheless insisted that a spiritual transaction occurred in the baptismal waters, even for infants who were sprinkled. He likewise argued that Christ was physically present in the Eucharist, even though the elements remained bread and wine.[40] Hence, Lutheranism retained some "high church" characteristics that other Reformation groups sought to eliminate.

During the second generation of reform, French émigré John Calvin (1509–64) addressed the church in a major section of his *Institutes of the Christian Religion* (Book 4). As leader of the reform movement in Geneva, Switzerland, Calvin owed a theological debt to Luther. At the same time, he was sympathetic with the efforts of Ulrich Zwingli (1484–1531) in Zurich, who diverged from Luther, especially on the sacraments. Zwingli's premature death in a religious war made Calvin the most important contributor to a Reformation tradition distinct from

---

[37] Martin Luther, "Appeal to the German Nobility," in Manschreck, *A History of Christianity*, 19.

[38] Luther, "The Babylonian Captivity of the Church," in *Three Treatises*, trans. A. T. W. Steinhäuser, rev. ed. (Philadelphia: Fortress, 1970), 113–260.

[39] In his *Small Catechism* (1529), Luther specifically refers to the sacraments of baptism and "the altar," but does not use the term "sacrament" in the section "Confession and Absolution." See Luther, "The Small Catechism," in Leith, *Creeds of the Churches*, 120–24.

[40] See Luther, "Martin Luther on the Marks of the Church," in *The Christian Theology Reader*, ed. Alister E. McGrath, 4th ed. (Malden, MA: Wiley-Blackwell, 2001), 418–19; Luther, "The Small Catechism," in Leith, *Creeds of the Churches*, 120–21, 123–24; and "The Augsburg Confession, 1530," in Manschreck, *A History of Christianity*, 44. Although Philip Melanchthon was the primary author of this confessional statement, it reflected Luther's beliefs.

Lutheranism. In ecclesiology Calvin displayed notable differences with the German Reformer.

Calvin, more consistently than Luther, upheld the distinction between the visible and invisible church. Picking up a thread from Augustine's ecclesiology, he wrote in the *Institutes* that "the church includes not only the saints presently living on earth, but all the elect from the beginning of the world." The visible church, however, included some "hypocrites who have nothing of Christ but the name and outward appearance."[41] For Calvin, then, looks could be deceiving. The concept of the church universal had to be balanced with the reality that visible congregations were composed of fallen human beings, not all of whom were even redeemed.

Calvin focused more attention on the visible church, affirming that the identity of the elect was evident "to the eyes of God alone." As a consequence, regenerate church membership and totally pure churches were impossible ideals; until the *parousia*, the churches of this world would be mixtures of wheat and tares (Matt 13:24–30, 36–43). Yet the inevitable impurities that characterized visible churches did not provide a rationale for schism—the unity of the visible church was a priority for Calvin.[42]

In the context of his warnings against unnecessary separation from a visible congregation, Calvin set forth the essential marks of a true church. Although he shared common ground with Luther on this matter, Calvin boiled the matter down to this declaration: "Wherever we see the Word of God purely preached and heard, and the sacraments administered according to Christ's institution, there, it is not to be doubted, a church of God exists."[43] If critics claimed that Calvin himself engaged in schism by leaving the Catholic Church, he would have responded that for centuries the Roman Church failed to preach the Word and properly celebrate the sacraments.[44] When a church did exhibit those two marks, however, it would constitute a sin to separate from it.

---

[41] John Calvin, *Institutes of the Christian Religion* 4.1.7.

[42] Calvin, *Institutes*, 4.1.7–8 and 12–13. There are echoes of Cyprian in Calvin. In *Institutes* 4.1.1–4 he spoke of both the "holy catholic church" and the visible church as "Mother." In 4.1.19 he cited Cyprian's interpretation of the parable of the wheat and the tares. The problem with using this parable to justify the church's mixed membership is that Jesus identified the "field" with the "world," not with the church (Matt 13:38).

[43] Calvin, *Institutes* 4.9.

[44] On the false nature of the Roman Church, see Calvin, *Institutes* 4.2.1–6.

On the sacraments, Calvin once again showed both similarities to and differences with Luther. Like Luther, Calvin clung to infant baptism; however, he did not view it in regenerative terms. He connected it to circumcision as a covenant sign that conveyed blessings.[45] He believed in greater continuity between the old and new covenants than did his Anabaptist opponents.

In reference to the Lord's Supper, Calvin rejected Luther's notion of the bodily presence of Christ, but he also moved beyond Zwingli's understanding of Communion as merely a memorial. Calvin's approach is generally described as spiritual presence. He believed that the Lord indeed was mysteriously present at the Eucharist in a manner different from his ordinary presence when two or three were gathered in his name. Hence, the Supper incorporated more than empty symbols and thus brought spiritual nourishment to believers: "The present distribution of the body and blood of the Lord would not greatly benefit us unless they had once for all been given for our redemption and salvation. They are therefore represented under bread and wine so that we may learn not only that they are ours but that they have been destined as food for our spiritual life."[46] Because of Communion's spiritual benefits, frequent—even weekly—observation of it was warranted.[47] Calvin's approach to the Eucharist set him apart from Catholics, Lutherans, Zwinglians, Anabaptists, and most Anglicans.

In the context of the Reformation, Calvin's ecclesiology was distinctive and, at points, even innovative. In particular, he gave more attention to the ordering of the visible church than Luther. Luther had no unique polity associated with his movement, but Calvin—with a bit of help from Zwingli—has often been considered the architect of Presbyterian church government. In Book 4 of his *Institutes*, he wrote at length about the organization of the church and its ministries. He designated four officers in each congregation: pastors, teachers, elders (presbyters), and deacons. In Geneva a consistory was made up of all the pastors in the city, along with twelve elders. This body handled church discipline. Elders were elected by the city council as part of a cooperative relationship between

---

[45] Calvin, *Institutes* 4.15–16.
[46] Ibid., 4.17.3. The broader framework for Calvin's consideration of the Lord's Supper is the entirety of 4.17. The Roman Mass is critically addressed in 4.18.
[47] Ibid., 4.17.43.

church and state, leading some to characterize Geneva as a theocracy. Actually, the clergy lacked political power, but magistrates exercised some coercion in the enforcement of Christian morals and orthodox doctrine, a pattern that the New England Puritans later followed in the forging of "God's New Israel."[48]

Calvin's polity included the notion that a congregation was not independent or autonomous but part of a larger institutional framework that included layers of authority beyond the local church. Ordained ministers in an area made up the presbytery. Beyond that, the Westminster Confession, which represented post-Reformation English and Scottish Presbyterianism, noted, "For the better government and further edification of the Church, there ought to be such assemblies as are commonly called synods and councils."[49] Some historians and theologians have discerned a federal pattern in presbyterian polity, suggesting that it influenced the American Founding Fathers in their incorporation of separation of powers and checks and balances into the US Constitution.[50] Though Calvin and his successors lacked ample biblical warrant for their form of church government, they rightly sought to build in safeguards against monarchical and tyrannical arrangements.

For the Anabaptists, neither Calvin nor the other magisterial Reformers went far enough. The Anabaptist movement produced the most radical ecclesiology of the Reformation period. Their revolution began in Zurich in 1525 when a small group of dissenters that became known as the Swiss Brethren opposed their mentor Zwingli by embracing believers' baptism, probably by pouring. Led by Conrad Grebel, George Blaurock, and Felix Manz, these early Anabaptists also challenged Zwingli on the close relationship that had been established between the church and the

---

[48] For Calvin's discussion of ministry and church structures, see *Institutes* 4.3–13, which shows that he was concerned with preventing the kind of ecclesiastical tyranny that he identified with papal Rome. On theocracy in colonial New England, see James Alan Patterson, "The Theocratic Impulse in American Protestantism: The Persistence of the Puritan Tradition," in *God and Caesar: Selected Essays from the 1993 Evangelical Theological Society's Convention at Washington, D.C.*, ed. Michael Bauman and David Hall (Camp Hill, PA: Christian Publications, 1994), 115–41.

[49] "The Westminster Confession of Faith (1646)," in Leith, *Creeds of the Churches*, 227. In the United States, the highest body in the mainline Presbyterian Church is the General Assembly.

[50] For example, see Douglas F. Kelly, *The Emergence of Liberty in the Modern World: The Influence of Calvin on Five Governments from the 16th through 18th Centuries* (Phillipsburg: P&R, 1992).

city council in Zurich. Indeed, sixteenth-century Anabaptists in general stood against the concept of a state church, pitting themselves against a tradition that had been the norm in Europe for centuries. In turn, the established churches of the Reformation era did not hesitate to use the secular sword as a weapon to suppress the Anabaptists. For example, Zwingli and the city council imprisoned Grebel and drowned Manz.[51]

The mainstream of the Anabaptist movement rejected any notion of Real Presence in the Lord's Supper and instead supported a memorial view similar to Zwingli's. Although early on they did not systematically articulate a church polity, they leaned toward congregationalism with a strong emphasis on regenerate church membership and discipline, including a formal ban that could be enforced against unrepentant sinners. The Schleitheim Confession, an early Anabaptist statement of beliefs and practices, revealed a sketchy ecclesiology; the author, Michael Sattler, focused mainly on believers' baptism, the Supper as a remembrance, pacifism, the evil of oaths, and the importance of maintaining a disciplined community separated from the world.[52]

More than a century later, Dutch Mennonites exhibited what had become a classic Anabaptist focus on the visible church. They said in the Dordrecht Confession that the visible church consisted of those who "have truly repented, and rightly believed; who are rightly baptized, united with God in heaven, and incorporated with the communion of the saints on earth."[53] The confession did not provide the level of detail that marked Calvin's writings on the proper ordering of the church, though it did list offices. The statement seemingly distinguished between bishops and pastors, and the reference to "circuits" implied connectionalism between the churches that was not explicit in earlier Anabaptism.[54] Nevertheless, the Dordrecht Confession illustrated Anabaptist priorities, centering on visible congregations made up of true believers who had undergone baptism after conversion. This set them apart from all the other Reformation bodies.

---

[51] On Anabaptist origins, see William R. Estep, *The Anabaptist Story*, rev. ed. (Grand Rapids: Eerdmans, 1975), 8–39. On their ecclesiology, see Dennis Bollinger, *First-Generation Anabaptist Ecclesiology, 1525–1561: A Study of Swiss, German, and Dutch Sources* (Lewiston, NY: Edwin Mellen Press, 2009).

[52] "The Schleitheim Confession (1527)," in Leith, *Creeds of the Churches*, 282–92. On Anabaptist congregationalism, see Estep, *The Anabaptist Story*, 190–91.

[53] "The Dordrecht Confession (1632)," in Leith, *Creeds of the Churches*, 299.

[54] Ibid., 300–301.

The Anabaptist movement remained small, persecuted, and somewhat sectarian. At the same time, these Reformation radicals at least indirectly influenced English Separatists and Baptists. Thus, they set the foundation for what is often labeled the "free church" tradition. Their voluntary, gathered congregations represented a much different model than the parish churches that dominated Roman Catholic and magisterial Reformation traditions. The Anabaptist perspective, in short, could be classified as "low church."

The "high church" Roman Catholic leaders responded with horror not only to Anabaptists but also to Lutherans and Calvinists. Not much changed in Catholic ecclesiology during the sixteenth century as the Roman Church dug in its heels against the onslaught of reform. The Council of Trent (1545–63) illustrated Rome's negative reaction to Protestantism as it sought to reaffirm the theology of the Middle Ages. The council declared that (1) the Roman Church was the only true one; (2) there were seven valid sacraments that imparted grace *ex opere operato*; and (3) the Mass—which needed to be in Latin—was a propitiatory sacrifice where the bread and wine were transubstantiated into the body and blood of Christ.[55] This understanding prevailed until Vatican II (1962–65). Even though certain reforms and a new spirit were evident at Vatican II, traditionalism continues to surface occasionally, such as in Benedict XVI's approval of a 2007 document restating the primacy of the Roman Church in relation to all other Christian communions.[56]

Anglicanism constituted another relatively "high church" tradition in the sixteenth century. Of all the reformations in the period, that involving the Church of England was the most ecclesiologically conservative, resulting in a kind of hybrid institution that blended Protestant doctrines with Roman Catholic rituals and practices. Indeed, the English Reformation stood in substantial continuity with the Roman Catholic tradition. Henry VIII's (reigned 1509–47) break with the pope in the

---

[55] "Canons and Decrees of the Council of Trent, 1545–1563," in Manschreck, *A History of Christianity*, 131–39.

[56] "Pope: Other Christian Denominations Not True Churches," Associated Press, July 10, 2007; accessed July 10, 2007, http://www.foxnews.com/printer_friendly_story/0,3566,288841,00.html. On Vatican II, see Walter M. Abbott, ed., *The Documents of Vatican II* (New York: Guild Press, America Press, Association Press, 1966). The Eastern Orthodox churches never had to confront a reformation or deal with modern pressures to implement significant changes; thus, Orthodoxy has had no councils equivalent to Trent or Vatican II.

1530s, for example, was not accompanied by substantive theological or liturgical changes. The Supremacy Act of 1534, however, opened the door for future reforms by declaring the king the supreme head of the English Church. This meant that the Reformation in England would be directed from the top down. With the rejection of papal authority, monarchs played a dominant role in the direction of ecclesiastical affairs. In a sense, Constantinianism reappeared, although the church-state situation might be more accurately described as Erastian.[57]

During the reign of Henry VIII's daughter, Elizabeth I (reigned 1558–1603), the Anglican tradition stabilized in its mildly "high church" format. The Church of England retained bishops who, it was claimed, stood in a line of apostolic succession dating to the early church. The archbishop of Canterbury held a position of special prominence under the monarch. The Thirty-Nine Articles (1563), which served as the church's primary doctrinal affirmation, incorporated many Reformation themes such as justification by faith and the supreme authority of Scripture. Several articles addressed ecclesiological issues, including a definition of the church that Calvin would have heartily endorsed. The creedal statement posited two sacraments, with interpretations of baptism and the Eucharist in language that was closer to Luther than to any other Reformer; however, it noted that "the Body of Christ is given, taken, and eaten, in the Supper, only after an heavenly and spiritual manner."[58] In summary, the Church of England under Elizabeth was noticeably Protestant, even if Catholic forms lingered in rituals, vestments, and other external matters.

Nevertheless, some members of the Church of England believed it was still too sacramental and sought additional reforms. Most Puritans, the "low church" party, pledged loyalty to the state church, although some preferred a Presbyterian polity. More radical Puritans and other dissenters moved into Separatism and advocated congregationalism. In this context, the English Baptist movement emerged under the leadership of

---

[57] See "The Supremacy Act, 1534," in Manschreck, *A History of Christianity*, 178–79. A similar bill early in the reign of Elizabeth I reaffirmed royal authority in the Church of England. See "Elizabeth's Supremacy Act, 1559," in Manschreck, *A History of Christianity*, 184. Thomas Erastus (1524–83) was a Swiss Protestant who promoted the right of civil authorities to exercise jurisdiction over the church. The theory assumed an established state church.

[58] "The Thirty-Nine Articles of Religion," in Leith, *Creeds of the Churches*, 276. The document included affirmations of royal prerogative in church life (280).

John Smyth (c. 1570–1612) and Thomas Helwys (c. 1575–c. 1615). These Separatist exiles in Holland transitioned to believers' baptism in 1609. Helwys eventually returned to England, where he planted the first Baptist congregation near London and pioneered the General Baptist denomination. Drawing on both Anabaptist and Separatist impulses, the Baptists championed autonomous congregational polity, religious liberty, and the separation of church and state. Immersion as the appropriate mode of baptism was adopted in the early 1640s.[59]

Baptists and other Protestants made ecclesiology much more complex than it had been before 1500. This held enormous implications for denominations in the New World and eventually—through the modern missionary movement—around the globe. Most of the thinking about the church after 1600 followed paradigms already established either in Catholicism/Orthodoxy or the Protestant communions.

At the same time, fresh breezes occasionally wafted through the Christian world, bringing new ecclesial challenges and opportunities. In Germany after the Thirty Years' War, for instance, the Pietist movement within the established Lutheran Church launched an innovative program of reform that featured small discipleship groups within larger congregations. In particular, Philip Spener (1635–1705) promoted *collegia pietatis*, or meetings for spiritual renewal that functioned as *ecclesiolae in ecclesia* (little congregations within the larger church).[60] In turn, Pietism helped spur the transatlantic revivals of the eighteenth century. In England, for example, John Wesley (1703–91) borrowed Spener's small-group approach and used it as a primary means of following up with new converts from his evangelistic meetings. Although the Methodist societies tended to compete with Anglican parish churches, Wesley remained in the Church of England and did not intend to father a new denomination. Eighteenth-century revivalism in both Great Britain and North America was generally church-based, even if new institutional forms sometimes resulted.[61]

---

[59] I have summarized Baptist history, including ecclesiological distinctives, in James A. Patterson, "Reflections on 400 Years of the Baptist Movement: Who We Are, What We Believe," in *Southern Baptists, Evangelicals, and the Future of Denominationalism*, ed. David S. Dockery (Nashville: B&H Academic, 2011), 191–230.

[60] Philip Jacob Spener, *Pia Desideria*, "Introduction," trans. and ed. Theodore G. Tappert (Philadelphia: Fortress Press, 1964), 19–20.

[61] See Mark A. Noll, *The Rise of Evangelicalism: The Age of Edwards, Whitefield and the Wesleys*, A History of Evangelicalism (Downers Grove: IVP Academic, 2004).

Modern Churches

In the nineteenth century, revivalism posed threats to a meaningful doctrine of the church because many popular evangelists were not associated with denominations or local congregations. Further, the growing parachurch agencies usually functioned without denominational accountability. John Nevin (1803–86), a German Reformed professor at Mercersburg Seminary in Pennsylvania, protested the damage that Charles Finney's (1792–1875) "new measures" were inflicting on the churches of America.[62] Nevin, however, stood as a lonely voice in the wilderness as most evangelical Protestants embraced revivalism as a tool for church growth.

In the Church of England, the Oxford or Tractarian movement represented a nineteenth-century variety of the "high-church" perspective. Under the leadership of John Henry Newman (1801–90), who later converted to Roman Catholicism; Edward Pusey (1800–1882); and John Keble (1792–1866), the Tractarians objected to liberal and secularizing trends in English church life. Furthermore, they conceived of Anglicanism as one of three "branches" in the "Catholic Church" (the other two being Roman Catholicism and Eastern Orthodoxy). This movement set the stage for an Anglo-Catholic party in the Church of England, which positioned itself as a contrast to the evangelical wing of Anglicanism.[63] As was the case in many modern Christian communions, pluralism held sway; therefore, it became increasingly difficult to pinpoint ecclesiological identity.

In the United States, frustration with pluralism led some to restorationism, i.e., the attempt to structure church life in conformity with the primitive church of the apostolic age. Alexander Campbell's (1788–1866) Disciples/Christian movement tried to displace denominations with an emphasis on Christian unity based solely on the New Testament—creeds were accordingly eschewed. Campbell and his followers affirmed a fairly simple democratic polity and believers' baptism

---

[62] J. W. Nevin, *The Anxious Bench* (Chambersburg, PA: printed at the office of the "Weekly Messenger," 1843). For a sympathetic treatment of Nevin, see D. G. Hart, *John Williamson Nevin, High-Church Calvinist*, American Reformed Biographies (Phillipsburg: P&R, 2005).

[63] C. Brad Faught, *The Oxford Movement: A Thematic History of the Tractarians and Their Times* (University Park: Pennsylvania State University Press, 2003).

by immersion, although their soteriological language implied that the baptismal water was regenerative.[64]

One of Campbell's notable adversaries, James Robinson Graves (1820–93), brought a restorationist spirit to Baptist life with his Landmarkist ecclesiology. Fearing that Baptists had lost sight of their central doctrines and principles, this feisty religious journalist argued that Baptist churches were the only true ones, in part because they had existed in an unbroken historical succession since the first century. Baptists needed to recover the "ancient landmarks," which included fencing the Communion table so that only members of a specific local church were welcome, and rejecting as invalid all baptisms not performed by Baptists. Moreover, Graves's definition of "church" focused exclusively on visible congregations. He repudiated the idea of the church universal. He gained a wide following among Southern Baptists, although his theories proved divisive.[65]

Ironically, Graves also espoused dispensational theology, which said little about the visible church and stressed the more ethereal church that would be raptured out of the world before the great tribulation. The popularity of dispensationalism in American fundamentalism and evangelicalism contributed to a more spiritualized, universal understanding of the church within those movements. This was reinforced by the many parachurch ministries in conservative Protestantism. Hence, thoughtful ecclesiology often took a backseat to prophetic speculation or missionary activism.[66]

In the twentieth century, the Protestant missionary enterprise helped spawn interest among the mainline denominations in Christian unity. This led to a prominent manifestation of the ecumenical movement, the World Council of Churches, officially organized in 1948. Although Eastern Orthodox and Protestant bodies affiliated with the WCC, the Roman Catholic Church and the Southern Baptist Convention never joined. It was never entirely clear what kind of unity was anticipated, and

---

[64] Nathan Hatch relates the Christian movement and other populist groups to the democratizing trends of the nineteenth-century frontier. See his *The Democratization of American Christianity* (New Haven: Yale University Press, 1989).

[65] See James A. Patterson, *James Robinson Graves: Staking the Boundaries of Baptist Identity* (Nashville: B&H Academic, 2012).

[66] For helpful background, see J. Michael Utzinger, *Yet Saints Their Watch Are Keeping: Fundamentalists, Modernists, and the Development of Evangelical Ecclesiology, 1887–1937* (Macon, GA: Mercer University Press, 2006).

the WCC has fallen on hard times in recent years because of its theological pluralism as well as radical economic and political agendas.[67]

Partly as a consequence of persistent efforts in world evangelization, Christianity became a global phenomenon. This in turn spawned new church forms, and thorny ecclesiological issues arose. For instance, the church in China faced major persecution beginning in 1950, resulting in a widespread but often endangered house-church movement. The institutional life and ethos are quite different in churches under oppression than in the comfortable churches of the West. The daily pressures that such churches face make systematic ecclesiology overwhelming.[68]

Global Christianity has become complex. The churches of the global South do not necessarily function like their counterparts in Europe and North America. Leadership models and church polity often are adjusted to fit particular cultural and ethnic contexts. Newer churches, even with some manifest vulnerabilities and excesses, lend an incredible richness to worldwide Christianity. In numerical terms, Christianity in the global South is slowly overtaking the more established communions of the West.[69] These developments will greatly influence ecclesiology over the next several decades.

Conclusion

Christians have thought in a multitude of ways about the church. Ecclesiological pluralism prevails in contemporary Christianity, but it differs only in degree—and not in kind—from that of earlier eras. The past highlights the inclination of Christian movements and denominations to absorb cultural influences into their ecclesiology. Institutional realities sometimes override scriptural principles in church life.

---

[67] For the connection between missions and ecumenism, along with significant WCC documents, see the chapter on "Missions and Ecumenicity" in Manschreck, *A History of Christianity*, 461–507. Reflecting its interest in the sacraments, the WCC's Faith and Order Commission adopted *Baptism, Eucharist, and Ministry* (Geneva: World Council of Churches, 1982) at its 1982 meeting in Lima, Peru, with the goal of stimulating "mutual recognition" agreements among churches. Results have been mixed.

[68] See Liao Yiwu, *God Is Red: The Secret Story of How Christianity Survived and Flourished in Communist China* (New York: HarperOne, 2011).

[69] Philip Jenkins, *The Next Christendom: The Coming of Global Christianity*, 3rd ed. (New York: Oxford University Press, 2011).

In light of the historical record, believers must think intently about the church and how it should incarnate itself in the modern world. Newer ecclesial models found in megachurches or emerging/emergent churches need to be evaluated in light of Scripture and church history. Perhaps most importantly, a review of Christian history ought to inspire people of faith to engage themselves more earnestly in their visible congregations.[70]

The concept of the church universal is a glorious one, but it should not cause Christians to downplay or be indifferent to the local churches in which they must participate. For the church to transcend the narrow pragmatism that has sometimes determined its agenda, its members need to commit themselves afresh to the Lord's commission. Institutional realities cannot be allowed to detract from the missional responsibility of his church, which has been assigned a pivotal role in the proclamation of his redemptive plan.

---

[70] See Robert W. Patterson, "In Search of the Visible Church," *Christianity Today*, March 11, 1991, 36–40.

CHAPTER 7

Beyond Mere Ecclesiology: The Church as God's New Covenant Community

Stephen J. Wellum

J esus said, "I will build My church" (Matt 16:18), but what exactly is the church? This is an important question to ask for a variety of reasons, not least because discussion of the church has fallen on hard times. Many factors contribute to this sad state of affairs, both outside and within the church. Outside, the pervasive influence of philosophical and religious pluralism makes talk of the church as unique and exclusive seem intolerant, just as talk of an exclusive Lord and Savior is dismissed. Within the church, we are preoccupied with pragmatism and downplay theology. Thus, to ask "What is the church?" is viewed as unnecessary and counterproductive to carrying out the church's mission. So we often ask instead: "How should we *do* church?" or "What *works* best in order for the church to carry out her mission in the world?" Obviously these questions are important. Yet we must first wrestle with what the church *is* before we can know what she should be *doing* in the world.

However, the most important reason to ask this question is the church's role in God's redemptive purposes. As Jesus' promise makes clear, the church is central to his saving work. He came in obedience to his Father to redeem a people for himself and hence the statement, "I will build My church." One only has to reflect on statements in Ephesians to see how central the church is to God's redemptive plan. For example, in Eph 1:22 the Father "put everything under His feet and appointed Him as head over everything *for the church*."[1] In other words, Christ's supremacy over the universe is for the benefit of his people. This is also borne out in 3:1–10, where Paul identifies the "mystery" of God. This was God's eternal plan hidden in ages past but now revealed in Christ. As Paul proclaims the "incalculable riches of the Messiah" (v. 8), the result is the growth of the church. The "mystery" is not an abstraction. In Christ and his church it takes on concrete shape before our eyes, as a new multiracial humanity is formed and grows, constituted by believing Jews and Gentiles. This displays nothing less than "God's multi-faceted wisdom" (v. 10). The church is the public demonstration of God's power, grace, and wisdom, and is central to his redemptive plan.[2]

Yet, sadly, even though Scripture is clear that the church is at the center of God's saving purposes, confusion still exists regarding the church's identity, as is reflected in many of our ecclesiastical and denominational divisions. This chapter will begin to provide a biblical-theological answer to this crucial question, but where shall we begin? One helpful entry point for at least two reasons is to think through the relationship between the NT "church" and OT "Israel," i.e., the relationship between the "people of God" in the OT and NT.

First, to begin with the Israel-church relationship allows us to formulate a "whole-Bible" theology of the church because this relationship unpacks the Bible's story line and allows us to think canonically about "the people of God." In fact, to begin our reflections on the church at this point is precisely where the NT commences. The question of the *identity* and *nature* of the church is an issue that the NT wrestles with at length in light of Christ's finished work.[3] Because our Lord fulfilled the OT in his life, death, and resurrection and thus inaugurated the new covenant era, the question of the *identity* of his people is raised. Is

---

[1] Italics are mine. See P. T. O'Brien, *The Letter to the Ephesians*, PNTC (Grand Rapids: Eerdmans, 1999), 138–52.

[2] See O'Brien, *Ephesians*, 240–52, and the helpful discussion of this text in John R. W. Stott, *The Message of Ephesians*, BST (Downers Grove: InterVarsity, 1996), 122–30.

[3] For example, remember how the early church wrestled with the Judaizers at the Jerusalem Council (Acts 15; see Galatians) and then later in regard to the "strong and weak" issue (Romans 14–15), circumcision (1 Cor 7:17–19), feast days (Col 2:16–23), and so on. Each of these discussions wrestles with the relationship between the biblical covenants and the larger Israel-church relationship.

Jesus' new community merely the continuation of Israel, hence a Jewish community that Gentiles may now join as long as they come under the demands of the old covenant? Or, is it more of a Gentile community, divorced from Israel of old, a kind of replacement of Israel? Or, is it, as I argue below, neither Jewish nor Gentile but a third entity—a *new* humanity—organically related to the dawning of the new creation and the new covenant age? In addition, what is the *nature* of the church, especially in relation to the OT people of God? Is the church's nature similar to Israel's, i.e., a "mixed" community constituted by believers and unbelievers, or is she constituted as a regenerate, believing community consisting of all professing faith in Jesus Christ? What precisely is new about the new covenant people of God?

Second, to begin with the Israel-church relationship also allows us to think carefully about the differences between the biblical-theological systems of dispensationalism and covenant theology. In regard to how "to put the Bible together," dispensational and covenant theology represent competing viewpoints. Most people associate the differences between these two views with the area of eschatology. However, often neglected are the more important *ecclesiological* differences that are foundational to the eschatological ones.

Each system roots its understanding of the Israel-church relationship in the larger discussion of the relationship between the old and new covenants, and different views of the *identity* and *nature* of the church result. So, in answering the question, what is the church? via the Israel-church relationship, we are able to accomplish three goals. (1) We are able to offer a "whole-Bible" answer to the question. (2) We are better able to see the ecclesiastical differences between dispensational and covenant theology and thus place ourselves in a better position to understand why evangelicals differ on ecclesiology. (3) In the course of our discussion, we are able to set the stage for a *via media* position between these two viewpoints. This will allow us to move beyond a mere ecclesiology and provide a more biblical grounding for a Baptist view of the church.

I will proceed in two steps. First, I will describe briefly the competing biblical-theological systems of dispensational and covenant theology in regard to the question, what is the church? Second, in light of that discussion, I will move beyond mere ecclesiology by offering five summary statements. These will present the church as God's regenerate, believing new covenant people—a new humanity and new creation—graciously called by the Father, born of the Spirit, and effectively brought into faith union with our new covenant mediator and head, our Lord Jesus.

What Is the Church?

Dispensational Theology

Dispensationalism is no monolithic biblical-theological viewpoint. Over the years it has gone through a number of revisions, although it remains united by a common core.[4] It first took shape in the Brethren Movement in early nineteenth-century England. Originally it was associated with such names as John Darby (1800–82), Benjamin Newton (1807–99), and George Müller (1805–98) and in North America with such names as D. L. Moody (1837–99), J. R. Graves (1820–93), and C. I. Scofield (1843–1921). The famous *Scofield Reference Bible* provided notes for its readers on how to interpret Scripture and put the whole canon together through the lens of its theology. The most extensive dispensational systematic theology was Lewis Sperry Chafer's eight-volume *Systematic Theology*.[5] It is difficult to classify all the differences among dispensationalists, but "three broad forms of dispensational thought"[6] are important to distinguish. "Classic" dispensationalism is represented by John Darby, Lewis S. Chafer, and the *Scofield Reference Bible*. "Revised" dispensationalists include John Walvoord, Charles Ryrie, J. Dwight Pentecost, and the editors of the revised *Scofield Bible*. "Progressive" dispensationalist authors include Craig Blaising, Darrell Bock, John Feinberg, Robert Saucy, and Bruce Ware.

"Dispensation" is a biblical term derived from *oikonomia* (see Eph 1:10; 3:2, 9; Col 1:25), which means "to manage, regulate, administer,

---

[4] For helpful summaries of the history and development of dispensational theology, see Craig A. Blaising and Darrell L. Bock, *Progressive Dispensationalism* (Wheaton: BridgePoint, 1993); Craig A. Blaising and Darrell L. Bock, eds., *Dispensationalism, Israel and the Church: A Search for Definition* (Grand Rapids: Zondervan, 1992); Robert L. Saucy, *The Case for Progressive Dispensationalism* (Grand Rapids: Zondervan, 1993); Herbert W. Bateman IV, ed., *Three Central Issues in Contemporary Dispensationalism: A Comparison of Traditional and Progressive Views* (Grand Rapids: Kregel, 1999); John S. Feinberg, ed., *Continuity and Discontinuity: Perspectives on the Relationship Between the Old and New Testaments* (Wheaton: Crossway, 1988).

[5] Lewis Sperry Chafer, *Systematic Theology* (1948; repr., Grand Rapids: Kregel, 1993).

[6] Blaising and Bock, *Progressive Dispensationalism*, 22.

and plan the affairs of a household."[7] Behind the term is the idea of God's plan or administration being accomplished in this world and how God arranges and orders his relationship to humans. "Dispensation," as Blaising explains, "refers to a distinctive way in which God manages or arranges the relationship of human beings to Himself."[8] Dispensationalists are well known for how they divide redemptive history into distinct "dispensations," arguing that during each of these periods of time, God works out a particular phase of his overall plan. However, Vern Poythress notes that there is a sense in which the word "dispensation" is *not* helpful for distinguishing dispensationalism from other views because "virtually all ages of the church and all branches of the church have believed that there are distinctive dispensations in God's government of the world, though sometimes the consciousness of such distinctions has grown dim. The recognition of distinctions between different epochs is by no means unique to D[dispensational]-theologians."[9]

Many contemporary dispensationalists acknowledge this point. For example, John Feinberg agrees that the uniqueness of dispensationalism is *not* tied merely to the word "dispensation," or even to the idea behind the word. If this were the case, then all Christians would be "dispensationalists" in this broad sense. Every believer recognizes that God's salvific plan across redemptive history involves various "dispensations." As God's plan reaches fulfillment in Christ, various changes take place.[10] This observation raises the question, what is unique about dispensational theology, given its diversity? What is its *sine qua non*? Much discussion and debate has taken place over this question, and the answer is not

---

[7] See ibid., 106–11; John Feinberg, "Systems of Discontinuity" in *Continuity and Discontinuity*, 68–9. Technically the word "dispensation" is the anglicized form of *dispensatio*, the Latin Vulgate rendering of *oikonomia*.

[8] Blaising and Bock, *Progressive Dispensationalism*, 11.

[9] Vern S. Poythress, *Understanding Dispensationalists*, 2nd ed. (Phillipsburg: P&R, 1994), 9–10.

[10] For a discussion of this point, see Feinberg, "Systems of Discontinuity," in *Continuity and Discontinuity*, 68–70. Feinberg rightly notes: "Since both dispensationalists and nondispensationalists use the term and concept of a dispensation, that alone is not distinctive to Dispensationalism. It is no more distinctive to Dispensationalism than talk of covenants is distinctive to Covenant Theology. Dispensationalists talk about covenants all the time" (69). In addition, Feinberg notes: (1) To prove "dispensationalism" requires more than showing the biblical evidence for "dispensations" (68–69), and (2) the number of "dispensations" one holds to is not essential to "dispensationalism" (70).

uniform. However, an excellent case can be made that its *sine qua non* is the Israel-church distinction, undergirded by an understanding of the covenantal differences between the ethnic nation of Israel under the old covenant and the church as God's people under the new.

For all varieties of dispensationalism, "Israel" refers to a physical, national people with a specific genealogical heritage and distinct privileges and promises. Further, it is *not* the case that the church is the NT replacement of historic Israel in God's plan of salvation, as, for example, covenant theology teaches. Thus, the salvation of Gentiles in God's plan is not the fulfillment of the promises made to Israel as a nation, specifically associated with the land promised to them. Rather the church, a *spiritual* people comprised of an international community, is distinctively new in God's redemptive purposes. It finds its origin in Christ and particularly in the baptism of the Spirit that Christ bestowed equally on all in the church at Pentecost. Thus, what constitutes the church as "new" are the blessings of the Spirit tied to the coming of Christ that are *qualitatively* different from the blessings of the Spirit in the OT. That is why for dispensational theology, the salvation experience of the person under the new covenant is qualitatively different from the salvation experience of the Israelite under the old covenant.[11]

Thus, dispensational theology sees more *discontinuity* from the old to the new covenant in regard to the *nature* of the covenant communities. The church is seen as distinctively *new* in the divine dispensations due to the work of Christ and the newness of the Spirit's permanent indwelling of the believer. Dispensationalists view the nature of the church, along with its structure and ordinances, as distinct from the nation of Israel under the old covenant. Often this discontinuity in nature is described as the difference between a "mixed" and "regenerate" community.[12] Israel, as the former, is constituted by believers and unbelievers; the church, as the latter, is comprised of all who have been born of the Spirit, united to

---

[11] See Feinberg, "Systems of Discontinuity," in *Continuity and Discontinuity*, 71–85; Blaising and Bock, *Progressive Dispensationalism*, 13–21, who unpack the unique features of dispensational theology primarily in terms of the Israel–church relationship.

[12] The "mixed" nature of the covenant communities refers to the belief that under both the old and new covenants, the locus of the covenant community and the locus of the elect are distinct. Covenant theology, for example, on the basis of this "mixed" view of the church, affirms the "visible–invisible" church distinction. Dispensational theology has argued, similar to Baptist theology, for the unique, *new* nature of the church as a regenerate community and thus structurally different from Israel of old.

Christ, and who profess this to be the case. Thus most dispensationalists affirm believer's baptism instead of infant baptism because to equate the sign of the old covenant (circumcision) with the sign of the new (baptism), given the Israel-church distinction, is simply a mistake. In addition, most affirm that the covenant sign of baptism must be applied only to those who have been born of the Spirit and profess faith union in Christ because the church is a regenerate people.[13]

Covenant Theology

Covenant theology, as a biblical-theological system, has its roots in the Reformation (Ulrich Zwingli [1484–1531], Heinrich Bullinger [1504–75], and John Calvin [1509–64]). In the post-Reformation era, Herman Witsius (1636–1708) and Johannes Cocceius (1603–69) systematized it. It is ably represented in the Westminster Confession of Faith (1643–49) as well as in other Reformed confessions.[14]

As the name suggests, *covenant* theology not only organizes the history of the world in terms of covenants, but it also contends that what brings together the diverse themes of Scripture is the theme of covenant. Michael Horton says it this way:

> What unites them [all the themes of Scripture] is not itself a
> central dogma but an architectonic structure of biblical faith and

---

[13] Although eschatology is not the focus of this chapter, it is also due to the Israel-church distinction that dispensational theology argues for a distinctive eschatology. Because Israel is *not* the church, coupled with God's unchanging promise to Abraham (and thus to Israel) that the Davidic king must rule in the land of Israel (which has not yet been realized), the land promise must receive its fulfillment in the future millennium when Christ returns as the Davidic king to rule in Jerusalem, thus bringing to pass all of God's promises to ethnic Israel. This distinct view of eschatology—known as "dispensational premillennialism"—has been promulgated through books, movies, and other forms of media. By contrast, covenant theology rejects a dispensational premillennial eschatology and holds to a variety of millennial viewpoints, including historic premillennialism, amillennialism, and postmillennialism. On this point see Anthony A. Hoekema, *The Bible and the Future* (Grand Rapids: Eerdmans, 1994).

[14] For some introductory books on covenant theology, see Michael Horton, *God of Promise* (Grand Rapids: Baker, 2006); Peter Golding, *Covenant Theology: The Key of Theology in Reformed Thought and Tradition* (Ross–Shire: Mentor, 2004); Geerhardus Vos, "The Doctrine of the Covenant in Reformed Theology" in *Redemptive History and Biblical Interpretation: The Shorter Writings of Geerhardus Vos*, ed. Richard B. Gaffin Jr. (Phillipsburg: P&R, 1979); O. Palmer Robertson, *The Christ of the Covenants* (Grand Rapids: Baker, 1980); William J. Dumbrell, *Covenant and Creation: A Theology of the Old Testament Covenants* (Carlisle: Paternoster, 1984).

practice. That particular architectural structure that we believe the Scriptures themselves to yield is the covenant. It is not simply the concept of the covenant, but the concrete existence of God's covenantal dealings in our history that provides the context within which we recognize the unity of Scripture amid its remarkable variety.[15]

Historically, covenant theology has taught that all of God's relations to human beings are understood in terms of three covenants: the pretemporal "covenant of redemption" (*pactum salutis*) between the persons of the Godhead, the "covenant of works" (*foederus naturae*) made with Adam before the fall on behalf of the entire human race, and the "covenant of grace" (*foederus gratiae*) made through Christ with all who are to believe, namely the elect.[16]

In covenant theology, the "covenant of grace"—an overarching theological category—subsumes all of the biblical covenants. When did the "covenant of grace" begin? It began immediately after the fall with the promise of grace in Gen 3:15. This promise was then progressively revealed and fulfilled in history through variously administered covenants with Noah, Abraham, Israel, and David. Ultimately it was brought to fulfillment in the new covenant inaugurated by our Lord in his victorious cross work on our behalf. In this view, although different covenants are described in Scripture, there is only one "covenant of grace." That is why covenant theology views the relationships between the biblical covenants in terms of an overall *continuity*. No doubt covenant theology allows for differences throughout redemptive history in the administration of the biblical covenants, and the nature of continuity in the covenant of grace varies among covenant theologians. Vern Poythress acknowledges this point: "Covenant theology has always allowed for a diversity of administration of the one covenant of grace." Yet, as Poythress continues, this diversity is largely accounted for by the "diversity of epochs in biblical history." The emphasis is "undeniably on the unity of *one* covenant of grace."[17]

---

[15] Horton, *God of Promise*, 13; see also his *Covenant and Eschatology: The Divine Drama* (Louisville: WJK, 2002) for a more extensive development of this idea.

[16] Within covenant theology there is disagreement regarding with whom the "covenant of grace" is made. Is it with the elect alone or with the elect and their children?

[17] Poythress, *Understanding Dispensationalists*, 40. Randy Booth, *Children of Promise* (Phillipsburg: P&R, 1995), 9, underscores this point when he comments on

Thus, under the old covenant administration, the covenant of grace was administered through various promises, prophecies, sacrifices, rites, and ordinances (e.g., circumcision) that ultimately typified and foreshadowed the coming of Christ. Now in light of our Lord's coming and work, the covenant of grace is administered through the preaching of the Word and the administration of the sacraments. However, in God's plan there are *not* two covenants of grace, one in the OT and the other in the NT, but one covenant differing not in substance but essentially the same across the ages.

Given covenant theology's stress on the *continuity* of the covenant of grace, it is important to ask: In Christ's inauguration of the new covenant, what is "new" about it? Within covenant theology, the answer to this question is not monolithic. However, despite various nuances, most would view the main difference in terms of "promise-fulfillment," i.e., what the older administration promised through types, ceremonies, and sacrifices has now come to fulfillment in Jesus the Christ. As such, "newness" is more a *renewal* of the covenant than a replacement of it.[18] That is why most within covenant theology argue that the new covenant administration simply expands the previous era by broadening its extent and application and bringing greater blessing. Yet it leaves intact the fundamental elements of the covenant of grace; hence the assertion of the continuity of the covenant of grace across the ages.[19]

---

the "newness" of the new covenant. He states, "the new covenant is but a new—though more glorious—administration of the same covenant of grace."

[18] See for example, Booth, *Children of Promise*, 51; Jeffrey D. Niell, "The Newness of the New Covenant," in *The Case for Covenantal Infant Baptism*, ed. Gregg Strawbridge (Phillipsburg: P&R, 2003), 127–55. Even though *renewal* is a common way to view the relationship between the old and new covenants, not all covenant theologians agree. Michael Horton, for example, does say that the new covenant is qualitatively different, if contrasted with the Sinai (old) covenant. As Horton (*God of Promise*, 53) states, "The point could not be clearer [from Jer 31:31–34]: the new covenant is not a renewal of the old covenant made at Sinai, but an entirely different covenant with an entirely different basis." Yet it is important to acknowledge that Horton views the Sinai covenant more in terms of the covenant of works and not the covenant of grace. When it comes to viewing the new covenant in relation to the Abrahamic and other biblical covenants, which he believes are "gospel" covenants given their unconditional, royal–grant nature, he does see much more continuity between the OT covenants and the new covenant.

[19] Specifically, but not limited to these points, covenant theology views the "newness" of the new covenant in the following ways: (1) On the basis of Christ's cross and through the application of it by the Spirit, a greater power of obedience is possible in the new covenant. (2) The knowledge of God extends to all nations, thus fulfilling the Abrahamic promise of blessings to the nations. (3) The promise of redemption is now

Note that covenant theology rarely discusses the newness of the new covenant in terms of a change in the *structure* and *nature* of the covenant community. Those who argue for such a change, such as Baptists, differ with covenant theology at this crucial point.[20] For Baptists, one thing that makes the church "new" is that she is structurally different from Israel. By definition *all* those within the "new covenant community" are people who profess to have experienced the regenerative work of the Spirit and forgiveness of sin. Jeremiah 31 points in this direction, and the NT confirms it. At this point different understandings of the nature of the church begin to emerge. The Baptist view of "newness" implies a *discontinuity* at the structural/nature level between the old and new covenants, a view rejected by covenant theology.

For this reason covenant theology insists on more *continuity* in the "Israel–church" relationship. It has always insisted that God has one plan of salvation and one people of God and that the similarities between Israel and the church as covenant communities are significant. Unlike dispensational theology, "Israel" is viewed as "the church" and vice versa.[21] That is why covenant theology has argued that there is *continuity* between Israel and the church in a host of ways. For example, the nature of the covenant communities is that they are comprised of believers and unbelievers (i.e., a "mixed" community) so that the locus of the covenant community and the locus of the elect are different. This emphasis has led to the famous

---

accomplished in Christ with the full payment of sin and thus the old Levitical administration, along with the ceremonial law, has now been fulfilled. (4) The new covenant is the final manifestation of God's redemptive plan. No more covenant administrations are to be revealed. See these points in: Booth, *Children of the Promise*, 63–66; Douglas Wilson, *To a Thousand Generations: Infant Baptism—Covenant Mercy for the People of God* (Moscow, ID: Canon, 1996), 22–34; and both Niell, "The Newness of the New Covenant," 127–74; and Richard L. Pratt Jr., "Infant Baptism in the New Covenant," in Strawbridge, *The Case for Covenantal Infant Baptism*, 127–74.

[20] As noted above, against covenant theology, dispensationalism agrees that the church is different from Israel. However, the reason for the difference is not always the same. Even though many Baptists are dispensationalists, this is *not* true of all Baptists. For example, I am not a dispensationalist. Instead, I argue for a Baptist view of the church by steering a middle course between dispensational and covenant theology.

[21] If one asks the question, "When did the church begin?" dispensational and covenant theology answer this question differently. For dispensational thought, the church is new in redemptive history and thus begins at Pentecost. For covenant theology, the church begins immediately after God's first promise of redemption in Gen 3:15, acknowledging redemptive–historical difference but basically conceiving of the two communities as the same.

"visible-invisible church" distinction, with the former referring to the "mixed" nature of the church and the latter referring to the elect throughout the ages.[22] In addition, covenant theology has argued for a continuity in covenant signs (i.e., circumcision spiritually signifies the same realities as baptism). It affirms the essential sameness of the salvation experience of old and new covenant believers, allowing some modifications for the final realities that Christ has achieved. In this way, within covenant theology, "Israel–church" are so linked that it becomes difficult not to say that the only major differences between the old and new covenant people of God is that the NT church is a racially mixed and nonnational Israel and that the "church" is a more knowledgeable version of the old covenant people of God. The work of the Spirit in terms of regeneration, indwelling, and sealing is basically the same across redemptive history.

Evaluation

At crucial points dispensational and covenant theologies differ in how they conceive the identity and nature of the church. I contend that insights and flaws are in both positions. What is ultimately needed is a *via media*, what I will contend is a proper Baptist view of the church.[23] I will agree with both progressive dispensationalism (in contrast to other forms of dispensational theology) and covenant theology that there is only *one*

---

[22] As noted above, this view is different from a Baptist or believer's view of the church, which maintains that the church, by definition, is a regenerate, believing community. Covenant theology contends that the church is constituted by both believers and unbelievers or, as they like to say, "believers and their children"—children who may or may not constitute the elect. It is not an accident that given this view of the church, covenant theology has strongly endorsed paedobaptism, parallel to the covenant sign of circumcision. For a discussion of the "visible–invisible" distinction, see Louis Berkhof, *Systematic Theology* (1939; Grand Rapids: Eerdmans, reprint, 1982), 566. Often appeal is made to the parable of the Weeds (Matt 13:24–30, 36–43) to justify the "mixed" nature of the church, which is exegetically unsustainable. See e.g., Horton, *God of Promise*, 182, 185; id., *The Gospel Commission: Recovering God's Strategy for Making Disciples* (Grand Rapids: Baker, 2011), 293, for an appeal to the parable in this way. See D. A. Carson, *Matthew*, EBC (Grand Rapids: Zondervan, 1984), 324–27, for a helpful response to the misuse of this parable.

[23] What follows is a shortened version of an argument that Peter Gentry and I have set forth for a *via media* between dispensational and covenant theology. We have sought to rethink the relationships between the biblical covenants across redemptive history as they find their fulfillment in Christ in a middle way between the two dominant viewpoints, what we label "progressive covenantalism." For the full discussion of the position, see Peter J. Gentry and Stephen J. Wellum, *Kingdom through Covenant: A Biblical-Theological Understanding of the Covenants* (Wheaton: Crossway, 2012).

people of God (the elect) throughout the ages and *one* plan of redemption centered in Christ. However, against covenant theology, the church is different from Israel in at least two significant ways.

First, the church is *new* in redemptive history precisely because she is the community of the *new* covenant. With the coming of our Lord Jesus Christ, all previous covenants have reached their fulfillment and end so that the salvation realities that Jesus achieves and applies to his people are *not* the same as under the old covenant.[24] Against all forms of dispensational theology, this is *not* to say that the church is different in essence from Israel. Rather, the *newness* of the church is a redemptive-historical newness, rooted in the coming and work of Jesus the Messiah, the last Adam and true Israel, who has inaugurated a new and better covenant. In his obedient life and triumphant atoning work, our Lord has achieved our eternal redemption, secured the new covenant promise and gift of the Spirit in his blood. He has given birth to a new community—a new creation—a people in faith union with him, receiving all the gracious blessings that result from union with their covenantal head.

Second, the church, unlike Israel, is *new* because she is comprised of a *regenerate*, *believing* people rather than a "mixed" group. True members of the new covenant community are only those who have professed that they have entered into union with Christ by repentance and faith and are thus partakers of all the benefits and blessings of the new covenant age. This is the primary reason Baptists vociferously contend that the covenant sign of the new covenant church (baptism) is reserved only for those who have entered these glorious realities by the work of God's grace in their lives. Although circumcision and baptism are both covenant signs, they do not signify the same realities because of their respective covenantal differences. Let us now turn to the biblical data that substantiates such a view and, in so doing, move beyond a mere ecclesiology.

---

[24] I am thinking of the salvation experience differences between old and new covenant believers. No doubt, old covenant believers were regenerated, saved by grace through faith in the promises of God, knew the Lord, and experienced forgiveness of sins under the old covenant structures in anticipation of the fulfillment of those types and shadows in Christ. But it is not the case that these salvation experiences were true of the *entire* old covenant community *and* that the OT saint experienced the same access to God, the indwelling of the Spirit, and other salvation experiences unique to the new covenant work of Christ.

Beyond Mere Ecclesiology

To state that the church is "God's new covenant community" requires some unpacking. Specifically, we must think through the Israel–church relationship, especially in terms of the continuity and discontinuity between the two communities. By doing so, we will capture more clearly two important points. First, the church is not a "mixed" community (against covenant theology) but a regenerate, believing people—neither Jew nor Gentile but a *new* humanity and a new creation, bringing both Jew and Gentile together on equal footing (against most forms of dispensational theology). Second, we will grasp better something of the glory of our Triune God, who has planned, accomplished, and applied our redemption in and through our new covenant head, our Lord Jesus Christ, the builder and head of the church. Let us turn to five statements summarizing the rich and diverse biblical data that begin to unpack the fact that the church is God's new covenant community.

1. The Church as the New Covenant Community Is Part of the One People of God

From the outset, against some forms of dispensational theology, it is important to establish that there is only *one* people of God (the elect) across time. Much data could be given at this point, but most today do not dispute this fact. In the OT era, people were saved by grace through faith in the promises of God. The same is true in the new covenant era, except that the promises of God are now Christologically defined with greater clarity. This is because of the progress of revelation and the unfolding of God's redemptive plan through the biblical covenants (see Gen 15:6; Rom 4:9–12; Gal 3:6–9; Heb 11:8–19). "Promise" has given way to "fulfillment." Now one cannot know God in salvation apart from faith in Christ (John 5:23; Acts 4:12; cf. 1 John 2:23; 4:2–3). Furthermore, Scripture assumes a genuine continuity between OT and NT saints (see Rom 1:1–2, 11; Phil 3:3, 7, 9), and language applied to Israel as God's covenant people is also applied to the church because of her identification with Jesus the Messiah. The language of "assembly" (*qāhāl* and *ekklēsia*) is applied both to Israel and to the church (e.g., Deut 4:10; Josh 24:1, 25; Isa 2:2–4; Matt 16:18; 1 Cor 11:18; Heb 10:25). Other OT language describing Israel (e.g., Exod 19:6; Deut 32:15; 33:12; Isa 43:20–21; 44:2; Hos 1:6, 9; 2:1, 23) and OT texts applied to Israel (e.g., Jer 31:31–34; Hos

1:10–11) are now applied to the church (e.g., Rom 9:24–26; Gal 3:26–29; 1 Thess 1:4; cf. Eph 2:12, 19; 3:4–6; Heb 8:6–13; 1 Pet 2:9–10). All this serves as strong evidence for the claim that there is only *one* people of God throughout the ages.[25]

However, affirming this point does *not* necessitate that Israel and the church are basically the same kind of community. Through Jesus, the church (comprised of Jewish and Gentile believers) may be viewed as the Israel of God (Gal 6:16).[26] Yet there are important differences. The church is *new* both redemptive-historically and in regard to its *nature* and *structure*. In other words, the church, unlike the community of Israel, is not a "mixed" entity; instead, it is best viewed as a regenerate, believing community. The evidence for this assertion is first found *within the OT* as the prophets anticipated the coming of Christ and a new community that would differ from the previous one. It is also borne out in the NT description of the church. This observation leads to the next point as we think through OT anticipation and NT fulfillment.

2. The Church as the New Covenant Community Is Really "New"[27]

The most famous OT "new covenant" text is Jeremiah 31, but instruction regarding the new covenant is not limited to this text. Anticipation of it is also found throughout the prophets, especially in the language of "everlasting covenant" and the expectation of the coming of the new creation, the Spirit, and God's saving rule and reign among the nations. Within the OT, the new covenant is viewed as both national (Jer 31:36–40; 33:6–16; Ezek 36:24–38; 37:11–28) and international (Jer 33:9; Ezek 36:36; 37:28).

---

[25] For a detailed development of this point, see G. K. Beale, *A New Testament Biblical Theology* (Grand Rapids: Baker, 2011), 651–749. Also see, Edmund P. Clowney, *The Church* (Downers Grove: InterVarsity, 1995), 27–36.

[26] For a defense of this identification, see Beale, *A New Testament Biblical Theology*, 670–72, 719–24; see also Andreas Köstenberger, "The Identity of the *Israel tou theou* (Israel of God) in Galatians 6:16," *Faith and Mission* 19, no. 1 (2001): 3–24.

[27] The word "new" is taken from the important new covenant text found in Jer 31:31–34. There is much debate over the meaning of the word (Hb., *hadas*; LXX, *kainos*) and hence the "newness" of the new covenant. Some argue that the word only means "renewed" (e.g., Lam 3:22–23) and others argue that it means "new" in a qualitatively different sense (Exod 1:8; Deut 32:17; 1 Sam 6:7; Eccl 1:10). Ultimately, the "newness" of the new covenant must be contextually determined. On this debate see Dumbrell, *Covenant and Creation*, 175, and James R. White, "The Newness of the New Covenant: Part 1," *Reformed Baptist Theological Review* 1, no. 2 (2004), 144–52; Beale, *A New Testament Biblical Theology*, 727–49.

In fact, its scope is viewed as universal, especially in Isaiah (42:6; 49:6; 55:3–5; 56:4–8; 66:18–24). The Isaiah texts project the ultimate fulfillment of the divine promises in the new covenant onto an "ideal Israel," a community tied to the Servant of the Lord located in a rejuvenated new creation (65:17; 66:22). This ideal Israel picks up the promises to Abraham and is presented as the ultimate fulfillment of the covenants that God established with Adam, the patriarchs, the nation of Israel, and David's son (Isa 9:6–7; 11:1–10; Jer 23:5–6; 33:14–26; Ezek 34:23–24; 37:24–28) and hence fulfills all of God's promises.[28]

Although Jeremiah 31 is not the only new covenant text, it does nicely describe the *new* covenant community in speaking of its change in *structure* and *nature* from Israel of old. First, *structurally* speaking, vv. 29–34 anticipates massive changes in the arrival of the new covenant community, which becomes the underpinning for the NT teaching of the "priesthood of all believers." Under the old covenant, as D. A. Carson has noted, God dealt with his people in a mediated or tribal-representative way.[29] Despite remnant themes and an emphasis on individual believers, the OT pictures God working with his people as a "tribal" grouping whose knowledge of and relations with him were uniquely dependent on specially endowed leaders. Thus, the OT emphasizes God's Spirit being poured out, not on each believer but distinctively on prophets, priests, kings, and other designated leaders. Given this hierarchical structure of the covenant community, when these leaders did what was right, the entire nation benefited. However, when they did not, the entire nation suffered for their actions. But Jeremiah anticipates that this tribal-representative structure will change: "In those days, it will never again be said: The fathers have eaten sour grapes, and the children's teeth are set on edge. Rather, each will die for his own wrongdoing. Anyone who eats sour grapes—his own teeth will be set on edge" (31:29–30). As Carson observes:

> In short, Jeremiah understood that the new covenant would bring some dramatic changes. The tribal nature of the people of God

---

[28] For an in-depth defense of these points, see Gentry and Wellum, *Kingdom through Covenant*.

[29] See D. A. Carson, *Showing the Spirit* (Grand Rapids: Baker, 1996), 150–58; cf. id., "1–3 John," in *Commentary on the New Testament Use of the Old Testament*, ed. G. K. Beale and D. A. Carson (Grand Rapids: Baker, 2007), 1065; Beale, *New Testament Biblical Theology*, 733–37, refers to it as "democratization."

would end, and the new covenant would bring with it a new emphasis on the distribution of the knowledge of God down to the level of each member of the covenant community. Knowledge of God would no longer be mediated through specially endowed leaders, for *all* of God's covenant people would know him, from the least to the greatest. Jeremiah is not concerned to say there would be no teachers under the new covenant, but to remove from leaders that distinctive mediatorial role that made the knowledge of God among the people at large a secondary knowledge, a mediated knowledge.[30]

This does *not* deny that the new covenant is a mediated covenant in and through our Lord Jesus Christ, the antitype of all the previous covenant mediators. Yet, it does entail that the covenant community he mediates is not *structurally* the same as Israel. Those who come under his mediatorial rule include both believing Jews and Gentiles, and one enters this relationship not by physical birth, circumcision, or the Torah but through spiritual rebirth and faith. Only those in faith union with their covenant head are his family, and *all* of his family know him and have access to the Father through him. Another way of stating this is that under previous covenants the genealogical principle prevailed, that is, the relationship between the covenant mediator and his seed was *biological/physical* (e.g., Adam, Noah, Abraham, Israel, David), but now, in Christ, under his mediation, the relationship between Christ and his people is *spiritual*, i.e., born of the Spirit. Thus *all* those within the new covenant community *know* the Lord in contrast to the "mixed" nation of Israel. Jeremiah 31:34 states, "No longer will one teach his neighbor or his brother, saying: Know the LORD, for they will all know Me, from the least to the greatest of them."

Intimately related to this anticipated *structural* change is the OT promise of the Spirit and his empowering work in the new covenant era, first on the Messiah (Isa 11:1–3; 61:1) and then on Messiah's people (see

---

[30] Carson, *Showing the Spirit*, 152. It is clear from the context that the knowledge spoken of here is a salvific knowledge so that *all* within the covenant community savingly know God. See Dumbrell, *Covenant and Creation*, 177–78; Paul R. House, *Old Testament Theology* (Downers Grove: InterVarsity, 1998), 317–21; cf. Pratt, "Infant Baptism in the New Covenant," in Strawbridge, *The Case for Covenantal Infant Baptism*, 159–61.

Ezek 11:19–20; 36:25–27; Joel 2:28–32; see Num 11:27–29)—all evidence that God's kingdom has been inaugurated and that last days have dawned.[31] In terms of the latter, no longer will the Spirit merely empower leaders within the community for acts of leadership and service; instead, there will be a *universal* distribution of the Spirit (Joel 2:28–32; cf. Acts 2:1–36). God will pour out his Spirit on *all* within the covenant community, which is precisely what occurs (Acts 2; Eph 1:13–14). *All* will have the Spirit in the empowering and gifting sense. In fact, the NT presents the Spirit as the agent who not only gives us life but also enables us to follow God's decrees and to keep God's laws, thus making us covenant keepers and not covenant breakers. The role Israel was supposed to play is now fulfilled in us, the church, by the Spirit.[32] In the NT, John the Baptist announces this coming age (Matt 3:11); the work of Christ procures and secures it (John 7:39; 16:7; Acts 2:33); and Pentecost proclaims that it is now finally inaugurated. The new covenant era is intimately associated with the Spirit because *all* within the new covenant community are given the Spirit as the seal, down-payment, and guarantee of their promised inheritance. To be a member of the new covenant community, the church, is to be united to Christ and to have the Spirit. In fact, *not* to have the Spirit is *not* to have Christ or to be among his people (Rom 8:9).

Second, alongside the anticipated structural changes, Jeremiah 31 also signals a change in the *nature* of the covenant people. The new community will *not* be like the old (v. 32) due to the work of Christ, our representative head and substitute. What Israel could only foreshadow will become reality because of the great mediator of the new covenant. In him and what he inaugurates, *all* will know the Lord directly; *all* will have the law written on their hearts (which is another way of saying "circumcision of the heart" or *regeneration* [see Deut 10:16; 30:6; Jer 4:4; 9:25]). Significantly, *all* will know the full forgiveness of sin (31:33–34). We are *not* to conclude from this that no OT saint knew God, was regenerated, or was forgiven of his sins. Instead, under the old covenant

---

[31] See Max Turner, "Holy Spirit," in *NDBT*, ed. T. D. Alexander et al. (Downers Grove: InterVarsity, 2000), 551–58; David F. Wells, *God the Evangelist* (Grand Rapids: Eerdmans, 1987), 1–4; Geerhardus Vos, "The Eschatological Aspect of the Pauline Conception of the Spirit," in Gaffin, *Redemptive History and Biblical Interpretation*, 91–125; Hoekema, *The Bible and the Future*, 55–67.

[32] See Thomas R. Schreiner, *Romans*, BECNT (Grand Rapids: Baker, 1998), 395–468.

these realities were true for the remnant (the elect) within the nation in a typological, shadowy, and anticipatory way. The OT believer had access to God but mediately *through* the priesthood and tabernacle/temple structures; it was not immediate as it now is under the new covenant. In the same way, the elect under the old covenant were regenerate, but this was *not* true of the entire community. Even the elect did not experience the full new covenant realities of the Spirit's work, especially in regard to the indwelling of the Spirit.[33] The sins of the elect were forgiven, and they were declared just before God (see Gen 15:6), not solely on the basis of the sacrificial system but as they believed God's promises and looked forward to God's provision of a greater sacrifice to come (see Rom 3:21–26; Hebrews 9–10).

What Jeremiah 31 is signaling, then, is that under the new covenant what was true of the remnant (the elect) within Israel will now be true of the entire covenant community, and in greater ways. Unlike Israel of old, which *in its very makeup and nature* was a "mixed" group, the anticipation is that the entire people will be characterized by the following: the saving knowledge of God, regeneration, and the declaration of justification. Furthermore, the people will be characterized by these realities in a greater way. They will have direct access to God and will be empowered and indwelt by the Spirit. The verdict of justification is definitive due to Christ's once-for-all-time work.

From this discussion one must conclude that the OT itself anticipates that the future new covenant community, which the NT identifies as the church, will be both *new* and constituted by a believing, regenerate people in contrast to the "mixed" constitution of Israel.[34] Under the old covenant, within national Israel, there was a distinction between the physical/biological (not necessarily true believer) and spiritual/true believer seed of Abraham (see Rom 9:6). Both "seeds" received the covenant sign of circumcision, and both were viewed as full covenant members in the

---

[33] See James M. Hamilton Jr., *God's Indwelling Presence: The Holy Spirit in the Old and New Testaments* (Nashville: B&H, 2006).

[34] See House, *Old Testament Theology*, 317–21, who rightly observes that Jeremiah 31 provides a profound shift in the definition of the elect. In Israel one can think of the nation as consisting of those who believe and nonfaithful persons, a situation that creates the notion of a remnant. However, in the new covenant, the idea of the remnant or the elect within the community is not what Jeremiah anticipates. Also see James R. White, who makes this same point ("The Newness of the New Covenant: Part 2," *Reformed Baptist Theological Review* 2, no. 1 [2005]: 88).

national sense. Yet, it was only the believers—the remnant—who were "true Israel" in a salvation sense. As James White reminds us, because of the nature of the old covenant community, "For every David there were a dozen Ahabs; for every Josiah a legion of Manassehs. Unfaithfulness, the flaunting of God's law, the rejection of the role of truly being God's people, the rejection of His knowledge, and the experience of His wrath, were the *normative* experiences seen in the Old Covenant."[35] However, this is *not* what is anticipated for those under the new covenant.

What implications result for our understanding of the church? In contrast to some forms of dispensational theology, the NT explicitly applies the new covenant of Jeremiah 31 to the coming of Christ and his work *and* to the church (Luke 22:20; see 1 Cor 11:25; 2 Cor 3:7–18; Heb 8:1–13; 9:15–28). Whatever complex relationships exist between Israel and the church, Carson aptly concludes that at least there is a typological relationship. The promise is made to "the house of Israel" and "the house of Judah" (Jer 31:31) but applied in the NT to the church.[36]

The church is God's new covenant community; it is *new*, yet not ontologically so, given its relation to Israel of old. However, in contrast to covenant theology, one must say that the church is a regenerate, believing community now. It is not enough to say that the church, as God's new covenant community, is here now but only in an inaugurated form, so that presently it is a "mixed" community, like Israel, but in the future it will be a *regenerate* community.[37] Of course, we still await the not-yet aspects of our redemption, but the community is already constituted as a believing, justified people, born of the Spirit and united to Christ, our covenant head.

The perfect passive form of the verb in Heb 8:6—he "has . . . enacted"—emphasizes the completed action although the full ramifications may be future.[38] What this means, then, against a "mixed" view of the church,

---

[35] White, "The Newness of the New Covenant: Part 2," 88.

[36] D. A. Carson, "Evangelicals, Ecumenism, and the Church," in *Evangelical Affirmations*, ed. Kenneth S. Kantzer and Carl F. H. Henry (Grand Rapids: Zondervan, 1990), 361.

[37] See Pratt, who makes this argument, "Infant Baptism in the New Covenant," in Strawbridge, *The Case for Covenantal Infant Baptism*. For detailed and helpful critique of Pratt, see White, "The Newness of the New Covenant: Part 2," 97–103.

[38] White, "The Newness of the New Covenant: Part 1," 157, captures this point well when he argues, "There is nothing in the text that would lead us to believe that the full establishment of this covenant is yet future, for such would destroy the present

is that by definition, the locus of the covenant community and the locus of the redeemed is one, unlike Israel. One simply cannot understand the argument of Hebrews (let alone the NT) without arguing for the redemptive-historical *newness* of the church *and* massive changes in both her *structure* and *nature*. In Christ's coming, the new covenant and community is here; the Spirit has been poured out on the entire community (Acts 2); *all* those in the community know God in a direct and immediate fashion (Eph 2:18; Heb 10:19–25); and *all* are declared forgiven of their sins before God (Rom 8:1). Even though we still long for the consummated realities of what has already begun, those realities are present and lived out in the church, God's new covenant community.

3. The Church as the New Covenant Community Is God's New Assembly

The previous observations are further buttressed by how the church is described in the NT. For example, the church is viewed as an eschatological and "gathered" (*ekklēsia*) community.[39] The church is identified with the dawning of the kingdom and the ushering in of the "age to come," which arrived in Christ and which will be consummated in his return. As such, the church is part of the running tension between the "already" and the "not yet" in the NT. Her identity is not with "this present age" (which is passing away) but with the "age to come" (which has now arrived in the saving reign [kingdom] of Christ).[40] As a result of Christ's work, those who have placed their faith in him are now citizens of the new, heavenly Jerusalem (our final destination linked to the dawning of the new creation). In one sense this Jerusalem is still future but in a profound sense is already here.

---

apologetic concern of the author; likewise, he will complete his citation of Jer. 31 by asserting the obsolete nature of the first covenant, which leaves one to have to theorize, without textual basis, about some kind of intermediate covenantal state if one does not accept the full establishment of the New Covenant as seen in the term *nenomothetētai* ['has enacted']."

[39] See Carson, "Evangelicals, Ecumenism, and the Church," in Kantzer and Henry, *Evangelical Affirmations*, 363–67, as well as the helpful discussion in P. T. O'Brien, "Church," in *DPL*, 123–31; and Clowney, *The Church*, 27–33.

[40] For a thorough discussion of inaugurated eschatology and its application to the church see, Thomas R. Schreiner, *New Testament Theology* (Grand Rapids: Baker, 2008), 41–116, 675–754.

This is the point of Heb 12:18–29. In contrast with the Israelites who assembled at Sinai (vv. 18–21), as new covenant believers we have already gathered to meet God at the "heavenly" Jerusalem (vv. 22–24) associated with the dawning of the new creation.[41] As the church (see Col 1:18; Heb 12:22–24),[42]—those who now participate in the "age to come" that Jesus has won—we are beginning to enjoy by faith the privileges of that city still to come (Heb 13:14). We still await the consummation of the ages in Christ's return, but as the gathered people of God we already experience the realities of the end, though not yet in their fullness.

Three entailments result from these important biblical truths for our understanding of the church. The first pertains to the relationship between the local church and the eschatological, heavenly gathering. D. A. Carson spells out this relationship by first saying what the local church is *not*. He writes, "Each local church is not seen primarily as one member parallel to a lot of other member churches, together constituting one body, one church; nor is each local church seen as the body of Christ parallel to other earthly churches that are also the body of Christ—as if Christ had many bodies."[43] Rather, we should think of the relationship in this way: "Each church is the full manifestation in space and time of the one, true, heavenly, eschatological, new covenant church. Local churches should see themselves as outcroppings of heaven, analogies of 'the Jerusalem that is above,' indeed colonies of the new Jerusalem, providing on earth a corporate and visible expression of 'the glorious freedom of the children of God.'"[44]

---

[41] "You have already come" (*proseléluthate*) is in the perfect tense, which stresses the point that believers have come to their final destination even now starting with our conversion. In other words, we *already* participate in new covenant realities as the gathered people of God, even though we await the consummation of those realities. On this point see P. T. O'Brien, *The Letter to the Hebrews*, PNTC (Grand Rapids: Eerdmans, 2010), 482–85.

[42] In the NT, *ekklēsia* is used in the plural and singular. Both forms can be used for specifying local assemblies, as in "the church at Corinth" (1 Cor 1:2) or "the churches" of Galatia (Gal 1:22). But the singular form can also be used in reference to our participation in the heavenly, eschatological church, i.e., the *heavenly* Zion or the *new Jerusalem*, which is identified with the "age to come" and which is now here. In this latter sense, the language of *heavenly* or *new* Jerusalem is not a spatial image but an eschatological one, identifying the people of God with the eschatological realities that Jesus has won for us in his finished work. See, O'Brien, "Church," *DPL*, 123–31.

[43] Carson, "Evangelicals, Ecumenism, and the Church," in Kantzer and Henry, *Evangelical Affirmations*, 366.

[44] Ibid. Also see O'Brien, "Church," *DPL*, 123–31.

If so, then a second entailment follows. This understanding of the church presupposes something about her *nature*. Those who are members of the church are a *regenerate, believing* people. Why? Because to have already come to the new/heavenly Jerusalem and to have begun to participate in its realities is another way of saying that those in the church are, by definition, part of the new creation, members of the new covenant, and people already raised and seated with Christ in the heavenly realms (see Eph 2:5–6; Col 2:12–13; 3:3). But, as noted above, biblically speaking, this reality is only possible for those who have been born of the Spirit and united to Christ by faith.

As new covenant people we receive the benefits of Christ's work in only one way: individual repentance toward God and faith in Christ. In salvation we are transferred by God's grace and power from being "in Adam" to being "in Christ" with all the benefits of that union.[45] To be "in Christ" (and thus in the new covenant, a member of his *ekklesia*) means that one is a regenerate believer. The NT knows nothing of one who is "in Christ" who is not regenerate, effectually called by the Father, born of the Spirit, justified, holy, and awaiting glorification. That is why it is so difficult to think of the church as a "mixed" entity.

There is a third entailment. If this biblical and theological understanding of the church is basically right, then, as Carson notes, "The ancient contrast between the church visible and the church invisible, a contrast that has nurtured not a little ecclesiology, is either fundamentally mistaken, or at best of marginal importance."[46] Why? Because the NT views the church as a *heavenly* (tied to the "age to come" and the new creation, not "in Adam" but "in Christ") and *spiritual* community (born of and empowered by the Spirit in faith union with Christ). She lives her life out now while she awaits the consummation, literally "the outcropping of the heavenly assembly gathered in the Jerusalem that is above,"[47] which assumes a regenerate people. The church is not viewed as a "visible" community in the sense that it is comprised of believers and unbelievers simultaneously until the end, like Israel of old (with the "invisible" church

---

[45] On the reality of union with Christ and all that it entails, see Sinclair Ferguson, *Holy Spirit* (Downers Grove: InterVarsity, 1996), 93–138; and Wayne Grudem, *Systematic Theology* (Grand Rapids: Zondervan, 1994), 840–50.

[46] Carson, "Evangelicals, Ecumenism, and the Church," in Kantzer and Henry, *Evangelical Affirmations*, 367.

[47] Ibid., 371.

as the true, believing, regenerate community of all ages). It may be true that the church is universal and "invisible" because there is only one people of God throughout the ages. But it is not the case that the "visible," local church is *constituted* in its very nature by a mixture of believers and unbelievers.

Instead, the NT church, unlike Israel under the old covenant, is *constituted* by those who profess that they have been transferred from death to life, from being "in Adam" to now "in Christ." They have become participants in the new creation bound up with the inauguration of the entire new covenant age. Surely not all those who profess faith in Christ are regenerate, and some admitted to membership in the church later show themselves not to have belonged. In the words of the apostle John, "If they had belonged to us, they would have remained with us. However, they went out so that it might be made clear that none of them belongs to us" (1 John 2:19). The NT knows of false professions and spurious conversions; in fact, the Scripture exhorts us to examine ourselves (2 Pet 1:10). Yet the NT also assures us that all those united to Christ and born of the Spirit will be preserved to the end. This contrasts greatly with those who affirm a "mixed" view of the church or assert that the visible church is constituted by believers and unbelievers until the end of the age. The NT may speak of the visible local church but not in this way. It is mistaken to think that the NT church is constituted the same as Israel of old.

4. The Church as the New Covenant Community Is God's New Temple

The tabernacle/temple theme looms large across the biblical covenants, especially under the old covenant.[48] At the heart of the covenant relationship is the Triune God dwelling with his people and vice versa. The tabernacle/temple was the means by which God in his holiness dwelt among a sinful people without destroying them. It was also the means by which atonement was made for the covenant people's sin, through the mediation of the priesthood and the sacrificial system.

When Jerusalem became the capital under David, and Solomon later constructed the temple, God's dwelling with his people took on a note of permanency. God is omnipresent, but the temple was the means by which

---

[48] For a development of the temple theme in Scripture, see G. K. Beale, *The Temple and the Church's Mission: A Biblical Theology of the Dwelling Place of God*, NSBT (Downers Grove: InterVarsity, 2004); R. J. McKelvey, "Temple," in *NDBT,* 806–11.

he manifested his unique covenantal presence among his people. In fact, God's presence in the midst of the nation distinguished Israel from all other nations (Exod 33:15–16). With the construction of the temple, the nation was now able to assemble annually in Jerusalem and go to the place where God dwelt (Pss 42:2; 63:2; 65:1–2). Worship was centered in a place, and the covenant community was able to meet with God at the temple though their interactions with him were mediated through the priests.

When the nation went into exile and the temple was destroyed, it was as if the entire covenant had come to an end. But in the midst of God's judgment on the nation, the prophets held out hope. They reminded the people that God's presence was not limited to a place; the temple itself was a type and pattern of something greater (see Exod 25:40; cf. Ezek 11:22–23; Heb 8:3–5). The hope for Israel was in God himself, who would act to keep his promises, to save his people, and ultimately to make all things new by definitively dealing with human sin through a new and better covenant (Isa 2:2–4; 53–55; Ezekiel 34, 36–37; Jer 31:31–34; see Hebrews 8). As noted above, in that new covenant, the Lord himself through the Davidic son would come; he would be present among his people as Immanuel; he would be anointed with the Spirit and would also pour out the Spirit on his people (Psalm 110; Isa 7:14; 11:1–5; 61:1–3; Joel 2:28–32; cf. Acts 2). He would secure everything necessary for our redemption, supremely associated with the forgiveness of sin and the inauguration of the new creation (Isaiah 53; 61:1–3; 65:17–25; Jer 31:34).

As we move from OT to NT, our Lord Jesus Christ fulfills all the hopes and expectations of the prophets in at least two important ways.[49] First, he is the fulfillment and replacement of the temple (John 1:14–18; 2:19–22).[50] As the Lord (who is also David's greater Son and the great High Priest of the new covenant [see Hebrews 5–7]), he is the very dwelling of God with us (Matt 1:23; John 1:14). In his life, death, and resurrection he ends the purpose and function of the earthly temple (Matt 27:51; Heb 9:1–10:18). Second, as the temple-builder and Lord of the house (3:1–6), Jesus now builds a people for himself, namely the church, from every nation, tribe, and tongue (Matt 16:18; Eph 2:11–22; see Rev 5:9–10). By God's grace, we his people become his house/temple by being transferred

---

[49] Edmund Clowney, "The Final Temple," *WTJ* 35 (1972–73): 156–89.
[50] See Paul M. Hoskins, *Jesus as the Fulfillment of the Temple in the Gospel of John* (Eugene: Wipf and Stock, 2007).

from one covenant head to another, from Adam to Christ. By the agency of the Spirit (who not only regenerates us but now indwells us, individually as Christians and corporately as Christ's church), we now have become God's *new* temple (1 Cor 3:16–17; 6:19; 2 Cor 6:16; Eph 2:21; Heb 3:6; 1 Pet 2:5). Now that Christ has come, no longer is the temple associated with a specific building in a particular place (Jerusalem); instead, the temple is identified with a person (the Lord Jesus) and then by virtue of our relationship to him with us, his people (the church, his body).[51] In Christ, we are his temple-people, who now have direct access to the Father through him by the Spirit (Eph 2:18; Heb 4:14–16; 10:19–22).

What is the significance of this truth for the church? First, to describe the individual Christian and the corporate people of God as his *new* temple highlights something of the *newness*, superiority, and glory of the new covenant. Nowhere in the OT is Israel as a people described as the temple of God in which God's Spirit dwells. Instead, Israel as a nation had a physical temple in their midst. They could travel to it, and their worship centered around it. God condescended to dwell in it. But never was Israel overtly described as God's temple. On the other hand, the church experiences a *greater* reality than Israel ever knew, precisely because Jesus has come and has brought all the types and shadows of the OT to their God-ordained end. In this important way, the church is something *new* in God's redemptive plan not in the ontological sense (against dispensational theology) but redemptive-historically. God's plan of salvation has now reached its fulfillment in Christ.

Second, one can only make sense of the individual Christian and the church being described as God's new temple if the church is constituted by a *regenerate, believing* people and not a "mixed" body (against covenant theology). Why? This description is true only of people brought from death

---

[51] The description of the church as God's new temple—because of our union with Christ, the true temple and our covenantal head, and indwelt by the Spirit—is quite close to another NT description of the church as "the body of Christ." Biblically and theologically, it is best to understand the body imagery in covenantal terms: Christ is our representative head and we are his body, i.e., his covenantal people. Headship has more to do with representation, primacy, and authority than merely that Christ is the top member of the body. This is clear from the fact that when Paul, for example, speaks of the members of the body, he includes ear, eye, and nose—technically all parts of the head (1 Cor 12:16–21). This is also borne out in the fact that Paul thinks of the church as a body in terms of one whole man in Christ, not merely in terms of one part of the body in relation to other parts.

to life by the call of the Father and the new birth of the Spirit. They have been united to Christ by faith, a union that is permanent and secure (Rom 8:28–39; Eph 1:3–14). The NT knows nothing of unbelievers described in this way—though it does describe those who profess faith but, in the end, demonstrate (by their not persevering in the faith) that they were never truly God's people in the first place (1 John 2:19; see Col 1:21–23; Heb 3:6, 14).

5. The Church as the New Covenant Community Is God's New Humanity

The description of the church as the "new man" or the "new humanity" is drawn from the important ecclesiological text Eph 2:11–22.[52] For our purposes, this title nicely captures something of the *continuity* and *discontinuity* of the church with Israel. It is linked with the new creation and emphasizes the church's newness in God's unfolding plan as everything is brought to fulfillment and culmination in Christ (1:9–10).

On the one hand, in regard to the *continuity* of the church with Israel, Paul teaches that Gentile Christians were once excluded from "the citizenship of Israel," "foreigners to the covenants of promise," and "with no hope and without God in the world" (2:11–12). But now, in Messiah Jesus, everything has changed. In Christ, because of God's sovereign grace and according to his eternal plan (3:1–13), Gentiles have been brought near. They are now recipients of God's promises, given first to Adam and then through Abraham to the nation of Israel. In Christ and in his reconciling cross, the law covenant has been brought to fulfillment and thus torn down. The result is the creation of the church so that both Jews and Gentiles together now have peace with the Triune God and covenantal access to him (2:14–18).[53] Incredibly, believing Gentiles have become (alongside believing Jews) "fellow citizens with the saints, and members of God's household, built on the foundation of the apostles and prophets, with Christ Jesus Himself as the cornerstone" (vv. 19–20). Together, as God's "one new man" (v. 15), they are being built as a new temple "for God's dwelling in the Spirit" (v. 22).

---

[52] For helpful exegetical treatments of this text, see O'Brien, *Ephesians*, 182–221; Stott, *Ephesians*, 89–112.

[53] It is best to view "the law consisting of commands and expressed in regulations" (Eph 2:15) as a reference to the old covenant as a whole. See O'Brien, *Ephesians*, 193–201.

On the other hand, in the reconciling work of Messiah Jesus, God's Son, massive *discontinuity* also is at work. The new community formed is *not* simply an extension of Israel. It is related to Israel and the covenants of promise, but it is a "new humanity," part of the dawning of the "new creation" associated in OT expectation with the inauguration of the "age to come." It is *not* merely some kind of amalgam made out of the best elements of Israel and the Gentiles. It is a *new* creation, a third entity that is neither Jewish nor Gentile but Christian (see 1 Cor 9:19–23). It is *not* merely a phase in God's redemptive plan but is what was always anticipated. Now that Christ has come and by virtue of his saving work, this new entity has been created. In this way, the "new humanity" transcends the two old entities, even though unbelieving Israel and disobedient Gentiles continue to exist. Believing Gentiles are now able to receive the blessings of God and have equal standing with believing Jews without having to submit to the old covenant (circumcision, food laws, and so on). In Christ the old covenant has come to its fulfillment and the "new humanity" is identified with the inauguration of a new and better covenant.

Of course, what makes all this possible is Messiah Jesus. One cannot understand the *identity* and *nature* of the church apart from him, and it is viewing the church in relationship to him that explains the *newness* of the people of God. Dispensational theology views Israel and the church as distinct without sufficiently accounting for Jesus as the last Adam and true Israel. He fulfills the role of both Israel and Adam, thus creating not an ontologically distinct people but *"one* new man." Covenant theology tends to move from Israel to the church too quickly without sufficiently accounting for the differences between the two communities due to the person and work of Christ. As we progress across redemptive history, we move from type to antitype, from covenant heads such as Adam, Noah, Abraham, Moses/Israel, and David to Christ. Our Lord's work brings with it massive change and thus *discontinuity.* The church is not simply the replacement of Israel—a kind of renewed instance of it. Because of her identification with Christ, the head of the new covenant and the new creation, she is the "one *new* man." This is why the church is identified with the "age to come" and not with the structures of the old era. This is why the church is viewed as the *new* assembly, the *new* temple, born, empowered, and indwelt by the Spirit. This is why the church must be viewed not as a "mixed" entity but as a regenerate, believing community.

Concluding Reflections

These five ways of describing the church ground a believer's view of her, which is what Baptist theology has affirmed; moreover, it does so by not aligning completely with either the biblical-theological systems of dispensational or covenant theology. To understand the identity and nature of the church, we must view her in light of Jesus' person and work. For it is in Messiah Jesus that all the biblical covenants reach their fulfillment. In him, as last Adam and true Israel, all God's purposes for creation are realized, including his purposes for Israel. The new covenant can be applied to the church in the NT even though in Jeremiah it is to the "house of Israel" (31:33) because in Christ (the antitype of Israel) all God's promises are yes and amen. Furthermore, we, as the church—God's *new* assembly, people, and temple—receive all the benefits of his glorious, effective, and triumphant work by virtue of our faith union with him. Thus, the NT views the church as a regenerate people because only those who truly are in faith union with Christ, born of his Spirit, and declared just, are his. Further, the NT does not view the church as consisting of some who are in faith union with Christ and others who are not, unless one drastically alters the NT teaching on what it means to be in union with him.

Much more needs to be said, but these are first steps toward a theology of the church that moves us beyond a mere ecclesiology and provides underpinning for a Baptist ecclesiology. These steps will not persuade everyone, especially my valued dispensational and covenant theology brothers and sisters in Christ. Yet I believe that this best explains the story line of Scripture, the covenantal relationship between Israel and the church, and the biblical data in regard to the identity and nature of the church.

As I conclude, I want to address one significant challenge that covenant theology raises in defending a "mixed" view of the church, namely the warning and apostasy passages of Scripture (e.g., Heb 6:4–6; 10:26–39). Their argument is that the warning texts demonstrate that the visible church is a "mixed" community, just like Israel of old. Thus, it is possible for a person to be a member of the new covenant community but then, sadly, to depart from the faith. Such departure demonstrates that a person was never a regenerate believer even though he was externally a member of the church.[54] I can only respond briefly to this challenge, but there are three problems with this view.

---

[54] See e.g., Wilson, *To a Thousand Generations*, 34; Strawbridge, "Introduction," in *The Case for Covenantal Infant Baptism*, 4–5.

First, the "mixed" community interpretation of the warning passages assumes that the nature of Israel and the church is basically the same, but this is precisely what needs to be demonstrated. In order for their argument to carry any weight, they must first prove that the nature of the covenant communities is essentially the same, but I have already given reasons to think otherwise. As one thinks through the relationship between the old and new covenants, it is difficult to view Israel and the church as structurally and by nature the same.

Second, this interpretation misses the biblical teaching regarding the nature of the new covenant church. Some assert that because the NT speaks of the possibility of apostasy, and, sadly, we witness it in our daily experience, this demonstrates that the church is a mixed community like Israel. The problem is that this goes against what the OT anticipates regarding the nature of the new covenant community and what the NT confirms. One must carefully distinguish between the *fact* of apostasy taking place and the *status* of the one who commits it. No one disputes the fact that apostasy takes place in the new covenant age. What is at dispute is the status of those apostates. Should they be viewed as "new covenant breakers" (assuming they were once full covenant members) or as those who *professed* faith, who identified with the church but who, by their rejection of the gospel, demonstrated that they were never one with us (1 John 2:19)? I am convinced the NT teaches the latter, but ultimately this conviction requires a full analysis of the biblical covenants. In my view, when one who professed Christ walks away never to return, we reevaluate the person's former profession and thus their covenant status, and we conclude that they were not of us. But note that this situation is *not* like unbelievers under the old covenant. The old covenant by its very nature allowed for a mixed group. R. Fowler White hits the mark when he asserts: "Unlike apostates from the Mosaic covenant (Heb 3:7–11, 16–19) who had heard God say of them that he had (fore)known them in their mediatorial forebears (cf. Deut 4:37; 7:6–8; 10:15), apostates from the Messianic covenant will hear the Lord of the covenant say to them, 'I never knew you' (see Matt 7:23; cf. 2 Tim 2:17–19)."[55]

With few exceptions, one was under the old covenant because of physical/biological relationships that did not assume regeneration and

---

[55] R. F. White, "The Last Adam and His Seed: An Exercise in Theological Preemption," *TJ* n.s. 6, no. 1 (1985): 72n19.

saving faith. But new covenant members are those who are "in Christ" and all that it entails.

In addition, often the charge brought against a regenerate view of the church is that it would require us to have infallible knowledge regarding someone's regeneration. This is incorrect. No doubt, the church has made many mistakes in this regard. However, we receive people into the church on the basis of their profession that they have trusted in Christ. This is quite different than the situation under the old covenant where many within that covenant did not profess faith toward God. Trying to discern true saving faith is a human epistemological problem, and we do our best to discern whether one's profession of faith is genuine. But this is a far cry from thinking that people who do not profess, particularly infants who are baptized, are new covenant members in faith union with Christ.

Third, the "mixed" community interpretation of these texts is a possible reading. But in light of a better way to understand the relations between the biblical covenants, the nature of the new covenant community, and what it means for someone to be in union with Christ, there are other legitimate ways of reading these texts. In my view, these do better justice to all the scriptural data.[56]

Mere ecclesiology is not enough. The church is too central to our Lord's saving work and all of our Triune God's redemptive purposes to be neglected. With conviction, joy, and commitment, we must confess and live out the reality of the church as God's regenerate, believing new covenant people, graciously called by the Father, born of the Spirit, and effectively brought into faith union with our new covenant mediator and head, our Lord Jesus Christ. May we see in our day a renewed love for the church, knowing that it is impossible to love the Lord of the church without also loving and committing ourselves anew to guarding, leading, and shepherding "the church of God, which He purchased with His own blood" (Acts 20:28).

---

[56] See Thomas R. Schreiner and Ardel B. Caneday, *The Race Set Before Us* (Downers Grove: InterVarsity, 2001); and Thomas R. Schreiner, *Run to Win the Prize: Perseverance in the New Testament* (Wheaton: Crossway, 2010).

CHAPTER 8

The Church and God's Glory

Christopher W. Morgan

We've all had the experience of going to the doctor and being told to take a pill for what ails us. It seems too small, too simple to be effective, but amazingly, once we toss back a dose or two, the pain is relieved, the infection is fought, and the full-capacity functioning resurfaces once more. Behind that pill is years of research, lots of biochemical brainwork done by guys so nerdy they're denied interaction with normal people, extensive clinical trials, failures and redesigns, hundreds of millions of dollars, and proven success. In short, concealed in that innocent-looking solution is the power to change everything.[1]

To those of us who are a part of it, the church often seems like that pill—too ordinary to be effective, too common to be of cosmic significance. But behind the church stands infinitely more than scientific research and investment funds; behind the church stands God himself. Because God has linked his ultimate end, eternal plan, historical acts,

---

[1] Henry Cloud, "Foreword," in Bill Hybels, *Axiom: Powerful Leadership Proverbs* (Grand Rapids: Zondervan, 2008), 9.

and the display of his covenant presence to the church, it is anything but common.

But how does the church fit into God's larger purposes? What is its role in glorifying him? The questions are overwhelming, as is the enormous amount of biblical data related to them. Because of this, we will frame the answers with Paul's teachings to the Ephesians. Using the letter's vast portrait of the church in God's purposes, we will lay out six major truths related to the church. Each builds upon the previous ones and helps define the church's identity.

1. God's Ultimate End Is His Glory

From the outset of Ephesians, Paul establishes that God's ultimate end is his glory. The apostle praises God for his comprehensive blessings of salvation and highlights the work of the Trinity in salvation (1:3–14). He also incorporates a refrain: to the praise of the glory of his grace (v. 6), to the praise of his glory (v. 12), and to the praise of his glory (v. 14). Paul's point is unmistakable: the ultimate end of God's work in human lives is not our salvation, as important as that is. God chose, adopted, redeemed, united, gave an inheritance to, and sealed us to glorify himself.

Paul continues this emphasis in Ephesians 2. Because of his love and grace, God makes us alive in Christ. Ephesians 2:7 explains the purpose of this act: "So that in the coming ages He might display the immeasurable riches of His grace in [His] kindness to us in Christ Jesus."

That God's glory is his ultimate end is also clear in Ephesians 3:

> This grace was given to me—the least of all the saints!—to proclaim to the Gentiles the incalculable riches of the Messiah, and to shed light for all about the administration of the mystery hidden for ages in God who created all things. This is so that God's multi-faceted wisdom may now be made known through the church to the rulers and authorities in the heavens. (vv. 8–10)

Here Paul stresses that his salvation, apostolic calling, and mission to the Gentiles have as their ultimate end the glorious display of God and his wisdom.

The doxology[2] in Eph 3:20–21 continues this theme: "Now to Him who is able to do above and beyond all that we ask or think—according to the power that works in you—to Him be glory in the church and in Christ Jesus to all generations, forever and ever. Amen." The prayer and praise of the church is that God will receive glory for all eternity.

Thus, God's glory is his ultimate end.[3] But what does this mean? Ephesians offers two explanations. First, God acts in order to receive worship and praise from his creation, especially his people (1:6, 12, 14). Second, God acts to display himself throughout creation. He displays his love, mercy, grace, kindness, creative work, and wisdom (2:4–10; 3:8–10). As he displays himself, he communicates his greatness and fullness and thereby glorifies himself. As we will see, this understanding of God's glory enables us to grasp the nature of the church.

Ephesians also reminds us of a pitfall in understanding the glory of God: that God acts with his glory as his ultimate end does not imply that other ends are excluded. Those ends remain important and should not be marginalized. For example, if someone asks, "Why does God save us?" we can rightly reply, "For his glory" (1:3–14; 2:1–10; 3:8–10).

But the Bible puts forward additional reasons. That another motive in saving us is God's love is set forth powerfully and regularly. Ephesians 1:3–6 is instructive:

> Blessed be the God and Father of our Lord Jesus Christ, who has blessed us with every spiritual blessing in the heavens, in Christ; for He chose us in Him, before the foundation of the world, to be holy and blameless in His sight. *In love* He predestined us to be adopted through Jesus Christ for Himself, according to His favor and will, to the praise of His glorious grace that He favored us with in the Beloved. [italics added][4]

---

[2] Most doxologies highlight God's glory. For example, Rom 16:27 proclaims: "To the only wise God be glory forevermore through Jesus Christ" (ESV). See also Rom 11:36; Gal 1:5; Phil 4:20; 2 Tim 4:18; Jude 24–25; Rev 1:5–6. Note also that some doxologies are directed toward Christ: Heb 13:21; 2 Pet 3:18.

[3] God's glory is the goal of creation; the exodus; Israel; Jesus' ministry, life, death, resurrection, and reign; our salvation; the church; the consummation; and all of salvation history. See Jonathan Edwards, "The End for Which God Created the World," in *God's Passion for His Glory*, ed. John Piper (Wheaton: Crossway, 1998), 125–36.

[4] Note the same emphasis in Deuteronomy 7.

Notice also Eph 2:4–7:

> But God, who *is abundant in mercy, because of His great love that*
> *He had for us,* made us alive with the Messiah even though we
> were dead in trespasses. By grace you are saved! He also raised us
> up with Him and seated us with Him in the heavens, in Christ
> Jesus, so that in the coming ages He might display the immeasur-
> able riches of His grace in [His] kindness to us in Christ Jesus.
> [italics added]

The same passages in Ephesians that teach God acts for his glory also
emphasize that God acts out of a genuine love for us. So our conviction
that God acts with glory as his ultimate end must be linked to our
recognition that God acts out of love for our good.

Other passages highlight this as well. John 3:16 states, "For God
loved the world in this way: He gave . . ." (see 1 John 4:9–10). Titus
3:4–7 ties our salvation to God's mercy. Romans 8:28 makes it clear that
redemptive history achieves good for God's people.

Exodus is noteworthy too. Why did God redeem his people from
slavery in Egypt? One might quickly reply, "For his glory." Certainly that
is correct, but other concerns also played a part. The book presents God's
multifaceted reasons for deliverance: to show love for his oppressed people
(3–4); to express faithfulness to the covenant promises made to Abraham,
Isaac, and Jacob (3:15; 4:5; 6:8; 32:13; 34:6); to permit Israel to serve him
(4:23); to demonstrate that he is the covenant Lord (6:7; 10:2; 13:1); to
give his people the Promised Land (6:8); to display his sovereignty to the
Egyptians (5:2; 7:5; 14:3–4, 15–18); to teach Pharaoh that he (God) is
incomparable (7:17; 8:10–18); to display his power and to proclaim his name
in all the earth (9:16); to pass down a heritage to successive generations of
Israelites (10:1–2); to multiply his wonders (11:9); to get glory over Pharaoh
and his army (14:3–18); and to benefit Israel (18:8). These multiple ends
do not detract from God's glory but highlight it. Indeed, in the exodus
God displays his love, covenant faithfulness, jealously, providence, and
power through his wonders, salvation, and judgment. In doing so, he
communicates himself and thus glorifies himself.

Understanding this truth is significant, as it helps us address a
common question concerning God's glory: "If God seeks his own glory
above all things, does this mean that he is selfish? After all, if we seek our
own glory, we are deemed selfish." The standard answer to that line of

questioning is that God is the ultimate being and the highest end, and we are not. Good behavior seeks the highest end, so God's making himself his own ultimate end is fitting. If we treat ourselves as the highest end, we act wrongly because we are not the highest end. That argument is valid, but it ignores God's genuine desire for the good of his creatures and fails to show how God's love and his glory are linked. A better answer is to stress that God saves us out of love, displays his kindness toward us for all eternity, and is glorified by putting his greatness, goodness, and fullness on display. God is self-giving and self-exalting, saving us for our good and for his glory. He gives himself to us and acts on our behalf, which simultaneously meets our needs and demonstrates his sufficiency. As we will see, this is crucial for our theology of the church.[5]

2. God's Ultimate End Generates His Eternal Plan

God's glory as his ultimate end is linked to his eternal plan. It both drives the plan and is its goal. Ephesians articulates this in multiple ways:

> For He chose us in Him, before the foundation of the world, to be holy and blameless in His sight. In love He predestined us to be adopted through Jesus Christ for Himself, according to His favor and will. (1:4–5)

> He made known to us the mystery of His will, according to His good pleasure that He planned in Him for the administration of the days of fulfillment—to bring everything together in the Messiah, both things in heaven and things on earth in Him. In Him we were also made His inheritance, predestined according to the purpose of the One who works out everything in agreement with the decision of His will. (1:9–11)

> The mystery was made known to me by revelation, as I have briefly written above. By reading this you are able to understand my insight about the mystery of the Messiah. This was not made known to people in other generations as it is now revealed to His

---

[5] For more on how God's self-giving and self-exalting cohere, especially in the mutual glorification of the persons of the Trinity, see Christopher W. Morgan, "Toward a Theology of the Glory of God," in *The Glory of God*, ed. Christopher W. Morgan and Robert A. Peterson, Theology in Community 2 (Wheaton: Crossway, 2010), 175–87.

holy apostles and prophets by the Spirit: the Gentiles are co-heirs, members of the same body, and partners of the promise in Christ Jesus through the gospel. I was made a servant of this [gospel] by the gift of God's grace that was given to me by the working of His power.

This grace was given to me—the least of all the saints!—to proclaim to the Gentiles the incalculable riches of the Messiah, and to shed light for all about the administration of the mystery hidden for ages in God who created all things. This is so that God's multi-faceted wisdom may now be made known through the church to the rulers and authorities in the heavens. This is according to the purpose of the ages, which He made in the Messiah, Jesus our Lord. (3:3–11)

So what is God's plan? From Eph 1:4–5 we find that it is linked to his choice of his people, his election. God's election is the first of many blessings related to our salvation, including our adoption, inheritance, and sealing. Note also that God's election is tied to our union with Christ. And because God chose us before the foundation of the world, election is eternal. Further, God elects us according to his own free and gracious will and out of his love. This election is not only unto salvation in general but also unto holiness, blamelessness, and our adoption into his family. God's election of us and the corresponding blessings of our salvation are all for the praise of his glory (1:6, 12, 14). Thus, God's plan encompasses the whole of our salvation: his election of his people from eternity, his accomplishment of our salvation through union with Christ, his blessings in the present, and the praise of his glory for all eternity.

According to 1:9–11, God's plan is also linked to the "mystery." This mystery is rooted in God's sovereign and effective will, revealed in the gospel, set forth in Christ, and administered in the fullness of time and includes our being made God's inheritance. The essence of God's plan is "to bring everything together in the Messiah, both things in heaven and things on earth in Him." Notice that "everything" is specified as "things in heaven and things on earth." This is comprehensive language for an eschatological uniting of the cosmos in Christ (see 2 Cor 5:14–21; Col 1:15–20). Peter O'Brien explains: "The emphasis now is on a universe that is centered and reunited in Christ. The mystery which God has graciously made known refers to the summing up and bringing together of the fragmented and alienated elements of the universe ('all things') in Christ as the focal point."[6]

Ephesians 3:3–12 discloses that God's plan came to the apostles and prophets through the Spirit's revelation, focused Paul's ministry, was hidden for ages, was administered at the intended time, was realized in Christ, and inspires our faith (see Col 1:21–29). Called "the purpose of the ages" (Eph 3:11) or "the eternal purpose" (ESV), God's plan centers on the salvation of the Gentiles and their full inclusion into the people of God. As much as the Jews, believing Gentiles share in adoption, are fully incorporated into the people of God, and are partners of the promise in Christ Jesus through the gospel (see 2:11–22).

God's eternal plan encompasses our salvation (1:4–6), the creation of the church as one new people (2:11–22; 3:3–12), and the ultimate reconciliation of the cosmos (1:9–11; 3:9–11). It is personal, corporate, and cosmic. This has massive implications for the church, as we will see.

Why did God devise this plan? That we do not fully know the reasons is evident from language like "according to His favor and will" (1:5) and "according to His good pleasure" (v. 9). But we do know the biblical story and, therefore, a fraction of the answer.

The biblical story begins with God creating everything in a way that pleases him and benefits his creatures (Genesis 1–2). The creation account underscores the goodness of God and the goodness of his creation, using the refrain "And God saw that it was good" (1:4, 10, 12, 18, 21, 25). Indeed, Genesis records that after personally creating Adam in his image, "God saw all that He had made, and it was very good" (1:31). By creating humanity in his image, God distinguishes us from the rest of creation and establishes a Creator-creature distinction. Genesis 1–2 depicts all this as good, as Adam

---

[6] See Peter T. O'Brien, *The Letter to the Ephesians*, PNTC (Grand Rapids: Eerdmans, 1999), 112–13. He adds, "Chrys Caragounis claims that as Paul proceeds to amplify and explain throughout the letter the meaning of bringing all things together, he concentrates on the two main representatives of these spheres, namely, the powers representing 'the things in heaven,' and the church, (particularly the unity of Jews and Gentiles in the body of Christ) representing 'the things on earth.' He further suggests that the two obstacles which need to be overcome before the divine purpose of bringing everything into unity with Christ can be fulfilled are: (a) the rebellion of the powers, and (b) the alienation of Jews from Gentiles (2:11–22, as well as the estrangement of both from God, 2:16). Much of the rest of Ephesians is given over to explaining, with reference to each of these two spheres, the steps in the process that God has taken in order to achieve this supreme goal" (112–13).

and Eve are blessed by an unhindered relationship with God, intimate enjoyment of each other, and delegated authority over creation.

Only one prohibition is set forth, but, sadly, it is violated. Rather than submitting to God and finding their pleasure in him, Adam and Eve want complete autonomy. They are proud and want to be godlike, rebelling against their good covenant Lord. Genesis 3:6 records the fall in rapid fashion: "she saw," "she took," "she ate," "she gave," culminating in "he ate." The couple immediately feels shame, realizing they are naked (v. 7), estranged from God (vv. 8–10), and fearful (vv. 9–10). They are also alienated from each other, as the woman blames the serpent and the man blames the woman and God (vv. 10–13). Pain, sorrow, and disruption of their relationship ensue (vv. 15–19). Even worse, the couple is banished from Eden and God's glorious presence (vv. 22–24). In sum, through their disobedience, sin entered the world and disrupted their relationship to God, to each other, and to creation.

Paul informs us that Adam's sin, while personal and historical, also plunged all humanity into sin (Rom 5:12–21). Returning to Ephesians, we find that Paul graphically depicts the human condition apart from Christ (2:1–3). We are spiritually dead, separated from the life of God. Our lives are characterized by sin and reflect our inner sinful nature, our sinful environment, and our evil opponent. All of us were by nature children of wrath. Sin is primarily understood vertically: we are fundamentally anti-God and have radically disordered our relationship to God. But sin also has horizontal ramifications. It disorders our relationships to others. One example of this is the division of Jews and Gentiles (2:11–22). Prior to the revelation of the mystery of the gospel, the Gentiles were largely excluded from being citizens of God's nation, Israel. They were foreigners to God's covenant of promise, without hope, and without the true and living God.

Ephesians also points to the cosmic disorder resulting from sin. While Paul does not use the language of creation groaning and awaiting redemption as he does in Rom 8:18–30, the idea of the cosmos awaiting final reconciliation is clearly present. Ephesians 1:9–11 reveals this cosmic concern, as do passages that speak of our blessings in Christ in the heavenlies (v. 3; 2:6), the summing up of all things in Christ (1:9–10), Christ's ultimate authority and victory over the powers (1:19–22), the influence of the prince of the power of the air (2:1–3), the display of God's wisdom to the powers (3:9–11), the evil days (5:16), and especially the cosmic battle against evil (6:10–20).

Intent on bringing peace out of this disorder, God is on a mission of reconciliation, forming a "new creation," making all things new (2:10). Whereas sin brought disorder and division, God's eternal plan for reconciliation brings peace and unity and addresses these personal, community, and cosmic consequences of the fall. His plan is to bring all things together in Christ (1:9–10), uniting people to himself, uniting people to one another, and even uniting the cosmos in Christ. And as we will see, the church's identity and purpose are shaped by this plan.

3. God Accomplishes This Eternal Plan of Reconciliation in History through Christ and His Saving Work

God's ultimate end of his glory sets in motion his eternal plan of cosmic reconciliation. God accomplishes his eternal plan that encompasses our salvation (1:4–6), the creation of the church as one new people (2:11–22; 3:3–12), and the ultimate reconciliation of the cosmos (1:9–11; 3:9–11) through Christ and his saving work.[7]

Ephesians displays this frequently:

> In Him we have redemption through His blood, the forgiveness of our trespasses, according to the riches of His grace. (1:7)

> He demonstrated [this power] in the Messiah by raising Him from the dead and seating Him at His right hand in the heavens. . . . And He put everything under His feet and appointed Him as head over everything for the church. (1:20–22)

> [God] made us alive with the Messiah. . . . He also raised us up with Him and seated us with Him in the heavens, in Christ Jesus. (2:5–6)

> But now in Christ Jesus, you who were far away have been brought near by the blood of the Messiah. For He is our peace, who made both groups one and tore down the dividing wall of hostility. In His flesh, He did away with the law of the commandments in regulations, so that He might create in Himself

---

[7] For a helpful overview of how Christ's saving work has personal, community, and cosmic dimensions, see Graham A. Cole, *God the Peacemaker: How Atonement Brings Shalom*, NSBT, ed. D. A. Carson (Downers Grove: InterVarsity, 2009).

one new man from the two, resulting in peace. [He did this so] that He might reconcile both to God in one body through the cross and put the hostility to death by it. (2:13–16)

For it says: When He ascended on high, He took prisoners into captivity; He gave gifts to people. But what does "He ascended" mean except that He descended to the lower parts of the earth? The One who descended is the same as the One who ascended far above all the heavens, that He might fill all things. (4:8–10)

And walk in love, as the Messiah also loved us and gave Himself for us, a sacrificial and fragrant offering to God. (5:2)

He is the Savior of the body. . . . Husbands, love your wives, just as also Christ loved the church and gave Himself for her, to make her holy, cleansing her in the washing of water by the word. He did this to present the church to Himself in splendor, without spot or wrinkle or any such thing, but holy and blameless. (5:23–27)

Ephesians' sweeping portrayal of Christ's saving work is stunning. In this brief letter, Paul refers to a wide range of Christ's saving acts, though he emphasizes his death.

- incarnation (4:8–10)
- death (1:7; 2:13–16; 5:2, 25)
- resurrection (1:20–22)
- ascension (4:8–10)
- enthronement (1:20–22)
- session (1:20–22; 2:5–6)

In order to communicate the significance of Christ's saving work, Paul utilizes several pictures.

- redemption (1:7)
- blood sacrifice/offering (1:7; 2:13; 5:2, 25)
- peace/reconciliation (2:13–16)
- victory (2:16)
- substitution (5:2, "for us"; v. 25, "for her")[8]

---

[8] For an expanded treatment of Christ's saving events and pictures, see Robert A. Peterson, *Salvation Accomplished by the Son: The Work of Christ* (Wheaton: Crossway, 2011).

Each picture highlights the dark reality of sin. We need forgiveness, so Christ comes as our Redeemer. We are unholy and need his blood sacrifice. We are at enmity with God and need him to bring peace. We are in bondage and need his victory. We are guilty before God and need him as our substitute.

Indeed, Christ's saving work both flows out of his identity and clarifies it for us. Ephesians identifies him as our peace (2:14), the head over everything for the church's benefit (1:22), and the head and Savior of the church (5:23). What Christ is for the church relates to his saving work for the church.

4. God Applies This Eternal Plan to Us in History through Union with Christ

To glorify himself, God eternally plans to save sinners (1:4–6), create the church as one new people (2:11–22; 3:3–12), and unite the cosmos (1:9–11; 3:9–11). Christ accomplishes this eternal plan in history through his saving work. Christ's objective work is subjectively applied to us by the Holy Spirit through our union with Christ.

We must bear in mind three principles related to Scripture's presentation of union with Christ. First, union with Christ sometimes refers to Christ's overall representation of us or to our overall relationship with him (e.g., Eph 1:20–22; 4:11–16; 5:22–33).[9] We were in Adam, now we are in Christ (Rom 5:12–21). We are united to him in a way illustrated by the union of a husband and wife in marriage.

Second, union with Christ often refers to the Holy Spirit's subjective application of Christ's work to us, so that we receive its benefits. John Calvin captured this memorably: "We must understand that as long as Christ remains outside of us, and we are separated from him, all he has suffered and done for the salvation of the human race remains useless and of no value for us. . . . To sum up, the Holy Spirit is the bond by which Christ effectually unites us to himself."[10] Ephesians 2:4–10 particularly

---

[9] Michael Horton reminds, "The church is always on the receiving end in its relationship to Christ; it is never the redeemer, but always the redeemed; never the head, but always the body." Michael S. Horton, *People and Place: A Covenant Ecclesiology* (Louisville: WJK, 2008), 77.

[10] John Calvin, *Institutes of the Christian Religion*, trans. Ford L. Battles, ed. J. T. McNeill (Philadelphia: Westminster, 1960), III.I.I.

stresses this aspect of being in Christ. Paul states that though we were dead in sin, God made us alive. But how did he do so? Paul explains he made us alive "together with Christ." In our salvation, we undergo a resurrection. How? We are raised together with Christ. We are also seated in the heavenlies. How? Again—it is together with Christ. Paul attaches the Greek preposition *sun* ("with") to each of these verbs to underline this reality: what God has accomplished in Christ he has also accomplished for us.[11] His life connects to us, and we have life. His resurrection brings forth our resurrection. His reign effects our reign (Rom 6:4, 8; Gal 2:20).

Third, sometimes union with Christ refers to the whole sphere of our salvation and its blessings. Ephesians 1:3–14 highlights this aspect of being in Christ. In only one passage, Paul refers to being "in" Christ eleven times. The whole of our salvation is said to be in Christ—every spiritual blessing we have is by our union with him (1:3). Union with Christ is specifically linked to our election (vv. 4–5), adoption (vv. 4–5), redemption (v. 7), inheritance (v. 11), and sealing (vv. 13–14).

In Ephesians, union with Christ relates to the three recurring spheres: personal, communal, and cosmic. In Christ, we as individuals are linked to Christ's death and resurrection and thus receive salvation (1:3–14; 2:1–10). In Christ, we together are linked to Christ's death and resurrection and thus are united to one another as God's people, the church (2:11–22; 3:1–6). And in Christ, the whole cosmos is linked to Christ's saving work and is being reconciled (1:9–10; 3:9–11).

To recap, Ephesians teaches us:

- God's ultimate end is his glory.
- God's ultimate end generates his eternal plan.
- God accomplishes this eternal plan of reconciliation in history through Christ and his saving work.
- God applies this eternal plan to us in history through union with Christ.

How does all of this relate to our understanding of the church? To that we now turn.

---

[11] O'Brien, *Letter to the Ephesians*, 166–67.

5. God Creates Us as the One Church to Showcase His Purpose of Cosmic Reconciliation

God's new creation—the church—is related to all three spheres of his plan for reconciliation. First, the church consists of believers who no longer live in separation from God but are united to Christ and live with full access to God. We are God's chosen people; we are God's holy people; we are God's worshipping people; we are the children of God, adopted into his family; we are the redeemed people; we are heirs with an inheritance (1:3–14; note all the Israel imagery). The church is identified as the new covenant people of God and as central to God's eternal plan. The church is reconciled to God.

Second, the church is also the people of God reconciled to each other. Being united to Christ means we are united to one another.

> But now in Christ Jesus, you who were far away have been brought near by the blood of the Messiah. For He is our peace, who made both groups one and tore down the dividing wall of hostility. In His flesh, He did away with the law of the commandments in regulations, so that He might create in Himself one new man from the two, resulting in peace. [He did this so] that He might reconcile both to God in one body through the cross and put the hostility to death by it. (2:13–16)

The enormous rift between Jews and Gentiles is well known. Jews had religious and cultural identifiers that distinguished them from everyone else: circumcision, food laws, Sabbath, holy days, and so forth. God's reconciliation of Jews and Gentiles together into one body would have been virtually unfathomable and viewed as nothing short of miraculous (see Rom 14:1–15:13; Gal 3:28; Col 3:11). As Andrew Lincoln observes, "In accomplishing this, Christ has transcended one of the fundamental divisions of the first-century world."[12]

Paul shows how God addressed this division in Eph 2:11–22. Speaking of the spiritual state of the Gentiles before Christ, he lists five interrelated problems: they were without Christ, excluded from being citizens of Israel, foreigners to the covenants, without hope, and without the true God (v. 12).

---

[12] Andrew T. Lincoln, *Ephesians*, WBC (Dallas: Word, 1990), 141.

Then Paul points to Christ as our peace, using three participles to show how he brings peace: making both Jews and Gentiles one, destroying the barrier between them, and abolishing the hostility. O'Brien ably explains the biblical concept of peace:

> The term "peace" in both Old and New Testaments came to denote well-being in the widest sense, including salvation, the source and giver which is God alone. "Peace" was used for harmony among people (Acts 7:26; Gal. 5:22; Eph. 4:3; Jas. 3:18) and especially for the messianic salvation (Luke 1:79; 2:14; 19:42). The term could describe the goal and content of all Christian preaching, the message itself being called "the gospel of peace" (Eph. 6:15; see Acts 10:36; Eph. 2:17). The biblical concept of peace has to do with wholeness, particularly with reference to personal relationships. Peace describes an order established by the God of peace (1 Cor. 14:33; see Rom. 15:33; 16:20; Phil. 4:9). Christ himself is the mediator of that peace (Rom. 5:1; Col. 1:20). He gives peace to believers (2 Thess. 3:16); indeed, he himself is that peace.[13]

Paul explains that Christ brings peace between Jews and Gentiles for two purposes: (1) to create in himself one new humanity out of the two and (2) to reconcile both to God.

Christ our peace both removes the hostility between Jews and Gentiles, and out of the formerly divided peoples, he creates a new and unified humanity. Paul has already used new creation language in Eph 2:10. There it primarily refers to the salvation of believers but may also include the larger sphere of the church. Here in vv. 13–16 the new creation language clearly refers to the church.

Paul is using imagery that is linked to Adam and the image of God. Being created in the image of God, Adam was to display God to the cosmos, serving God through leading and serving creation (Gen 1:26–28; 2:15). Instead, Adam revolted, rebelling against God's authority, refusing to bear God's purposes, and failing to reflect God's glory.

But God's purposes continued as he saved and commissioned Noah. Indeed, new creation imagery abounds in the flood narrative, as Genesis depicts Noah as a new Adam, in the image of God (9:6), blessed

---

[13] O'Brien, *Letter to the Ephesians*, 193.

to be fruitful and multiply (vv. 1–7), walking with God (6:9), serving creation (7:15).[14] God's purpose of bringing restoration continued through Abraham. God blessed him to go and be a blessing to the nations, and the Lord built a great nation through him (12:1–3).[15]

God's image and mission drove the deliverance of his people from bondage in Egypt. Israel is likened to Adam, even being called God's "firstborn son" (Exod 4:22) and portrayed as fruitful and multiplying (Gen 12:2–3; 17:2–8; 22:16–18; 26:3–24; 28:3; 35:11–12; 47:27; 48:3–4; Exod 1:6–10).[16] One major purpose of the exodus was to make God's name known throughout the earth (Exod 8:22; 9:14, 29). Exodus 19:5–6 links the idea of Israel's being God's treasured possession with God's ownership of the whole earth. Israel is his possession in order to serve as a kingdom of priests and a holy nation. Like Abraham, "Israel is commissioned to be God's people on behalf of the earth which is God's."[17] As the image of God, Israel is called to embody his holiness, which is not only essential to their worship but also to their mission; they accurately reflect God to the nations only as they live in a way that resembles him (Deut 28:9–10). Israel often failed to do this, and the prophets pointed to a time when Israel would rightly display God's glory and the nations would be gathered (see Isa 56:1–8; 60; 66).

In Christ the eschatological hopes of Israel have become historical reality. The Messiah has come, and thus the kingdom and new age have broken into history. Christ is the new Adam, the new Israel, the firstborn, the Son of God, and the perfect image of God. Therefore, the new creation has come (Rom 5:12–21; 8:26–30; 1 Cor 15:20–58; 2 Cor 3:18; 4:4–12; Phil 2:5–11; Col 1:15–20). As the focal point and inaugurator of the new creation, Christ "who as the Son of God bears the divine image is also the one who by virtue of his death and resurrection is now re-creating a people into that same image."[18] Gordon Fee explains:

---

[14] Bruce K. Waltke with Charles Yu, *An Old Testament Theology: An Exegetical, Canonical, and Thematic Approach* (Grand Rapids: Zondervan, 2007), 292–302.

[15] For more on this important passage, see Christopher J. H. Wright, *The Mission of God: Unlocking the Bible's Grand Narrative* (Downers Grove: InterVarsity, 2006), 191–221.

[16] Waltke, *An Old Testament Theology*, 297. See also "Adam" in *Dictionary of Biblical Imagery*, ed. Leland Ryken, James C. Wilhoit, and Tremper Longman III (Downers Grove: InterVarsity, 1998), 11–13.

[17] Wright, *The Mission of God*, 225.

[18] Gordon D. Fee, *Pauline Christology: An Exegetical-Theological Study* (Peabody, MA: Hendrickson, 2007), 515. See also Richard B. Gaffin Jr., "The Glory of God in

For here the one who is himself the "image" of God, who is the Father's own "firstborn," and by virtue of his resurrection the "firstborn" with regard to the new creation, is now the one who "re-creates" broken and fallen humanity back into the divine image that he himself has perfectly borne. The Creator of the first creation, who himself bears the Father's image, now is seen as the Creator of the new creation, as he restores his own people back into the divine image.[19]

In light of the significance of the image of God in the biblical story, how monumental it is for Paul to refer to unity of the Jews and Gentiles as the creation of the one new humanity! Because of Christ's saving work and through our union with him, we as the church are now the image of God. We are the one new people, the new humanity, the people called to display God to the world, the new creation in the image of God, called to reflect Christ and embody God's holiness (Eph 2:14–16; 4:13, 24).

Notice also the church's relationship to Israel here. In some ways, the church stands in strong continuity with Israel—the church is the people of God, chosen, adopted, possessing an inheritance (land imagery), included in the covenant, citizens of the kingdom of God, and bearers of the image of God. Yet Paul does not equate Israel and the church here. Neither do the Gentiles become Jews, nor does Israel continue with a new identity. Instead, both Gentiles and Jews are reconciled together and become a new entity, the new humanity—the church.[20] As this one new humanity, Jews and Gentiles together form God's nation, God's family, and God's temple:

So then you are no longer foreigners and strangers, but fellow citizens with the saints, and members of God's household, built on the foundation of the apostles and prophets, with Christ Jesus Himself as the cornerstone. The whole building is being fitted together in Him and is growing into a holy sanctuary in the Lord, in whom you also are being built together for God's dwelling in the Spirit. (2:19–22)

The church is also described as the body of Christ (1:23; 2:16; 4:4, 12; 5:23), the fullness of Christ who fills all things (1:23), and the bride of

---

Paul's Epistles," in Morgan and Peterson, *The Glory of God*, 127–52.
    [19] Ibid.
    [20] See Stephen J. Wellum's chapter in this book (p. 183).

Christ (5:22–33). Though the images of nation, family, temple, body, fullness, and bride have nuanced meanings, they share much in common, especially the emphasis on God's presence in the church and God's glory displayed by the church.

Third, the church plays a key role in the cosmic dimension of God's plan—a point that is often missed. As the people reconciled to God and to one another, the church points to God's plan of cosmic reconciliation. Paul portrays this astonishing purpose of the church:

> This grace was given to me—the least of all the saints!—to proclaim to the Gentiles the incalculable riches of the Messiah, and to shed light for all about the administration of the mystery hidden for ages in God who created all things. This is so that God's multi-faceted wisdom may now be made known through the church to the rulers and authorities in the heavens. This is according to the purpose of the ages, which He made in the Messiah, Jesus our Lord. (Eph 3:8–11)

The unity of Jews and Gentiles as the one new humanity is an incredible testimony of God's broader purposes. Notice the intended audience of this showcase: the rulers and authorities in the heavenly realms, likely referring both to angels and demons. The point seems to be that beings in the heavenly realms are put on notice: God is going to do cosmically what he has already done for individuals in Christ; and God is going to do cosmically what he has done corporately with the Jews and Gentiles. All things in heaven and on earth will be brought together in Christ; all things will highlight Christ as the focal point of the cosmos. Not only is Christ the Savior of sinners and the head of the church; he is the goal of the entire cosmos. Paul's idea here is similar to that of Col 1:16, where he says all things are created by Christ and for Christ.

The church is God's visible exhibition that proclaims these cosmic purposes. In a sense, the church preaches Christ not only to humanity in the verbal proclamation of the gospel but also to the entire cosmos through the visible display of unity. Bryan Chapell captures Paul's point:

> This grafting of the redeemed is so amazing that it was God's intent to use it to display his wisdom to the heavenly beings. Thus Paul's words create a celestial stage to display the wonders of grace. . . . [I]n union with other sinners made perfect, and as

members of one body, we who come from every tribe and nation, people and personality, are on display as a church before the heavenly hosts as a testimony to the wisdom of God. . . . Just as Paul's sin makes the grace of God more apparent, the uniting of sinners in the body of Christ makes the grace of God more brilliant—even to the hosts of heaven. By our unity in Christ's body, the church, we are preaching to the angels about the power, wisdom, and glory of God who made us.

This is the apex of Paul's thought about the church. . . . [H]ere we learn that the church is intended not only to transform the world but also to transfix heaven.[21]

As we showcase God's eternal purpose of cosmic unity to the world, we demonstrate that the kingdom of God has already broken into history. Certainly, there is a "not yet" aspect of the kingdom still to come. God's eternal purpose of cosmic reconciliation is not perfectly realized yet—sin and injustice still occur. Yet sin will not have the last word; disorder and division will not last forever. Though the present age can be characterized to some extent as "not the way things are supposed to be,"[22] God will bring about a new creation.

Paul asserts that God's new creation is already underway—in the church. As the firstfruits of the new creation, we are the foretaste of more to come—a genuine embodiment of the kingdom, a glimpse of the ways things are supposed to be, and a glimpse of the way the cosmos ultimately will be; we are a showcase of God's eternal plan of cosmic unity.

6. God Creates Us as the Church to Display Himself and Thus Glorify Himself

God not only creates the church as the one new humanity to display his eternal plan of cosmic reconciliation, but he also creates the church to display himself, and thus glorify himself. We previously stressed that God's ultimate end is his glory. We learned from Ephesians that he acts

---

[21] Bryan Chapell, *Ephesians*, Reformed Expository Commentary (Phillipsburg: P&R, 2009), 144–45. See Timothy G. Gombis, *The Drama of Ephesians: Participating in the Triumph of God* (Downers Grove: InterVarsity, 2010), 134–37.

[22] Cornelius Plantinga Jr., *Not the Way It's Supposed to Be: A Breviary of Sin* (Grand Rapids: Eerdmans, 1995), 2–27.

for the praise of his glory (1:6, 12, 14) and that he acts to display himself, particularly his love, mercy, grace, kindness, creative work, and wisdom (2:4–10; 3:8–10). As we connect these dots, we find that God eternally planned to glorify himself by displaying himself through the church.[23] As he displays his greatness, he glorifies himself.

In the creation of the cosmos, God revealed himself. Psalm 19 makes this plain:

> The heavens declare the glory of God,
> and the sky proclaims the work of His hands.
> Day after day they pour out speech;
> night after night they communicate knowledge. (19:1–2)

In the new creation of the church, God reveals himself in an even greater way.

In the formation of Israel, God displayed himself. Israel was called to embody God's holiness (Exod 19:5–6; Deut 28:9–10). As a kingdom of priests, Israel was to exhibit his presence throughout the earth; and as a holy nation, Israel was "to be a people set apart, different from all other people by what they [were] and [were] becoming—a display people, a showcase to the world of how being in covenant with Yahweh changes a people."[24] In the new creation of the church, God displays himself in an even greater way.

The church, too, is rightly described as "a display people, a showcase to the world of how being in covenant with Yahweh changes a people." In Ephesians, Paul often underlines that God saves and creates the church to display himself, and examples of this include:

> So that in the coming ages He might display the immeasurable riches of His grace through [His] kindness to us in Christ Jesus. (2:7)

> For we are His creation—created in Christ Jesus for good works, which God prepared ahead of time so that we should walk in them. (2:10)

---

[23] Note that Israel and the church deserve treatment under the doctrine of revelation.

[24] John I. Durham, *Exodus*, WBC (Waco: Word, 1987), 263. I first noticed this quote in Cole, *God the Peacemaker*, 94.

This is so that God's multi-faceted wisdom may now be made known through the church to the rulers and authorities in the heavens. (3:10)

Repeating the verb "walk" (*peripateō*), Ephesians notes several ways in which the church showcases God. Before knowing Christ, we walked according to the world, the flesh, and Satan (2:1–3). But God graciously stepped in and rescued us through the saving work of Christ. Through uniting us to Christ, God makes us alive (vv. 4–7). In turn, our entire walk is transformed (v. 10). We used to resemble the world, but now we walk in good works, in a way that resembles our good God. We have been recreated by God to display his goodness to the world. This is all according to his eternal plan (v. 10). We are to walk in unity, in a manner worthy of our calling (4:1). We are to walk in holiness (v. 17), reflective of being created anew as God's image. We are to walk in love, as Christ loves us (5:2). We are to walk in truth and holiness, as children of light (v. 8). We are to walk wisely as we understand the times (v. 15).

Paul speaks of other ways that God's people are a "display people." Note five examples.

1. *Our salvation glorifies God by displaying the inexhaustible nature of his grace throughout the age to come (2:7).* Recreating dead, enslaved, condemned sinners into living, active image-bearers points both to the invincible power of God's grace as well as its boundless supply. Our election, adoption, redemption, unity, inheritance, and sealing in Christ all redound to his glory (1:6, 12, 14).

2. *Our very existence as the church glorifies God by displaying his wisdom.* As we previously saw, through the church the infinite multidimensional wisdom of God is being made known to the rulers and authorities in the heavenly places (3:10).

3. *Our unity glorifies God by displaying his oneness (4:1–6).* That God is one and not many means he is the only God and is alone worthy to receive worship (Deut 6:4–5). Being the only God also means he deserves to be worshipped universally. The sheer diversity of believers makes it appear unlikely that unity would characterize God's people. But in his eternal plan, he reflects his oneness through the unity of his church. Our church unity declares that there is one God, who is over all, through all, and in all. That the church is one body is grounded in and declares that there is one Lord, one Spirit, one faith, one hope, and one baptism. The church's

oneness also points to its universality, which results from and displays God's universality.

4. *Our love glorifies God by displaying his love.* God's love for us not only drives him to save us (Eph 1:3–6); it also manifests itself in the church (3:14–19; 4:11–16; 1 John 4:7–12). As we walk in love, we reflect the love of Christ, who loves us and gave himself for us (5:2). As husbands love their wives, they embody Christ's love for his church (vv. 22–33).

5. *Our holiness glorifies God by displaying his holiness.* God chose to save and create the church so that we would be holy and blameless before him (1:4). Our election is not only unto salvation but also unto the creation of a holy people. Christ's husbandlike self-sacrifice was not only for our salvation but also to make us a holy bride. As God's new creation, his holy people are to put on the new self, created after his likeness in true righteousness and holiness (4:24). Further, the church is not only characterized by holiness now but will be presented to Christ as perfectly holy on the final day (5:25–27).

That God's people are a "display people" has significance for our ecclesiology. First, notice that although these realities mark the church as a whole, they also mark the local, visible church. The reconciliation of Jews and Gentiles into one new humanity is across a vast scale. It is sweeping, salvation-historical, global, and requires belief in some sort of universal church. Yet the very fact that the reconciliation of the Jews and Gentiles into this one new humanity serves as a showcase of God's eternal purposes of cosmic unity also requires the church's visibility and thus the local church.

Second, the marks of the church stressed by Ephesians—unity, universality, holiness, truth, love—communicate and reflect God's goodness, which is why such attributes are sometimes called God's communicable attributes. These marks are present precisely because the church displays God's goodness. That the church is able to display God is even more surprising when we consider how often Paul describes God and his attributes in superlatives: the riches of God's grace lavished upon us (1:8); the riches of his glorious inheritance (v. 18); the immeasurable greatness of his power and the working of his great might (v. 19); the head over all things (v. 22); the One who fills all in all (v. 23); the richness of God's mercy (2:4); the great love with which he loves us (v. 4); the immeasurable riches of his grace (v. 7); the unsearchable riches of Christ (3:8); the manifold wisdom of God (v. 10); the riches of his glory (v. 16);

the love of Christ that surpasses knowledge (v. 19); ability to do beyond far more than we can ask or imagine (v. 20); who is over all, through all, and in all (4:6); and love so radical that it is self-sacrificing (5:2, 25). One might assume that a God this infinite would be unknowable. The Creator-creature distinction remains, to be sure, but genuine revelation occurs nonetheless. Just as Paul prays that the church would know the love of Christ that surpasses knowledge, he also urges the church to display the reality of, nature of, and purposes of the infinitely glorious God. While Christ and his infinite love are beyond our full comprehension, through his gracious self-communication and self-condescension, our knowledge of him can be truthful and genuine, even if partial. Similarly, while God's perfections cannot be *fully* communicated to or through creatures, the church can still *truthfully* and *genuinely* display our great and glorious God.

Third, the marks of God's "display people" characterize both the church as a whole as well as the local, visible church. Yet the visible church is exhorted to be ever more holy and faithful—maintaining unity, living in accord with holiness, teaching truth, and embodying love. The church is to live up to its high calling, and, in so doing, it showcases God. As such, the marks of the church reveal a strong relationship between what the church is and how the church should behave. Ephesians regularly points to this already/not yet (and indicative-imperative) aspect of the church. The church already is the fullness of Christ (1:23), but Paul prays that it will be filled with the fullness of Christ (3:19; cf. 4:13).[25] The church already is the one new humanity (2:14–18) but is to grow into a mature humanity (4:13) and put on the new humanity (vv. 20–24). The church already is under its head, Christ (1:22–23), but is to grow up into Christ, who is the head (4:15). The church already is one, united in Christ (2:12–22; 4:1–6); yet it is to maintain the unity of the Spirit (4:3). The church already is holy (2:19–22) but is to walk in holiness, put on the new humanity and holiness, become more and more holy, and one day be presented to Christ as holy (4:20–24; 5:2–21, 27). The church already is grounded in truth and built on Christ as the cornerstone, with the apostles and prophets as its foundation (2:19–22); yet it is to teach truth, speak truth in love, walk

---

[25] For how the already and not yet relates to the church as temple, see the insightful work by G. K. Beale, *The Temple and the Church's Mission: A Biblical Theology of the Dwelling Place of God*, NSBT (Downers Grove: InterVarsity, 2004), 392–93.

in truth, and stand firm as an army for truth (4:5, 11, 14–15, 21; 6:10–18). The church is glorious now as the fullness of Christ (1:22–23), but one day it will be presented to Christ as glorious (5:25–28). Thus, the church is an eschatological community of Christians that exists in the already and not yet. The church is to display God and the realities of the new creation but still await the culmination of history, the final stage of the new creation.

So is the church too ordinary to be effective, too common to be of cosmic significance? Not at all! The church has its origin in the eternal purposes of God, its basis in the saving work of Christ, its life from union with Christ, and its end as the glory of God. The church is God's showcase for his eternal plan of bringing forth cosmic reconciliation and highlighting Christ as the focal point of history. The church is also God's "display people," showcasing not only his purposes but even his person. In and through the church, God shows his grace, wisdom, love, unity, and holiness. And as God displays himself, he glorifies himself. It is no wonder Paul proclaims: "Now to Him who is able to do above and beyond all that we ask or think according to the power that works in us—to Him be glory in the church and in Christ Jesus to all generations, forever and ever" (Eph 3:20–21).

CHAPTER 9

The Church in the Mission of God

Bruce Riley Ashford

The mission of God is both a central theme in the unfolding biblical narrative and vital to a biblical theology of the church.[1] This chapter seeks to articulate God's mission and the church's role within that mission. In particular, we will argue that *God's mission* provides the impetus, framework, and trajectory for *the church's mission* to glorify God among the nations by proclaiming and promoting the good news that God is redeeming a people for himself and bringing all things under his good rule. This thesis includes a particular view of *missio Dei* (mission of God). Before arguing this thesis, then, we offer a brief historical overview of the church's discussion of *missio Dei*.

---

[1] Christopher Wright recently has argued that the Bible is about the mission of God, and that mission is the key to unlocking the "grand narrative" of the Bible. Christopher J. H. Wright, *The Mission of God: Unlocking the Bible's Grand Narrative* (Downers Grove: IVP Academic, 2006). Similarly, Kevin Vanhoozer argues that God is a "missionary" and therefore "the whole theodrama is essentially missional," and Timothy Tennent argues for the missional nature of the biblical narrative and all theology (Vanhoozer, "'One Rule to Rule Them All?' Theological Method in an Era of World Christianity," in *Global Theologizing*, ed. Harold Netland and Craig Ott [Grand Rapids: Baker Academic, 2006], 110; Tennent, *Invitation to World Missions: A Trinitarian Missiology for the Twenty-First Century* [Grand Rapids: Kregel, 2010], 60–61).

A Brief Historical Overview

The notion of *missio Dei* is both new and not new. On the one hand, early theologians discussed and debated the mission of God. The classical treatment of this topic is books II–IV of Augustine's *On the Trinity*, in which the bishop of Hippo argues that each of the persons of the Trinity must be involved together in any "sending" in the divine mission. On the other hand, the discussion of *missio Dei* is new. After the patristic period, *missio Dei* received little attention until the twentieth century. Karl Barth placed the doctrine of election under the doctrine of God,[2] thereby locating the concept of mission in the Godhead. Being influenced by Barth, Karl Hartenstein argued that the *missio Dei* issues forth in a *missio ecclesiae* (mission of the church); in fact, the church ceases to be the church if she loses her mission.[3] Toward the end of the twentieth century, numerous theologians and missiologists have located the concept of mission within the Godhead. They therefore started with the mission of God before moving to the mission of the church.[4]

The resurgence of discussion about *missio Dei* has ignited a debate about *missio ecclesiae* and the relation of these two concepts. As Scott Moreau has noted, three competing streams of thought dominate the evangelical landscape.[5] The first stream equates mission with evangelism, while the second—represented by John Stott's work—offers a more holistic view of mission, including both evangelism and advancement of social

---

[2] Karl Barth, *Church Dogmatics II/2*, ed. G. W. Bromiley and T. F. Torrance (Peabody, MA: Hendrickson, 2010), 76–93; Colin Gunton, "Karl Barth's Doctrine of Election as Part of His Doctrine of God," in *JTS* 25 (1974), 381–92; Stephen R. Holmes, "Trinitarian Missiology: Towards a Theology of God as Missionary," in *IJST* 8, no. 1 (January 2006): 72–90.

[3] Hartenstein's views were set forth in his report on the Willingen Conference, which is recorded in George Vicedeom, *The Mission of God: An Introduction to the Theology of Mission* (St. Louis: Concordia, 1965), 5.

[4] Lesslie Newbigin, *The Open Secret*, rev. ed. (Grand Rapids: Eerdmans, 1995); David Bosch, *Transforming Mission* (Maryknoll, NY: Orbis, 1991); Wright, *Mission of God*; Tennent, *Invitation to World Missions*; Michael W. Goheen, *A Light to the Nations* (Grand Rapids: Baker, 2011). Also, see Keith Whitfield: "The Triune God: The God of Mission," in *Theology and Practice of Mission*, ed. Bruce Riley Ashford (Nashville: B&H, 2011), 17–34.

[5] A. Scott Moreau, "Mission and Missions," in *Evangelical Dictionary of World Missions* (Grand Rapids: Baker, 2000), 636–38. For the first stream, Moreau lists the Global Consultations on World Evangelization (GCOWE) as representative. For the second stream, he lists John Stott. For the third stream, he lists Ron Sider, Rene Padilla, and Samuel Escobar.

justice but giving priority to evangelism. The third stream also offers a holistic view but, unlike Stott, makes no distinction between evangelism and social justice in terms of centrality or priority. Each stream represents an attempt to locate the church and her mission within the framework of God's mission. This essay argues for a holistic view of mission in which the church glorifies God among the nations by proclaiming and promoting the good news that God is redeeming a people for himself *and* bringing all things under his good rule. In order to understand the church's mission, one must first reflect on God's mission.

The Mission of God

The Bible is about the mission of God, a mission that stems from his character and permeates the biblical witness. As Christopher Wright argues, one must build one's view of mission on an indicative (God's character as revealed in Scripture) and not merely on imperatives (the Great Commission). Thus, to read the Bible missionally "is nothing more than to accept that the biblical worldview locates us in the midst of a narrative of the universe behind which stands the mission of the living God."[6] In order to investigate the church's role in the mission of God, therefore, we must trace God's self-revelation throughout the biblical canon. This narrative contains four plot movements: creation, fall, redemption, and restoration.[7] Within that framework we will focus on particular aspects of each plot movement relevant to articulating the *missio Dei* as God's mission to glorify himself by redeeming his image bearers and renewing his good creation, restoring both to their intended shalom.

Creation

The story of creation sets the trajectory for the mission of God, for he created a people with a mission to be accomplished in his world. Before the fall, the mission was not one of redemption but of God's image bearers glorifying him by living under his rule in proper relationship to him,

---

[6] Wright, *Mission of God*, 64.

[7] More than a few theologians have treated the canonical material as narrative or drama. See Craig G. Bartholomew and Michael W. Goheen, *The Drama of Scripture* (Grand Rapids: Baker, 2004); Albert M. Wolters, *Creation Regained* (Grand Rapids: Eerdmans, 2005); Wright, *The Mission of God*; N. T. Wright, *The New Testament and the People of God* (London: SPCK, 1992), 139–43.

to creation, and to one another. Four elements of the creation account are especially significant to the mission of God.

First, the narrative identifies God as the one and only Creator and, therefore, distinct from his creation. Although he is referred to as *Elohim* (generic for deity) in Gen 1:1, he is later referred to as *Yahweh Elohim* (a particular term associated with the God of Israel who makes covenants and redeems people) in 2:4.[8] With this reference, God is distinguished from other gods as the only God, the source of all creation, distinct from all creation, and personally related to his creation. The created order is the stage for this unfolding drama of God's mission, and God and humanity are the central actors. God is distinct from his creation because in his initial creative act he calls forth creation from nothing, and does so by means of his word. God's creative word, therefore, serves as a boundary line between the Creator and the created. God is related to the world, but the world is not God and does not emanate from God. At the same time, creation must turn itself toward God to maintain its proper order, giving its Creator proper glory.

Second, God affirms that his creation is good and that it glorifies him. After the initial creative act, he shapes his created material in six successive movements (Gen 1:3–2:1). God affirms that his creation is good (1:10, 12, 18, 21, 25, 31), and at the end of his creative acts, he affirms that it is very good (v. 31). Indeed, it glorifies him (cf. Psalm 148). Not only is this doctrine repeatedly affirmed in Genesis; the apostles also indicate its significance for Christian doctrine and life (1 Tim 4:4).[9] The fact that the Son redeemed us by taking on human flesh indicates that created material is not inherently evil. God's material creation—both human flesh (John 1:14) and the material cosmos (Romans 8)—is good. There are, to be sure, clear scriptural warnings about the world and things on earth, such as when Paul writes, "Set your minds on what is above, not on what is on the earth" (Col 3:2), and John writes, "Do not

---

[8] *Elohim* is an appellative rather than a personal name. Its use in this context implies that God is not merely Israel's tribal deity but, rather, is Lord of the entire universe. See Jean L'Hour, "Yahweh Elohim," *RB* 81 (1974): 524–56; Gordon J. Wenham, *Genesis 1–15*, WBC 1 (Waco: Word, 1987), 15, 56–57.

[9] This doctrine of the good is an important consideration in the doctrine of the incarnation. Athanasius made this connection in *On the Incarnation*, affirming that the goodness of God's creation is directly related to the incarnation and, therefore, to Christian redemption. Athanasius, *On the Incarnation* (New York: St. Vladimir's, 1996), 4:2.

love the world or the things that belong to the world" (1 John 2:15). But these teachings are not in conflict. The biblical writers view the world/ earth positively when referencing the material cosmos God created but negatively when referencing evil, evil humanity, and evil powers. When referenced ontologically, the world/earth is understood to be good, but when referenced morally, it is understood to be bad. From this good earth, God formed his image bearers.

Third, God created man and woman in his image and likeness. On the sixth day, God created man and woman (Gen 1:26–28) and marked this act as a special moment. Instead of creating man and woman "according to their kind," he created them in his image and likeness. Though the image/likeness is not defined, v. 28 gives an exegetical clue by tying this image/likeness to the task of dominion. "It is not that having dominion is what *constitutes* the image of God, but rather that exercising dominion is what being made in God's image enables us to do."[10] Man is to be God's vice-regent, lovingly ruling God's good creation under the oversight of its King. God gives three further commands that provide insight into the nature and mission of his image bearers. He tells Adam to be fruitful and multiply (v. 28), to work the garden (2:15), and not to eat from the tree of the knowledge of good and evil (v. 17).[11] Taken together, these commands imply that God gifted humans to image him in a holistic manner (via spiritual, moral, rational, creative, relational, and physical capacities) in order to fulfill a unique role in his good world. When God's image bearers function under his rule and fulfill their proper role, God's peace reigns over his creation.

Fourth, God's good creation was marked by shalom. Although the Genesis account does not use the Hebrew word *shalom* to describe the original state of affairs, later biblical use of the term makes clear that the original state was one of shalom. The concept of shalom denotes "universal

---

[10] Christopher J. H. Wright, *The Mission of God's People* (Grand Rapids: Zondervan, 2010), 50.

[11] The biblical teaching concerning God's command to till the soil is significant, to which we return later. This tilling of the soil is in fact a statement about man's original calling as a worker and a culture maker. Thus von Rad writes, "Work was man's sober destiny even in his original state" (Gerhard von Rad, *Genesis*, rev. ed. [Philadelphia: Westminster, 1972], 80). Likewise Brueggemann refers to the basic anthropology given in 2:15–17 and includes vocation as central (Walter Brueggemann, *Genesis* [Atlanta: John Knox, 1982], 46).

flourishing, wholeness, and delight"[12] and is hinted at in the creation account when God places man and woman in the garden of "Eden," which means "delight." This garden included water, vegetation, and gold, which some commentators have argued points to the glory of God's presence and previews the new heavens and earth.[13] God's intended shalom sheds light on his mission, and in particular on his intentions for his image bearers, intentions that are uniquely relational. Indeed, man's unique nature and calling involve four significant relationships: relationship with God, with one another, with God's creation, and with himself. We take each in turn.

First, because God created us, our purpose in life stands in direct relation to him. Scripture makes clear that humanity's highest call is to love the Lord God (Deut 6:5; Matt 22:37; Mark 12:30; Luke 10:27). Even the created order praises God (Pss 145:10, 21; 148; 150:6) and testifies that he exists and is to be worshipped (Rom 1:19–20). Yet, God did not create man only for relationship with him.

Second, the Lord God said that it was not good for man to be alone. Thus, God made a helper who would be "his complement" (Gen 2:18). Man and woman are created to flourish in interdependence, reflecting God's triune being; they are created to depend on each other, as they both depend on God. The movement from loving God to loving others is underscored throughout the Bible. When Jesus spoke of loving God, he spoke of the second command like it, to love neighbor (Matt 22:39; Mark 12:31; Luke 10:27). Such love for others is essential to being a Christian (John 13:34–35; 15:12–17; 1 John 3–4).

Third, God made man to work the ground (Gen 2:5–15). Note that God asked man to change, and even enhance, his good creation. It is good for man to work, to develop and bring out the potential in God's good creation. Moreover, God gives man stewardship over the whole created order (1:26–30). Humanity and the created order flourish in interdependence, giving glory to their Creator.

Finally, shalom is incomplete apart from man's proper relation to himself. For when man desires that which is most satisfying for himself, namely God, he fulfills that for which he was created, dependence

---

[12] Cornelius Plantinga Jr., *Not the Way It's Supposed to Be: A Breviary of Sin* (Grand Rapids: Eerdmans, 1995), 10.

[13] John Sailhamer, *The Pentateuch as Narrative* (Grand Rapids: Zondervan, 1992), 98–100.

on God. As man lives in this dominion of dependence, the creation maintains its proper order, and God receives his rightful glory. This state of affairs, however, did not last long.

Fall

After the creation account, the biblical narrative takes a dark turn as Adam and Eve rebel against their Creator. Instead of giving him glory, they seek glory for themselves. Though this story of Adam and Eve's fall is told in a mere twenty-four verses, its consequences are deeply felt throughout the remainder of the biblical story.

In the midst of the many trees in Eden, God had placed the tree of life, whose fruit was good for Adam and Eve, and the tree of the knowledge of good and evil, whose fruit they were forbidden to eat and would lead to death. Satan used a serpent as his spokesman in order to cast doubt on God's good word and good intentions (Gen 3:1–5). Eve listened to the serpent, choosing his word over God's. She offered the fruit to Adam, who also ate (vv. 6–7). In so doing, they sinned. They sought to elevate themselves to the position of arbiter of good and evil and to seize for themselves power and happiness. They sought independence instead of recognizing their dependence. They worshipped and served themselves rather than God. They sought to rule the earth as kings, rather than exercising dominion as vice-regents under the Creator-King. Thus, "what had been a story of trust and obedience," Walter Brueggemann writes, "now becomes an account of crime and punishment."[14] Adam and Eve's sin resulted not only in their fall from God's good will but in the fall of the entire created order. Human sin broke the shalom of God's good creation. Thus, as the Bible recurrently makes clear, man suffered in his relationship to God, others, himself, and the world.

First, and most importantly, Adam and Eve's sin resulted in a broken relationship with God (Gen 3:8–10). Rather than remaining in loving fellowship with him, they became his enemies, competing with him in an attempt to be lords over his world. Rather than living wisely, they became fools. Instead of living in innocence, they now stood guilty before the divine judge. Now things were not as they were created to be. Adam and Eve had sought goodness and happiness on their own, apart from God; but when they ate of the fruit and their eyes were opened, they saw

---

[14] Brueggemann, *Genesis*, 48.

their own nakedness. They were naked before him and unable to clothe themselves, not just physically but in every respect.

Adam and Eve could not limit the consequences of their sin to themselves. Their own child Cain murdered his brother Abel, and Cain's descendent Lamech also committed murder. Human wickedness on the earth became great as "every scheme [man's] mind thought of was nothing but evil all the time" (Gen 6:5). This wickedness is evident across human history and in every fiber of man's existence. Humanity must now live amidst societal evils such as rape, murder, war, and betrayal.

Further, man's relationship with himself was broken. He loves himself more than he loves the Creator (Ps 115:1; Phil 3:18–19). He is curved in on himself (as Martin Luther put it) and thus not fully alive (Irenaeus).[15] Because of sin, man is less than fully human. His brokenness can be seen in every dimension of his humanness, as he becomes a slave to sin rather than to God. In his rational dimension, he allows his idolatrous will to corrupt his mind. In his moral dimension, he does not love what is good. In his social dimension, he exploits others and loves himself inordinately. In his creative dimension, his imagination leads to idolatry rather than worship of the true God. In his physical dimension, he experiences deficiency, sickness, and death. "His life," Bavinck writes, "is nothing other than a short and vain battle with death."[16] This death extends to humanity's relationship with creation.

Genesis tells us that because of Adam and Eve's sin they were removed from the land of blessing and sent into exile. Creation itself was affected by human sin (3:17–18), marring God's design of man and the created order flourishing in interdependence. Childbirth would be marked by pain (v. 16); work would now be marked by strife (vv. 17–19). Adam and Eve's great folly resulted in a broken relationship with a broken created order, and the outworking of this brokenness can be seen throughout Scripture and the world. Man's interdependence with the rest of God's

---

[15] Luther argues that man is *incurvatus in see*, "curved in on his own understanding." See Jaroslav Pelikan, ed., *Luther's Works* (St. Louis: Concordia, 1955–86), 25:426. For Irenaeus, there is no "complete" or "perfect" man without the Spirit. Christ, through his incarnation, bestows the Spirit and enables man to be truly alive. See Dominic Unger, trans., *Against Heresies* (New York: Paulist Press, 1992), 5.6.1 and 5.9.2. Indeed there is only one man who is fully man, the Lord Jesus Christ, whose righteousness not only expresses divinity but also expresses his full humanity.

[16] Herman Bavinck, *Our Reasonable Faith* (Grand Rapids: Eerdmans, 1956), 256.

creation was marred; there would be floods, earthquakes, famines, and the like. Further, mankind consistently desired to worship the created instead of the Creator (Rom 1:18–32). Rather than unbroken harmony and delight, their lives would now be marked by brokenness and pain. However, God wanted to preserve his creation and continue his mission, bringing us to the story of redemption.

Redemption

Genesis treats the movement from creation to fall to redemption in three short chapters. In the third chapter, immediately after the fall, God disclosed his redemptive plan. He gave Adam not only a promise of death (2:17) but also a promise of life (3:15). The woman would bear children, and although the serpent would bruise the heel of her seed, her seed would crush the serpent's head. Life would be sustained by God's gracious provision, and life is here associated with the promise of an offspring. Paul understood these promises about the seed to point ultimately to Christ (Gal 3:16), who is God's Son, "born of a woman" (4:4). The biblical story is redemptive; it's a story in which we discern God's mission by examining Israel, Jesus, and the church. Each one manifests, in a particular way, God's mission to glorify himself by redeeming his image bearers and renewing his good creation, restoring them both to their intended shalom.

God called Israel to be a missional people. He called Abraham and promised that he would bless his descendants, making them a great nation and a blessing to all people (Gen 12:1–3; 15; 17). Later, he promised Israel that he had chosen it to be a kingdom of priests, a holy nation that displayed his glory (Exod 19:5–6), and the bearer of an eternal king who would rule on David's throne forever (2 Sam 7:12–16). He promised the Israelites that he would make a new covenant with them although they had broken the Mosaic covenant (Jer 31:31–33). Along the way, God repeatedly promised that he would send a Messiah. This messianic promise began with the prophecy that a woman's seed would defeat the serpent (Gen 3:15). Then it narrowed to Abraham's seed (22:18), the tribe of Judah (49:10), the stem of Jesse (Isa 11:1), the house of David (2 Sam 7:12–16), and eventually to Yahweh's suffering servant (Isa 52:13–53:12). God's covenant love was reflected in the Law, which showed the people of Israel how to live faithfully under God's kingship in their particular era and context. His love was shown also through the prophets, who called the people back to covenant faithfulness. God's covenant love, his law, and his prophetic word were all intended to shape them as a missional people.[17] Israel's mission was to keep the covenants, live by God's law, and adhere to God's word through the prophets in order to be a light to the nations (see Isa 42:6).

God sent his Son to lead his missional people. God fulfilled his promise to Israel and sent his Son Jesus to provide the salvation promised since Genesis 3. Every aspect of Jesus' life and ministry confirmed that he was God and Messiah, reflecting something of the mission of the triune God. He was born of a virgin, which signaled that he was God in flesh (Matt 1:18–25; Luke 1:26–38). He taught God's word and lived God's law. He encountered Satan's temptation to be a populist, wonder worker, and violent revolutionary (Matt 4:1–11), and yet he rejected those paths in order to take "the hard road into the kingdom: the road of humble service, self-giving love, and sacrificial suffering."[18] He came announcing a kingdom, commanding repentance (Mark 1:14–15), and offering salvation to all who would believe in him (John 3). He performed miracles that revealed the nature of that kingdom. He showed his power over nature, demons, sickness, and death. In every instance his miracles demonstrated that he was indeed God (for example, only God can raise the dead) and previewed the nature of his kingdom (one in which there will be no death). He welcomed the sick and the sinful, enjoying fellowship with them (Luke 14:1–24). He taught the truth about God, salvation, and the nature of his kingdom. Throughout his life, he was sustained by prayerful fellowship with the Father and the ministry of the Spirit. He was crucified (his heel being bruised by the serpent), and on the third day he rose again (bruising the head of the serpent). Through his crucifixion and resurrection, he accomplished the mission of God: he inaugurated the kingdom by claiming victory over Satan, sin, and death, and he secured redemption for God's image bearers and restoration for his cosmos.

God gathers the church to be his missional people. Following Jesus' life, death, and resurrection, he ascended to the right hand of the Father. Soon after, on Pentecost, he poured out his Spirit on the disciples (Acts

---

[17] Wright, *The Mission of God's People*, 72, puts it well: "God's election of Israel is instrumental in God's mission for all nations. Election needs to be seen as a doctrine of *mission*, not a calculus for the arithmetic of salvation. If we are to speak of being chosen, of being among God's elect, it is to say that, like Abraham, we are chosen for the sake of God's plan that the nations of the world come to enjoy the blessing of Abraham."

[18] Bartholomew and Goheen, *Drama of Scripture*, 133–34.

2:1–4). The Spirit then became the main actor in the book of Acts. His first act was to form the church, which bears witness to God's salvation and lives as a sign of God's in-breaking kingdom (2:40–47). Through the church the word of God spread in Jerusalem (3:1–6:7), in Judea and Samaria (8:8–11:18), and farther (11:19–28:31; see 1:8). Thus, God does not merely save individuals; he redeems a whole multiethnic people for his own possession (see 1 Pet 2:9). This people of God is the body of Christ (Eph 4:16) and the temple of the Holy Spirit (1 Cor 6:19), whom God will make into a kingdom of priests (Exod 19:4–6) to serve him and glorify him forever. Through this redeemed community, its proclamation (Matt 28:18–20; Rom 10:14–17), and spiritual ministries (Acts 2:42–47), God unleashes his gospel on the world. The church thus carries forward God's mission for his glory by proclaiming and promoting the good news that he is redeeming a people for himself and bringing all things under his good rule.

Humanity reconciled. One of the terms Scripture uses to describe the salvation wrought by Christ Jesus is "reconciliation." Paul writes that God has through Christ reconciled us to himself and given us "the ministry of reconciliation" (2 Cor 5:18). Depraved man is an enemy of God and guilty before him. Through his death and resurrection, the Messiah enabled peace between man and God by taking man's sin on himself and absorbing the wrath of God (Rom 3:21–26). Those who believe in Christ are thereby justified and reconciled to God—no longer alienated from him—and become ministers of that same reconciliation. Followers of Christ experience God's reconciliation both in this age and in the future (Heb 11:16). We live between the times of the first and second comings of Christ. Our lives during this age, then, are lived with a certain purpose, one that aims to please the God of reconciliation (2 Cor 5:8) and takes seriously Paul's instruction that "those who live should no longer live for themselves, but for the One who died for them and was raised" (5:15). The church's mission is one of reconciliation.

Cosmos restored. Although God saves and reconciles those who believe in him (John 3:16), and although he redeems a people for himself (1 Pet 2:9), his redemption extends even further—to the entire *cosmos*. The biblical narrative opens, "In the beginning God created the heavens and the earth" (Gen 1:1). It closes with the new heavens and new earth (Rev 21:1; see also Isa 65:17). Christ's redemptive work extends through God's people to God's *cosmos*, so that in the end "creation itself will also be set free from the bondage of corruption into the glorious freedom of God's children" (Rom 8:21). This renewed creation will be a world "where righteousness will dwell" (2 Pet 3:13), a final restoration of God's good order for his world. The church's mission, therefore, does not denigrate the creational aspect of human life; it takes place in the midst of creational life and is accomplished as its members bring all of life—including its material-cultural aspects—under the lordship of Christ for the sake of the world.

Redemption in man's relationship with God and others. Jesus' atoning sacrifice restores one's relationship with God and then extends to the restoration of one's relationships with others, redefining them: "From now on, then, we do not know anyone in a purely human way. Even if we have known Christ in a purely human way, yet now we no longer know Him in this way" (2 Cor 5:16). In our fallen nature, we may see the "other" as a competitor, an inferior, a means to serve self, or even as an enemy. But the cross of Christ dispels such animus. In fact, the blood of Christ destroyed it (Eph 2:16). Now we owe others the gospel (Rom 1:14) and Christian love (13:8). Rather than loving ourselves and exploiting others, we are called to give of ourselves and love others.

Redemption in man's relationship to the created order. The reconciling work of Christ also affects one's relationship with the world itself. The cosmos has been distorted by the fall of Adam and the work of Satan and his fallen angels, such that it is characterized by struggle and turmoil (Gen 3:17–19). These organized powers and principalities (Eph 6:12) are committed to hostility with God. We ourselves once walked in accord with these powers (2:1–3), but as followers of Christ, we no longer do so. Instead, we set our affections on God and align ourselves with him in order to share in his reconciling ministry. Thus, the church's ministry includes first and foremost the gospel ministry of reconciling others to Christ, but it also includes bringing the creational-cultural aspects of our lives into submission to his lordship and into accord with his creational design (Gen 1:26–31). In so doing, as John Dickson puts it, we promote the gospel with our lives in addition to proclaiming it with our lips.[19]

Redemption in man's relationship with himself. Likewise, the reconciling ministry of the cross affects one's relationship with oneself. As the work

---

[19] John Dickson, *The Best Kept Secret in Christian Mission* (Grand Rapids: Zondervan, 2010), 23.

of Christ reconciles us to God, it brings healing in the soul, making the corrupt sinner a new creation (2 Cor 5:17). Just as in Christ I must look at other people differently, I must look at myself differently too. What is old (corrupt man) has become new (redeemed man). We sinful humans are being transformed into the image of Christ (3:18; Rom 8:29) as we undergo the sanctifying work of the Spirit of God. Not only are we being changed within; we also have new aims for life (2 Cor 5:8). We live for something, for someone, beyond ourselves (v. 15), and we understand that Christ's ministry of reconciliation to us has made us ministers of reconciliation to others; as ambassadors of Christ we plead for others to be reconciled to God (vv. 18–21).

Restoration

God's work of redemption will reach its goal in the end when Christ returns, as God saves for himself a people and restores his good creation. The entire biblical narrative moves toward this end. As Russell Moore writes,

> All of Christian theology points toward an end—an end where Jesus overcomes the satanic reign of death and restores God's original creation order. . . . In Scripture the *eschaton* is not simply tacked on to the gospel at the end. It is instead the vision toward which all of Scripture is pointing—and the vision that grounds the hope of the gathered church and the individual believer.[20]

Scripture's final plot movement, restoration, involves three significant themes: the renewed creation, the redemption of the nations, and the great divide.

The new heavens and earth. God's redemption through Christ goes beyond his image bearers and extends even to the created order. God proclaims through Isaiah, "For I will create a new heaven and a new earth; the past events will not be remembered or come to mind" (Isa 65:17). Peter reminds us to "wait for the new heavens and a new earth, where righteousness will dwell" (2 Pet 3:13).[21] In Rev 21:1–5, John receives a

---

[20] Russell D. Moore, "Personal and Cosmic Eschatology," in *A Theology for the Church*, ed. Daniel Akin (Nashville: B&H, 2007), 858.

[21] The 2 Peter passage also speaks of the present heavens and earth being reserved for fire on the day of judgment. Although some commentators take Peter to mean that the present universe will be consumed by fire, Richard Bauckham compellingly argues

vision of a new heaven and a new earth, where there is no pain or tears. The doctrine of creation has come full circle. The God whose good creation is groaning in the wake of the fall will renew and restore that creation.[22] In this new universe, God's image bearers will not experience sin or its consequences. We will no longer use our rational capacities to speak falsehoods or our creative capacities to construct idols. We will never again use our relational capacities to suppress others and promote ourselves, or our moral capacities to slander, rape, or murder. We will no longer live in an environment where tsunamis and floods destroy or where pollution poisons the ground and air. Instead, we will live in unbroken relationship with God, with others, with the new universe, and with ourselves.

The redemption of the nations. God's redemption extends to all tribes, tongues, peoples, and nations. This is a theme that pervades the biblical witness. Jesus promises, "This good news of the kingdom will be proclaimed in all the world as a testimony to all nations. And then the end will come" (Matt 24:14). John depicts a scene in which worshippers from all nations gather around the throne, singing to our Lord:

> You are worthy . . .
> because You were slaughtered,
> and You redeemed [people]
> for God by Your blood
> from every tribe and language
> and people and nation. (Rev 5:9)[23]

The ingathering of the nations is a truth to be proclaimed.

The great divide. A time will come when man's relationship with God is finalized: "It is appointed for men to die once, but after this the judgment" (Heb 9:27 NKJV). Those who die apart from Christ will receive eternal

---

that the purpose of the fire in these verses is not obliteration but the purging of the cosmos (of sin and its consequences, including its ecological consequences). Richard J. Bauckham, *2 Peter and Jude*, WBC 50 (Waco, TX: Word, 1983), 316–22.

[22] The "restoration" spoken of in this chapter is not a "repristination" in which God returns creation to its original Edenic state. Instead, God will restore creation by delivering it from sin and bring out its hidden potential by blessing it with social and cultural developments that were not present in Eden. The new creation will have not only a garden but also a city replete with art, architecture, and music.

[23] Sinful humans killed the Son of God, but it is also true that God the Father's plan was to put his Son on the cross.

torment (Matt 5:22; 8:12) while those who die in Christ will receive eternal life (Rev 21:2–4). This is a great motivator for Christians, as we hold three truths together: there is no name other than Christ by which men are saved; all who die apart from Christ abide in eternal torment; and God has given his church the responsibility to proclaim and embody the good news for them.[24] God's promised Messiah has come to provide redemption, and he will come again. In his first coming, he provided the firstfruits of that redemption. In the second coming, he will provide the consummation of it. We find ourselves living between those two comings, called to be ambassadors for the God who created us and purchased us with the blood of his Son.

Summary

In this restoration, wherein the heavens and earth are renewed and the redeemed of the nations worship the King, God's kingdom will be consummated and his mission realized. Having sent his Son to receive his due glory (2 Thess 1:9–10), he will fill the earth with the knowledge of his glory (Isa 6:1–3; Hab 2:14). Then, "at the name of Jesus every knee will bow—of those who are in heaven and on earth and under the earth—and every tongue should confess that Jesus Christ is Lord, to the glory of God the Father" (Phil 2:10–11). At this time, after winding its way through creation, fall, redemption, and restoration, God's mission will have found its fulfillment. He will have glorified himself by redeeming his image bearers and renewing his good creation, restoring them both to their intended shalom. God the Creator is God the Redeemer who redeems humanity so that they can glorify him and extend his mission through their whole human lives—in their spiritual, moral, rational, creative, relational, and physical aspects, and in their personal, social, and cultural dimensions. He reverses the alienation they have experienced in relation to God, each other, the created order, and even self. God's redemption is powerfully comprehensive and restorative. The church's mission, therefore, is also holistic and restorative.

---

[24] See Christopher W. Morgan and Robert A. Peterson, eds., *Faith Comes by Hearing: A Response to Inclusivism* (Downers Grove: InterVarsity, 2008); id., *Hell under Fire: Modern Scholarship Reinvents Eternal Punishment* (Grand Rapids: Zondervan, 2004).

The Church in God's Mission

The mission of God, as we noted previously, provides the foundation, the framework, and the trajectory for the mission of God's people. The missions of both Israel and the church included a call to look upward to him as the source of their mission, inward to themselves as they sought to manifest his mission, outward to the nations as they proclaimed and promoted his salvation, backward to his creational design for shalom, and forward to his promised kingdom.[25] Yet God's missional calling for each was uniquely applied to their particular role in God's redemptive plan. The church's mission, therefore, is articulated within the framework of God's mission (creation, fall, redemption, restoration), in relation to Israel (manifesting both continuity and discontinuity), and via the five aspects of its missional calling (upward, inward, backward, forward, outward). God's people draw on the entirety of themselves (spiritually, morally, rationally, creatively, relationally, physically) in order to be instruments and signs of his reconciliation (to God, others, creation, self). In both its institutional and organic aspects, the church's mission is holistic and restorative, just like God's mission. The church's mission is to glorify God among the nations by proclaiming and promoting the good news that God is redeeming a people for himself and bringing all things under his good rule.

Looking Upward

The biblical narrative is a theocentric, dramatic narrative. Its *theocentric* nature is manifested in biblical language about God's glory, his renown, and his name.[26] In all his resplendent glory, God is the center of the biblical witness and of history. This theocentric, dramatic narrative is anchored

---

[25] I owe the idea for this organizational scheme to Michael W. Goheen, *A Light to the Nations: The Missional Church and the Biblical Story* (Grand Rapids: Baker Academic, 2011). Goheen argues that both Israel and the church were called to look backward to creation, forward to the consummation, and outward to the nations. To these three directional categories (backward, forward, outward), I have added two (upward, inward).

[26] For more on the glory of God and the church, see the chapter by Christopher W. Morgan in the present work (p. 213); see also Christopher W. Morgan and Robert A. Peterson, eds., *The Glory of God*, Theology in Community (Wheaton: Crossway, 2010); John Piper, *God's Passion for His Glory* (Wheaton: Crossway, 1998), who draws on Jonathan Edwards's *The End for Which God Created the World* to argue that God's ultimate end is the manifestation of his glory in the happiness of his creatures; James

in God's gracious will to glorify himself, undergirded by his Word, and enabled by the salvation that he alone provides. In its *dramatic* nature, the narrative calls the church, like Israel, to enter into the drama for the sake of God's glory, calling the nations to rejoice in the Lord (Psalm 67) rather than in idols. Like Israel, the church proclaims that God's purpose to be glorified enables man's purpose to be satisfied.[27] The psalmist writes,

> God, You are my God; I eagerly seek You.
> I thirst for You;
> my body faints for You
> in a land that is dry, desolate, and without water. (63:1)

Our deepest thirst turns out to be God's highest goal—for man to glorify him with all he is and in everything that he does. The path that leads to God's glory and the path that leads to human flourishing (shalom) are not divergent but convergent; they are one. The message we bring to the nations is profoundly good news. Just as Israel was called to gaze upward toward God, and just as Jesus modeled that upward gaze, the church must allow worship to be both the fuel and the goal of her mission.[28]

Looking Inward

As God's mission unfolds in the biblical narrative, it becomes clear that God does not intend merely to redeem individuals but also a people for himself, and through that people to bless the nations. In the OT, that people was Israel. God previewed his intentions for Israel when he promised to make Abraham's seed into a great people through which he would bless all nations (Gen 12:1–3). He further revealed his intentions in the Mosaic covenant, when he promised Moses and Israel that he had chosen them in order for them to be a kingdom of priests and a holy nation who displayed his glory to a watching world (Exod 19:5–6). Indeed, God intended for Israel to provoke the nations to jealousy by their corporate and social life enabled by their love for God (Deut 4:5–8).

In the NT, that people is the church. Scripture provides images and analogies that help us to understand the church and, as Michael Goheen

---

M. Hamilton Jr., *God's Glory in Salvation through Judgment* (Wheaton: Crossway, 2010), 37–65, in which Hamilton argues that God's glory is the center of biblical theology.

[27] John Piper, *Let the Nations Be Glad*, 2nd ed., rev. and exp. (Grand Rapids: Baker, 2003), 31.

[28] Ibid., 17.

has argued, several of these images reveal how the church's inner life is part of her mission.[29] In 1 Pet 2:9–10, Peter describes the church as the *people of God*, underscoring the fact that the church is a cohesive community rather than an aggregate of individuals; this community is God's possession. This image draws on the language used to describe Israel's missional nature (Exod 19:5–6) in order to set forth the church's missional nature. Goheen writes, "'The people of God' then, as the term is applied to the church, must be understood in terms of the Old Testament story: this is a people chosen, redeemed, bound to God in covenant, holy, with God dwelling in its midst *for the sake of the nations*."[30] In several passages, Paul describes the church as the *body of Christ*. Sometimes he uses the image to refer to the church universal (see Ephesians, Colossians) and sometimes to the church local (see Romans, 1 Corinthians). In both cases the image helps us to understand that we are many members but one body, that each of us belongs to the other members of the body and that we "embody the life of Jesus for the sake of the world."[31] Third, we are told that the church is the *temple of the Spirit*, living stones built into a spiritual house (1 Pet 2:5). Gregory K. Beale, Goheen, and others have shown how God created the garden of Eden (Genesis 1–2) as a temple, then gave Israel a physical tabernacle and temple in order to declare his glory to the nations, and finally now considers his church to be the new temple, which is no longer in one location but scattered throughout the world. The Spirit empowers mission (Acts 1:8; 2:1–4). All three of these images portray the church as a missional people, whose mission is enabled and exemplified by its inner life.[32]

Because God's people are defined in relation to Christ, the church's members are connected to one another in a way that furthers Christ's mission. We are told to live in harmony with one another (Rom 12:16), forgive one another (Col 3:13), and refrain from passing judgment on one another (Rom 14:1). We must admonish and encourage one another (1 Thess 5:14), care for one another (1 Cor 12:25), and comfort

---

[29] Goheen, *A Light to the Nations*, 155–89. Goheen demonstrates the missional nature of five biblical images for the church: people of God, new creation, body of Christ, temple of the Holy Spirit, and diaspora.

[30] Ibid., 161.

[31] Ibid., 173.

[32] Gregory K. Beale, "Eden, the Temple, and the Church's Mission," *JETS* 48, no. 1 (March 2005): 5–31; Goheen, *A Light to the Nations*, 173–80.

one another (2 Cor 13:11). Perhaps the "one another" commands could be summed up in 1 Thess 5:15: "Always pursue what is good for one another and for all." This connection is also made clear in the practice of the Lord's Supper, ordained by Christ for the purpose of remembering him in fellowship with one another. As God's people love one another, they display God's love to a watching world. As their inner life is marked by grace and mercy, they provide the world with a tangible picture of God's grace and mercy. This provides a foretaste of the shalom that will be experienced in the new heavens and earth. Mark Dever writes, "Christian proclamation might make the gospel audible, but Christians living together in local congregations make the gospel visible (see John 13:34–35). The church is the gospel made visible."[33] In other words, the church is a shop window for God. For those who are "window shopping," who want to see Christ and his gospel, the church is God's chosen means to display them.

Looking Backward

The mission of God is first revealed in the creation account, which teaches God's good intentions for the creation in general and for his image bearers in particular. God's glory was manifested in his good creation, which was marked by shalom (a universal flourishing, peace, and Godward delight). At the apex of his creation were his image bearers, man and woman, whom he called to lovingly rule his good creation as vice-regents, to be fruitful and multiply, and to till the soil. In other words, he called them to live every aspect of their lives in submission to his loving lordship and in accord with his creational design. As the biblical story unfolds, it becomes clear that God equipped them to fulfill this task by endowing them with certain capacities—spiritual, moral, rational, creative, relational, and physical.

After the fall, as God's redemptive plan unfolded through Israel, God reaffirmed the holistic and comprehensive nature of the mission for his people and riveted that mission to his original creational intentions. As Goheen notes, the Torah reveals God's creational design for human life and does so in a way specific to Israel and the ancient Near Eastern

---

[33] Mark E. Dever, "The Church," in Akin, *A Theology for the Church*, 767. See also the previous chapter by Christopher W. Morgan, as well as Jonathan Leeman, *The Church and the Surprising Offense of God's Love* (Wheaton: Crossway, 2010) for a treatment of the way in which church membership and discipline proclaim and promote God's love to the world.

context.[34] As the people of Israel organized their lives according to God's law, they embodied God's original design for humanity and for the created order, thereby living as a contrast community whose life was distinct from the pagan nations. Goheen writes, "If we are to understand the missional calling of Israel and the church, we must give attention to the tie of law to creation. God's mission since Eden had been to restore the good creation from its sinful pollution."[35] The Torah, then, functioned as the means by which Israel could experience freedom from the sinful pollution of the world, bringing life to creation. God's mission—and his people's mission—was to make Israel thrive under his reign and according to his creational design.

Similarly, the NT people of God are called to live under his reign, looking backward to his creational design for direction in each area of our lives. "Therefore," Paul writes, "whether you eat or drink, or whatever you do, do everything for God's glory" (1 Cor 10:31). Abraham Kuyper writes, "There is not a square inch in the whole domain of our human existence over which Christ, who is Sovereign over all, does not cry: 'Mine!'"[36] And again, "The Son [of God] is not to be excluded from anything. You cannot point to any natural realm or star or comet or even descend into the depth of the earth, but it is related to Christ, not in some unimportant tangential way, but directly."[37] The whole human life matters to God. His mission extends beyond the walls of a congregational gathering, touching every facet of human existence. As God's people, we are to live Christianly as the church gathered and the church scattered. We must take seriously our work and our leisure and our participation in the arts (music, literature, cinema, architecture, etc.), the sciences (biology, physics, sociology, etc.), the public square (journalism, politics, economics, etc.), the academy (schools, universities, seminaries, etc.), the marketplace (business, marketing, etc.)—indeed, in every social and cultural endeavor.[38]

---

[34] Goheen, *A Light to the Nations*, 39–42.

[35] Ibid., 40.

[36] Abraham Kuyper, "Sphere Sovereignty," in *Abraham Kuyper: A Centennial Reader*, ed. James D. Bratt (Grand Rapids: Eerdmans, 1998), 488.

[37] Abraham Kuyper, *You Can Do Greater Things than Christ*, trans. Jan Boer (Jos, Nigeria: 1991).

[38] See Carl F. H. Henry, *The Uneasy Conscience of Modern Fundamentalism* (Grand Rapids: Eerdmans, 1947) for a treatment of the evangelical imperative to address meaningfully the social and intellectual needs of the world. See Abraham Kuyper, *Lectures on*

Anything under the sun can be directed toward God or away from him. In the beginning, his command was for man and woman to direct all of creation toward him and his glory, according to his creational design. In the aftermath of the fall, however, man and woman have become idolaters, misdirecting the personal, social, and cultural aspects of their lives (Rom 1:18–32). Although God's creation remains structurally good, since the fall it is directionally corrupt. The church's mission includes discerning God's creational design in every area of life, ascertaining the idolatrous misdirection in those areas, and seeking renewal and restoration.[39] In so doing, it is able to proclaim the gospel in word and deed.

Looking Forward

As the church points backward to God's creational design, she always points forward to the consummation of God's kingdom. The gospel of the kingdom affirms both an *anthropic* and a *cosmic* salvation. God's salvation extends beyond his image bearers to the entire created order. This theme stretches through the biblical narrative and is taught in summary form in such passages as Col 1:13–23 and Eph 1:1–14. In Colossians, Paul writes that Christ is the Creator and the reconciler of all things; God will "through [Christ] . . . reconcile everything to Himself" (Col 1:20). In Ephesians, Paul declares that we have redemption through Christ's blood and that God will "bring everything together in the Messiah, both things in heaven and things on earth in Him" (Eph 1:10). Indeed, Scripture points us forward to a new heavens and earth in which God's kingdom will be realized. At the beginning of the narrative, he created the heavens and the earth (Gen 1:1); at the end, he will give us a new heavens and a new earth (Isa 65:17; Rev 21:1). At the beginning, there is a garden; in the end, there is also a beautiful city with all its culture, replete with precious metals and jewels and the treasures of the nations. Christ's redemptive work extends through God's *people* to God's *cosmos*, so that in the end "creation itself will also be set free from the bondage of corruption into the glorious freedom of God's children" (Rom 8:21). This world will be one in which righteousness dwells (2 Pet 3:13), thus fulfilling God's good purposes.

Calvinism (Grand Rapids: Eerdmans, 1931) for a treatment of the church's imperative to bring various cultural spheres under the lordship of Christ.

[39] Michael W. Goheen and Craig G. Bartholomew, *Living at the Crossroads: An Introduction to Christian Worldview* (Grand Rapids: Baker, 2008), 135–37.

Because God's promised redemption includes both *anthropos* and *cosmos*, and because his kingdom is both spiritual and material, the church's mission is holistic, including all that man does. The church must not only proclaim the gospel with lips but also promote it with lives. "The difference between the Christian hope of resurrection and a mythological hope," writes Dietrich Bonhoeffer, "is that the Christian hope sends a man back to his life on earth in a wholly new way."[40] As the church brings all of life into submission to Christ's lordship, she points simultaneously back to God's design in creation and forward to the consummated kingdom. Her life is a sign of that kingdom, a foretaste of the feast, a preview of the new heavens and earth.

Looking Outward

The church is both a sign and an instrument of God's kingdom. She puts God and his gospel on display (sign of the kingdom) so that the nations will embrace their God and his gospel (instrument of the kingdom). This theme of God's people being a light to the nations is prominent throughout the biblical text. God promised Abraham an offspring who would in turn bless the nations (Gen 12:1–3); he redeemed Israel from slavery so that they would display his excellencies before the nations (Exod 19:3–6); he established his temple so that it would be a house of prayer for the nations (Isaiah 26); he called the nations to be glad and rejoice in him (Psalm 67); and he commanded his disciples to take the gospel to the ends of the earth (Matt 28:18–20). Like Israel, the church is called to "be a distinctive people displaying an attractive lifestyle to God's glory before the surrounding nations," so they might worship Israel's God, the church's Lord, and the Creator of all things.[41]

In the consummated kingdom, God will be given his due honor and glory by worshippers from every tribe, tongue, people, and nation (Revelation 5; 7). The redeemed of the nations will sing,

You are worthy . . .
because You were slaughtered,
and You redeemed [people]
for God by Your blood

---

[40] Dietrich Bonhoeffer, *Letters and Papers from Prison*, ed. Eberhard Bethge (New York: Simon & Schuster, 1953), 336–37.

[41] Goheen, *A Light to the Nations*, 25.

> from every tribe and language
> and people and nation. (Rev 5:9)

This ingathering of the nations is no mere appendix to Christian doctrine, nor is it a subject to be relegated to departments of missiology and applied theology. It is at the heart of God's promises. God sacrificed his Son on the cross in order to purchase redemption for the nations. The multinational nature of God's kingdom proclaims to the world that the God of Israel is not a tribal deity. He is the Creator, King, and Savior of the nations, and we will not know him in his full splendor until we know him as the King of the nations.

Summary

As the church worships God instead of idols (upward), she declares to the nations that God alone is worthy of worship. As the church proclaims and promotes the gospel through her inner life (inward), she provokes the nations to jealousy so that they also will embrace the Savior. As the church lives every aspect of her social and cultural life in accordance with God's creational design (backward), she shows the nations the nature of God's shalom. As the church proclaims and promotes the gospel as a sign of the kingdom (forward), she gives the nations a foretaste of the future banquet and a preview of the new heavens and earth. As the church takes God's gospel to the ends of the earth (outward), she does so by drawing on the upward, inward, backward, and forward dimensions of her life before God.

Distinctions and Conclusion

A proper conception of the church's mission also includes important distinctions. First, although there is great continuity between the missions of Israel and the church, as articulated above, there is also discontinuity.[42] Notably, the church is a postresurrection community composed of regenerate and Spirit-filled members (both Jew and Gentile; see Eph 2:11–22) with a centrifugal and centripetal mission.

Second, the church in both its universal and local aspects has a missional calling both when gathered and when scattered, as an institution

---

[42] For careful treatment of the relationship of Israel and the church, see the previous chapter by Stephen J. Wellum (p. 183).

and as an organism. The church's mission includes activities that are prescribed (and described) in Scripture: teaching and learning, fellowship, worship, and witness in word and deed (Acts 2:40–47). However, those activities are applied in different manners depending on whether one is referring to the local church gathered or to the church scattered. When the local church is gathered, the church diffuses the ministries into Scripture reading, preaching, prayer, song, baptism, the Lord's Supper, and so forth.[43] As the members of the body go as the church scattered into their workplaces and leisure activities, they do so in the hopes of redirecting those activities toward their creational design. They will approach their activities—in the home, the arts, the sciences, the marketplace, the public square, the academy, sports, and entertainment—with the intent of bringing them under submission to the lordship of Christ in order to be a sign of the kingdom. They will proclaim Christ with their lips and with their lives.

Third, the elements of the church's mission work in harmony but are not all equal in importance. The mission can be viewed as a wheel with a hub, spokes, and rim.[44] The hub—or the center—of the church's mission is verbal proclamation of Christ's saving work and his offer of salvation to those who believe in him. If Christ and his atonement are removed from the center, the wheel collapses. The spokes and rim of the church's mission are the promotion of Christ's gospel through our personal, social, and cultural submission to his lordship. If the spokes and rim are removed, the wheel loses traction. God's intention for his church is for the whole wheel to work together so that his gospel is proclaimed and promoted in harmony as a sign and an instrument of his kingdom.

Articulated through the biblical narrative of creation, fall, redemption, and restoration, God's mission is to glorify himself by redeeming his image bearers and renewing his good creation, restoring them both to their intended shalom. God's mission provides the impetus, the framework, and the trajectory for the church's mission: to glorify God among the nations by proclaiming and promoting the good news that God is redeeming a people for himself and bringing all things under his good rule.

---

[43] For an extensive list, see John Frame, *Worship in Spirit and Truth* (Phillipsburg: P&R, 1996), 55–60.

[44] I owe the wheel analogy to Christopher Wright, who suggested it in conversation.

Selected Bibliography

Allison, Gregg R. *Historical Theology: An Introduction to Christian Doctrine.* Grand Rapids: Zondervan, 2011.

———. *Sojourners and Strangers: The Doctrine of the Church.* Wheaton: Crossway, 2012.

Anyabwile, Thabiti M. *Finding Faithful Elders and Deacons.* Wheaton: Crossway, 2012.

———. *What Is a Healthy Church Member?* Wheaton: Crossway, 2008.

Ashford, Bruce Riley, ed. *Theology and Practice of Mission.* Nashville: B&H Academic, 2011.

Augustine. "The City of God." In *Nicene and Post-Nicene Fathers.* Vol. 2, *St. Augustine: The City of God and Christian Doctrine.* Grand Rapids: Eerdmans, 1997.

Badcock, Gary D. *The House Where God Lives: Renewing the Doctrine of the Church for Today.* Grand Rapids: Eerdmans, 2009.

Banks, Robert. *Paul's Idea of Community: The Early House Churches in Their Cultural Setting.* Peabody: Hendrickson, 1994.

Bannerman, James. *The Church of Christ: A Treatise on the Nature, Powers, Ordinances, Discipline, and Government of the Christian Church.* Vol. 1. 1869. Reprint, London: Banner of Truth, 1974.

Basden, Paul, and David S. Dockery, eds. *The People of God: Essays on the Believers' Church.* Nashville: Broadman, 1991.

Beale, Gregory K. *The Temple and the Church's Mission: A Biblical Theology of the Dwelling Place of God.* New Studies in Biblical Theology. Edited by D. A. Carson. Downers Grove: InterVarsity, 2004.

Berkhouwer, G. C. *Studies in Dogmatics: The Church.* Grand Rapids: Eerdmans, 1976.

Blaising, Craig A., and Darrell L. Bock, eds. *Dispensationalism, Israel and the Church.* Grand Rapids: Zondervan, 1992.

Bloesch, Donald. *The Church: Sacraments, Worship, Ministry, Mission.* Downers Grove: InterVarsity, 2005.

Carson, D. A. *Becoming Conversant with the Emerging Church: Understanding a Movement and Its Implications.* Grand Rapids: Zondervan, 2005.

———, ed. *Biblical Interpretation and the Church: Text and Context.* Exeter: Paternoster, 1984.

———. *Christ and Culture Revisited.* Grand Rapids: Eerdmans, 2008.

———, ed. *The Church in the Bible and the World: An International Study.* Grand Rapids: Baker, 1987.

———. "Evangelicals, Ecumenism, and the Church." Page 361 in *Evangelical Affirmations.* Edited by Kenneth S. Kantzer and Carl F. H. Henry. Grand Rapids: Zondervan, 1990.

Chambers, Andy. *Exemplary Life: A Theology of Church Life in Acts.* Nashville: B&H Academic, 2012.

Chute, Anthony L., Christopher W. Morgan, and Robert A. Peterson, eds. *Why We Belong: Evangelical Unity and Denominational Diversity.* Wheaton: Crossway, 2013.

Clowney, Edmund. *The Church: Contours of Christian Theology.* Edited by Gerald Bray. Downers Grove: InterVarsity, 1995.

Cornett, Daryl C. "Baptist Ecclesiology: A Faithful Application of New Testament Principles." *Journal for Baptist Theology and Ministry* 2 (Spring 2004): 22–44.

Dagg, John L. *A Treatise of Church Order.* Charleston, SC: Southern Baptist Publication Society, 1858. Reprint, Harrisonburg, VA: Gano Books, 1990.

Dever, Mark. "Baptist Polity and Elders." *Journal for Baptist Theology and Ministry* 3 (Spring 2005): 5–37.

———. *The Church: The Gospel Made Visible.* Nashville: B&H Academic, 2012.

———. *A Display of God's Glory: Basics of Church Structure, Deacons, Elders, Congregationalism and Membership.* Washington, DC: Center for Church Reform, 2001.

———. *Nine Marks of a Healthy Church.* Wheaton: Crossway, 2000.

———, ed. *Polity: Biblical Arguments on How to Conduct Church Life.* Washington, DC: Center for Church Reform, 2001.

Dever, Mark, and Paul Alexander. *The Deliberate Church: Building Your Ministry on the Gospel.* Wheaton: Crossway, 2005.

DeYoung, Kevin, and Ted Kluck. *Why We Love the Church: In Praise of Institutions and Organized Religion.* Chicago: Moody, 2009.

Dieter, Melvin E., and Daniel N. Berg, eds. *The Church: An Inquiry into Ecclesiology from a Biblical Theological Perspective.* Wesleyan Theological Perspectives IV. Anderson: Warner, 1984.

Dockery, David S. "Baptism." In *Dictionary of Jesus and the Gospels.* Edited by Joel B. Green, Scot McKnight, and I. Howard Marshall. Downers Grove: InterVarsity, 1997.

———. "The Church, Worship and the Lord's Supper." In *The Mission of Today's Church.* Edited by Stan Norman. Nashville: B&H Academic, 2006.

———. "Life in the Spirit in Pauline Thought." Pages 142–50 in *Scribes and Scriptures.* Edited by D. A. Black. Winona Lake: Eisenbrauns, 1993.

———. "A Theology of Baptism." *Southwestern Journal of Theology* 43 (Spring 2001): 4–16.

Dockery, David S., Ray Van Neste, and Jerry Tidwell, eds. *Southern Baptists, Evangelicals, and the Future of Denominationalism.* Nashville: B&H Academic, 2011.

Dulles, Avery. *Models of the Church.* Bantam: Doubleday, 2000.

Dunn, James D. G. "'The Body of Christ' in Paul." Pages 146–62 in *Worship, Theology and Ministry in the Early Church.* Edited by Michael J. Wilkins and Terence Paige. Sheffield: JSOT Press, 1992.

Ferguson, Everett. *The Church of Christ: A Biblical Ecclesiology for Today.* Grand Rapids: Eerdmans, 1995.

Gentry, Peter, and Stephen J. Wellum. *Kingdom through Covenant: A Biblical–Theological Understanding of the Covenants.* Wheaton: Crossway, 2012.

Giles, Kevin. *What on Earth Is the Church? An Exploration in New Testament Theology.* Downers Grove: InterVarsity, 1995.

Goheen, Michael. *Light to the Nations: The Missional Church and the Biblical Story.* Grand Rapids: Baker Academic, 2011.

Goldingay, John. *Old Testament Theology, Volume One: Israel's Gospel.* Downers Grove: InterVarsity, 2003.

Hafemann, Scott J. "The Covenant Relationship." Pages 20–65 in *Central Themes in Biblical Theology: Mapping Unity in Diversity.* Edited by Scott J. Hafemann and Paul R. House. Grand Rapids: Baker Academic, 2007.

Haight, Roger. *Christian Community in History: Historical Ecclesiology*. Vol. 1. New York: Continuum, 2004.

———. *Christian Community in History: Comparative Ecclesiology*. Vol. 2. New York: Continuum, 2005.

———. *Christian Community in History: Ecclesial Existence*. Vol. 3. New York: Continuum, 2008.

Hammett, John. *Biblical Foundations for Baptist Churches: A Contemporary Ecclesiology*. Grand Rapids: Kregel, 2005.

Hammett, John S., and Benjamin L. Merkle, eds. *Those Who Must Give Account: A Study of Church Membership and Church Discipline*. Nashville: B&H Academic, 2012.

Harper, Brad, and Paul L. Metzger. *Exploring Ecclesiology: An Evangelical and Ecumenical Introduction*. Grand Rapids: Brazos, 2009.

Hellerman, Joseph H. *The Ancient Church as Family*. Minneapolis: Augsburg Fortress, 2001.

———. *When the Church Was a Family: Recapturing Jesus' Vision for Authentic Community*. Nashville: B&H Academic, 2009.

Horton, Michael S. *People and Place: A Covenant Ecclesiology*. Louisville: Westminster John Knox, 2008.

Howard, James M. *Paul, the Community, and Progressive Sanctification: An Exploration into Community-Based Transformation within Pauline Theology*. Studies in Biblical Literature 90. New York: Peter Lang, 2007.

Husbands, Mark, and Daniel J. Treier, eds. *The Community of the Word: Toward an Evangelical Ecclesiology*. Downers Grove: InterVarsity, 2005.

Kärkkäinen, Veli-Matti. *An Introduction to Ecclesiology: Ecumenical, Historical and Global Perspectives*. Downers Grove: InterVarsity, 2002.

Knox, D. B. *Selected Works, Volume Two: Church and Ministry*. Sydney: Mathias Media, 2003.

Kraus, H. J. *The People of God in the Old Testament*. World Christian Books 22. London: Lutterworth Press, 1958.

Küng, Hans. *The Church*. New York: Sheed and Ward, 1967.

Leeman, Jonathan. *Church Discipline*. Wheaton: Crossway, 2012.

———. *Church Membership.* Wheaton: Crossway, 2012.

———. *The Church and the Surprising Offense of God's Love.* Wheaton: Crossway, 2010.

Lohfink, Gerhard. *Jesus and Community: The Social Dimension of Christian Faith.* Philadelphia: Fortress, 1984.

Longenecker, Richard, ed. *Community Formation: In the Early Church and in the Church Today.* Peabody: Hendrickson, 2002.

MacArthur, John, Jr. *The Master's Plan for the Church.* Chicago: Moody, 2008.

Malone, Fred A. *The Baptism of Disciples Alone.* 2nd ed. Cape Coral: Founders Press, 2007.

Martin, Ralph P. *The Family and the Fellowship: New Testament Images of the Church.* Grand Rapids: Eerdmans, 1979.

———. *Worship in the Early Church.* Grand Rapids: Eerdmans, 1975.

Martins, Elmer A. "The People of God." Pages 225–308 in *Central Themes in Biblical Theology: Mapping Unity in Diversity.* Edited by Scott J. Hafemann and Paul R. House. Grand Rapids: Baker Academic, 2007.

Minear, Paul. *Images of the Church in the New Testament.* London: Lutterworth Press, 1961.

Morgan, Christopher W., and Robert A. Peterson, eds. *The Glory of God.* Theology in Community 2. Wheaton: Crossway, 2012.

———. *The Kingdom of God.* Theology in Community 4. Wheaton: Crossway, 2012.

Newbigin, Lesslie. *The Household of God: Lectures on the Nature of the Church.* New York: Friendship Press, 1954.

Patzia, Arthur G. *The Emergence of the Church: Context, Growth, Leadership and Worship.* Downers Grove: InterVarsity, 2001.

Phillips, Richard D., Philip G. Ryken, and Mark E. Dever. *The Church: One, Holy, Catholic, and Apostolic.* Phillipsburg: P&R, 2004.

Radmacher, Earl D. *What the Church Is All About.* Chicago: Moody, 1978.

Robertson, Palmer. *God's People in the Wilderness.* Fearn, Scotland: Mentor, 2009.

Saucy, Robert L. *The Church in God's Program.* Chicago: Moody, 1972.

Schreiner, Thomas R., and Matthew R. Crawford, eds. *The Lord's Supper: Remembering and Proclaiming Christ Until He Comes.* NAC Studies in Bible & Theology 10. Nashville: B&H Academic, 2011.

Schreiner, Thomas R. and Shawn D. Wright, eds. *Believer's Baptism: Sing of the New Covenant in Christ.* NAC Studies in Bible & Theology 2. Nashville: B&H Academic, 2006.

Smith, David L. *All God's People: A Theology of the Church.* Wheaton: Bridgepoint, 1996.

Snyder, Howard. *The Community of the King.* Downers Grove: InterVarsity, 1977.

Stibbs, Alan. *God's Church.* Great Doctrines of the Bible. Leicester: InterVarsity, 1959.

Stott, John R. *The Living Church: Convictions of a Lifelong Pastor.* Downers Grove: InterVarsity, 2007.

Twelftree, Graham H. *People of the Spirit: Exploring Luke's View of the Church.* Grand Rapids: Baker, 2009.

Van Engen, Charles Edward. *God's Missionary People: Rethinking the Purpose of the Local Church.* Grand Rapids: Baker, 1991.

Van Gelder, Craig. *The Essence of the Church: A Community Created by the Spirit.* Grand Rapids: Baker, 2000.

Vlach, Michael J. *Has the Church Replaced Israel? A Theological Evaluation.* Nashville: B&H Academic, 2010.

Watson, David. *I Believe in the Church.* Grand Rapids: Eerdmans, 1978.

Webster, John. *Word and Church: Essays in Christian Dogmatics.* New York: T&T Clark, 2001.

Wilson, Jonathan R. *Why Church Matters: Worship, Ministry, and Mission in Practice.* Grand Rapids: Brazos, 2006.

Wright, Christopher J. H. *The Mission of God's People.* Grand Rapids: Zondervan, 2010.

———. *The Mission of God: Unlocking the Bible's Grand Narrative.* Downers Grove: InterVarsity Academic, 2006.

———. *Old Testament Ethics for the People of God.* Downers Grove: InterVarsity, 2004.

Wright, N. T. *The New Testament and the People of God.* Minneapolis: Fortress, 1992.

Yarnell, Malcolm B., III. *The Formation of Christian Doctrine.* Nashville: B&H Academic, 2007.

Contributors

Bruce Riley Ashford is provost and dean of faculty, associate professor of Thelogy and Culture, and fellow for the Bush Center for Faith and Culture at Southeastern Baptist Theological Seminary.

David S. Dockery is president and university professor of Christian thought and tradition at Union University.

Kendell H. Easley is professor of biblical studies and director of the School of Theology and Missions Programs graduate programs at the Stephen Olford Center at Union University.

Paul R. House is professor of divinity at Beeson Divinity School.

Andreas J. Köstenberger is senior research professor of New Testament and Biblical Theology at Southeastern Baptist Theological Seminary.

Christopher W. Morgan is dean and professor of theology of the School of Christian Ministries at California Baptist University.

James A. Patterson is associate dean and university professor of Christian thought and tradition of the School of Theology and Missions at Union University.

Ray F. Van Neste is professor of biblical studies and director of R. C. Ryan Center for Biblical Studies at Union University.

Stephen J. Wellum is professor of Christian theology at The Southern Baptist Theological Seminary.

Name Index

Subject Index

Scripture Index

277